THE
SEVEN THUNDERS

And when the seven thunders had uttered their voices,
I was about to write: and I heard a voice from heaven saying unto me,
Seal up those things which the seven thunders uttered, and write them not.

But in the days of the voice of the seventh angel, when he shall begin
to sound, the mystery of God should be finished, as he hath declared
to his servants the prophets.

Revelation 10:4; 7 (KJV)

THE
SEVEN THUNDERS

The Unveiling of Revelation 10:4

John Henry Holloway

WESTBOW
PRESS
A DIVISION OF THOMAS NELSON

WestBow Press books may be ordered through booksellers or by contacting:

WestBow Press
A Division of Thomas Nelson
1663 Liberty Drive
Bloomington, IN 47403
www.westbowpress.com
1-(866) 928-1240

ISBN: 978-1-4497-2542-6 (sc)
ISBN: 978-1-4497-2543-3 (hc)
ISBN: 978-1-4497-2541-9 (ebk)
Library of Congress Control Number: 2011914936

Printed in the United States of America

WestBow Press rev. date: 08/26/2011

To

The Elect of God

CONTENTS

ACKNOWLEDGEMENTS

A special thank you to all my friends and family, past and present, who contributed in one way or another to the writing and success of this book.

A deep sense of gratitude is also felt in particular towards:-

Deon Ward whose faith was challenged more than once;

Shirene Martiz, whose friendship is greatly appreciated;

My cousin Clint and his wife Annette Schuster who were there for me when I needed them the most;

James M. Moore along with all the other staff members of Thomas Nelson Westbow Press Publishers who constantly encouraged and motivated me telephonically and via email to continue in my quest to be the best I can be;

And last but not least, my daughter Justine who is my constant companion.

Your contributions are invaluable! God bless you all.

INTRODUCTION

Of all the books that have ever been written, the Bible, although the most widely read, must remain one of the most misunderstood. Various writers and Bible scholars of all walks of life have written on the subjects of the Bible in an earnest attempt at unraveling its mysteries and yet for many, it still remains a book that is completely sealed. This is a mystery indeed, for surely it is God's intention that people understand his word in order to know what it is that he desires of them? How then is it that which is given to be understood so hard to understand? Why is it that so many misunderstand the book that was given as a "road map" to eternal life?

Well, because the truth of matter is, the Bible was not written for everyone to understand. Only those who have the capacity to understand spiritual things will understand the mysteries of the Kingdom of God; those who from eternity past have been foreknown and called by Eternity Himself. It is written that the mysteries of the kingdom of heaven are not given to everyone to understand and unless a person is born again (spiritually resurrected or regenerated) he will not be able to see (or understand) the kingdom of God. The word of God is not for everyone to understand but for those who have the Spirit of God dwelling in them to guide them into all truth. No matter how learned you may think you are, you will have no understanding of the hidden "manna" if you are not lead by the Spirit of God in all the truth of his holy word.

It is true that not all "Christians" are born again but all those who are born again, are Christians (or citizens of the kingdom of God). And only those, so born again, may "see" the kingdom of God and understand its mysteries. It is therefore not necessary for me to deal exegetically with the subject matter in order for one to have understanding but to allow the Spirit of God to reveal the truth of his own word to you.

The Seven Thunders covers a wide range of spiritual issues beginning with the concept of who and what God is and going through the Luciferian rebellion and ending with the New Jerusalem and the Millennial Reign of Christ. It is my sincere prayer that the subject matter that will be dealt with in this study will go a long way to enlightening all my precious brothers and sisters in the Lord who have such an unquenchable thirst for the truth of God's word; because there is a great famine in the land, not of bread and water, but of hearing the pure unadulterated word of God.

Many of the things that will be dealt with in this study are extremely controversial and I have no doubt that I will draw many critics from the "learned" scholars of the Bible as well as those from the upper echelons of theology. There may even be many who will abuse the message herein to justify the desires of their own flesh and being contemptuous of spiritual things because they have no capacity to understand the things of the Kingdom of God. However, be that as it may, it remains nevertheless encumbered upon me to speak boldly of that which I believe to be the truth and to leave the rest in God's capable hands.

Before we commence with this study it is needful to draw your attention to the fact that there are two very important principles of truth that need to be understood to in order for one to gain proper insight into the deeper things of the Kingdom of God. Without applying these principles, the written word of God will continue to remain a closed book even though one is born again by the Spirit of God. It is vitally important that we first of all understand the spiritual principles that must be applied in order to interpret the word of God as these two principles act as primary keys that unlock the mysteries that are hidden beneath the pages of the Bible.

The first principle we need to keep in mind is that the word of God is to be spiritually understood. Scripture must be compared with scripture and spiritual things with spiritual things. "Line upon line and precept upon precept, here a little and there a little". The Bible is a spiritual book and therefore must be understood with the spiritual mind (the mind of Christ). And the only way that one is to gain a spiritual mind in order to understand the word of God is through being born again into the Kingdom of God (in other words, to be translated, through spiritual birth, from the power of the kingdom of darkness into the Kingdom of God's dear Son; also known as the first resurrection). Without going through this process of regeneration by the acceptance, by faith, of the Lord Jesus Christ as one's personal Lord and Savior it is a useless exercise to try and understand the deep mysteries of the Kingdom of God.

The second principle that must be kept in mind is that a person who has experienced this process of regeneration must start his journey through God's word by first feeding on the milk (basic teaching) of God's word before venturing into the deeper understanding of the mysteries of God, for such a person is yet unskillful in the word of righteousness. Deep spiritual truths are only reserved for them that are spiritually mature; those who have been weaned from the milk (basic doctrines) of God's word and are now ready for more advanced teaching in the oracles of God, and who by reason of use, have their senses exercised to discern both good and evil, both light as well as darkness.

If therefore you are a brother or sister who has only just recently come to know the Lord Jesus Christ as your personal Lord and Savior then it is strongly advised that you approach this study cautiously with the assistance of those who are more advanced in spiritual matters in order to avoid becoming confused and discouraged.

May I respectfully hasten to add however, that spiritual maturity does not mean that one necessarily has a degree in theology or is a pastor or some senior member of a denominational church; for even such may yet be babes in Christ! The exercising of the spiritual senses through great trial and suffering is the only thing that brings about spiritual maturity. It is the ability to receive, with an attitude of gratitude, not only the good things from the hand of God but also the bad and through all of this still love him. Not because he is good (although he is) but because he is God.

It is therefore only those who have developed an ear (spiritual hearing) through much tribulation and suffering who are able to hear what the Spirit says to the churches.

May the Lord therefore guide you by his Holy Spirit into all truth and protect you as you dare to venture deeper into the river of God, for the closer you come to know "the whole counsel of God", the more you will suffer.

CHAPTER ONE

"THE FIRST THUNDER SOUND"

GOD

INTRODUCTION

Because this book is really a study of God's Word, it is necessary to commence firstly with the understanding of who and what God is.[1] There are so many different points of view of who God really is and because of this, members of the universal church of Jesus Christ often fight among themselves, divided and confused.[2]

THE TRINITY, UNITY AND SINGULARITY OF GOD

Some Christians sincerely believe that God is a trinity comprising of three persons namely, the Father, the Son and the Holy Spirit[3]. Others again believe that he is a unity comprising only of the Father and the Son[4] and yet others that he is a singularity comprising only of the Father.[5] Because of this the church in general has in many instances become nothing more than a social club of people who come together from time to time in order to socialize and to gossip about one another[6] not really knowing or understanding who and what God really is.

The truth of the matter is, in a strange sort of way, all of them are right and yet at the same time in other instances all of them are wrong. God is neither a person[7] nor something.[8] He is both and at other times not. He is a person[9] when he chooses to be and a substance[10] at other times. God is Spirit[11] and Spirit is not restricted to personality, shape, form, time, dimension, or space. He is I AM THAT I AM. He is God and is whatever he chooses to be when and where he chooses so to be. He can do anything he chooses to do when and where he so chooses.

He is the God of Abraham (the past), Isaac (the present) and Jacob[12] (the future) the same yesterday, today and forever.[13] He is God and nothing is ever impossible for him.[14]

THE MOTIVE OF MOSES REGARDING THE NAME OF GOD

When Moses once asked God what his name[15] was, he was in effect asking God how is he to be defined or understood in order to determine what his limitations were. In other words, to what extent he was able to do what he said he was going to do. It was difficult for Moses to accept that any being could exist that was limitless. To Moses everyone had his limits, even Pharaoh.[16] But now, for the first time in his life, he finds himself face to face with someone who claims to have no limits. God's answer to Moses was simply that he had no limits and as such, he could be and do whatever he chose to be and do whenever and wherever he so chose to be and do.

THE "I AM"

God is I AM and not I WAS or I WILL BE but I AM THAT I AM. God is eternal, without beginning or end. He is and everything is in him. God does not only abide in space in the form of his Holy Spirit and Word; he is the space that his Spirit and Word abide in. God contains all things that exist in space for he is the space of all things. Space is eternal and endless as God is and there is nothing that exists outside of space. It cannot be defined, weighed, measured, or understood for it has no form, shape or size. There is space between all things in as much as all things exist in space. However, please don't be confused! Space is not God; God is space. Just as much as

4

life, light and love are not God, God is nevertheless life, light and love. And as much as God is life, light and love so he is also space. God is everything and anything he wants to be when he wants to be and nothing is impossible for him; ever! He is I AM THAT I AM. In other words I AM whatever, whenever and however I AM.

God is 'us', 'he' and 'it' at the same time and at other times not.[17] He is the angel of the Lord[18] as well as a consuming fire[19] and at other times neither.[20] He is a trinity,[21] unity[22] and singularity.[23] He is the Alpha and Omega,[24] the beginning and end,[25] light and darkness,[26] life and death[27] and everything else in between.[28] He is the Father expressed as the Word of God and Spirit of God and manifested as the Son of God and at other times not.[29] God is God, when, where and how he chooses to be . . . period.

THE EXPRESSIONS AND MANIFESTATION OF GOD

However, although God is whatever and whenever he chooses to be, he has nevertheless expressed himself in two primary ways in eternity. As the Word of God[30] and the Spirit of God[31] and only manifested himself in one primary way in time and that is in the flesh as the Son of God.[32] His expressions as the Word and Spirit of God are when the Father speaks and performs that which he speaks and the two are one. He who speaks is also he who performs.[33] He who sends,[34] is also the one who is sent.[35]

God is in everything and everything in him[36] while at the same time God is not everything and everything is not God. He holds everything together by the word of his power[37] and nothing exists, unless it exists within God. God does not only dwell in heaven[38] but heaven also exists in God.[39] He is the container of all things.[40]

THE FATHER SPEAKS AND WORKS

It was God the Father, as the Word of God, that was manifest in the flesh and called Jesus Christ the Son of God.[41] It was the Father in the Son while on earth reconciling the world unto himself and now it is the Son in the eternal Father while in heaven ruling from the throne of God! It was God who prepared a body for his own nature in eternity known as the Word of God[42] and clothed that expression with flesh and called it the Son of God and the Word became flesh. And, as much as the Word of God became flesh, so also in every sense did the Spirit of God, for the two are one being. It is not so much that Jesus (the man) is the Father, Son, and Holy Spirit as some may believe, but God, who is the Father, Son and Holy Spirit called Jesus![43]

While it was the Father as the Word of God in Christ that spoke the words that he spoke, it was the same Father as the Spirit of God in him that did the work that he did. Jesus claimed that he said and did nothing unless he first heard and saw the Father saying and doing it because the saying and doing was not him but the Father in him through his nature as the Word and Spirit of God![44]

The Word of God does not perform unless the Spirit of God is active[45] and the Spirit of God does not speak unless the Word of God is vocal.[46] The Father says nothing unless he says it through his Word and does nothing unless he does it by his Spirit. The fullness (the Word and Spirit of God) of the Godhead (the Father) dwells bodily in Jesus Christ the Son of God.[47]

THE LIMITLESS GOD

God cannot be limited in anyway because he is eternal; without beginning or end. He is what he is when and where he is. He is the source and culmination of all things. There is only one thing that God cannot be and do and that is he cannot be false to his own nature and do things contrary to it. In other words, God cannot, not be God.

It has always been the understanding of some that God is only light and not darkness only life and not death for we are taught that the devil is death and God is life as though God is the beginning and the devil is the end. There is no basis in scripture that sustains this kind of doctrine because it is God alone who is the beginning and end of all things.

When scripture says that in him there is no darkness[48] it simply means that in God's nature there is no unrighteousness, ignorance or sin and not that there is no darkness as a creature or dimension in him. All things are from him, through him and back to him.[49] All things have their being and existence in the omnipresence of God and although he dwells in light that no man can approach,[50] he also at the same time dwells in thick darkness,[51] because the darkness is the same as the light to him.[52]

THE BEGINNING AND END OF GOD

The beginning of God is not light but darkness, because it is out of darkness that God expressed himself as the light.[53] Not life but death for it is out of death that he expresses himself as life.[54] God is the

7

second death (the lake of fire) spoken of in scripture. In fact God is the Life of life and the Death of death.

Scripture does not say that the devil is death but the destroyer.[55] The one having the power of death.[56] Not the power of spiritual death, but of physical death. And it is this death that will be cast in to the lake of fire[57] which in scripture is also called the second death. It is in this regard that God is the Death of death.

PHYSICAL AND SPIRITUAL DEATH

Physical death is temporal and is the separation of all physical beings from temporal physical life. This is the first death and is also called in scripture the last enemy of Christ.[58] It will be this death that will be placed under the Lord's feet. For all things in the physical dimension is the footstool of the great King.[59]

Spiritual death is eternal[60] (everlasting) as only God is eternal[61] and is the separation of all spiritual beings from eternal spiritual life. This is the second death and is the nature of God for he alone gives and takes life, physical or spiritual.[62] He alone has the power that can separate any creature eternally from itself.

VENGEANCE BELONGS TO GOD

It is erroneous thinking to believe that the devil is the one who punishes those in hell. Vengeance does not belong to the devil but to God.[63] It is God himself who is the lake of fire that consumes all and sundry. Our God is a consuming fire wherein all things are consumed, the devil included.[64] It is only God that after killing the body has the

8

power to cast the soul into hell (another word synonymous with the lake of fire) and keep it there in a state of oblivion, for all eternity.[65]

The lake of fire is not a literal physical substance created by atomic combustion or running volcanic lava but the very Spirit of God expressed as the all consuming fire that dissolves the existence of all spirit life and returns it to God who gave in the first instance.[66] Those who are cast into the lake of fire do not consciously exist eternally therein as though they have eternal life spent in conscious anguish but rather that they are eternally consumed therein and their memory of existence eternally wiped out.[67] Although fire often refines and purges,[68] its primary nature is to consume up until there is nothing left but ashes.[69]

THE PROCESS OF DYING

It will only be the process of this dying that will bring 'eternal' anguish and not the end thereof. The lake of fire is not a place wherein the wicked live forever but a state of spiritual existence in God where their worm (the cause of their pain) will never die and the fire (the source of their destruction) will never be quenched.[70] It is therefore not so much the length (quantity) of the dying but the strength (quality) thereof that makes the difference and it is for this reason that man is no so much afraid of death as he is of dying.

To die by fire is said to be the most excruciating process of death in the physical dimension and, as it is in the physical, so is it in the spiritual. It is also for this reason that many have said that they would like to die in their sleep rather than go through any excruciating pain before death. There is no man on earth that truly believes that the dead rest in pain but rather in peace and it is for reason that the letters R.I.P on tombstones do not mean "Rest in Pain" but rather "Rest in Peace".

THE PAINLESS DEATH

There is no pain in death after dying for the dead know nothing.[71] Dying is only the journey while death is the destination. Once the destination has been reached the journey is ended. It will therefore be the process of death and not death itself that will be painfully experienced by those who are cast into the lake of fire.[72] For God, that process will be but a fleeting moment. But for all those who go through it, it will be experienced as though it is an eternity, for time is only a relative concept with God.[73] Time only exists in the mind of God as the figment of his imagination and experienced by man as reality.

Only man and angels have consciousness of time and existence and experience both as reality. Animals have no self-consciousness at all. They live entirely by instinct[74] and do not possess the knowledge of their own existence. A dog does not know that he is a dog although highly intelligent. Nor does it know anything about the existence of God. Animals are very much like new born babies. Although babies (at a certain age) appear to be acting consciously they have no conscious thought and act entirely by inherent instinct. Such also is death, an existence in God without any conscious knowledge or memory thereof.

THE WATER OF LIFE

It is a fearful thing to fall into the hands of the Almighty God.[75] However, as much as he is a God of vengeance he is also a God of mercy. And it is for this reason that he invites all and sundry (from every tribe, tongue and nation) to come now and drink freely of the water of life while time still exists. [76] Those who come to the Lord Jesus Christ and accept him as their Lord and personal Savior now are those who are drawn by God's Spirit to come and who prove that they are those who have been given, by the foreknowledge of God,[77] to God's Son before the foundation of the world.[78] It is also for this reason that Jesus Christ gave his life in eternity and in time, so that all who God gave to him before time began should believe in him and by believing in him should not die but have everlasting life.[79] This is who and what God really is.

CHAPTER TWO

"THE SECOND THUNDER SOUND"

THE MANIFESTATION OF GOD

INTRODUCTION

Although God has always been active in many different ways and forms,[1] the only true revelation of himself was when he was manifested in the flesh in time,[2] in the body of our Lord and Savior, Jesus Christ.[3] He and he alone is the express image of the Father[4] and in him alone dwells the fullness of the Godhead bodily.[5]

THE SPIRIT AND WORD OF GOD

Neither the Word of God nor the Spirit of God are manifestations of God but the divine nature of God.[6] It is for this reason that all who worship God must worship him according to his nature; in Spirit[7] (the Holy Spirit of God) and in Truth[8] (the Word of God).

The Word and Spirit of God do not manifest or reveal God as Father unless it is through the Son of God for only he is the express image of God.[9] In other words God does not reveal himself to his creation unless he does so through Jesus Christ.[10] Not through any saint, prophet, or angelic being, but through his Son. This is true in time and has always been true in eternity.

The Word and Spirit of God represent the person of God (in other words who God is) and it is therefore that the Holy Spirit is said to be blasphemed and lied to.[11] Not because he is a person in his own right, separate from the Father, but the nature of God in the person of the Father.[12] Whatever is true therefore of the Spirit of God is also true of the Father for such is the Father. Whoever therefore blasphemes against the Holy Spirit blasphemes against the Father because the Spirit of God is God!

GOD IS GOD BY THE SPIRIT OF GOD

Without the Spirit of God there can be no God for the Spirit of God is not only the divine nature of God but also the divine power of God[13] that enables God to be God.[14] And although the prophets of old had the Word and the Spirit of God come *unto* and *upon* them in one way or another, they never had the revelation in them that God was their Father.[15] It was not the place of the attributes of God to reveal this truth to them save through the image of God. Jesus Christ, the Son of God.[16]

Only the Son of God reveals God to us as Father.[17] It was for this reason that Jesus said "he who has seen me has seen the Father"[18] and "no man comes to the Father but by me".[19] No man can therefore have a relationship with God as Father unless he has it through the Son. And as much as the Word and the Spirit of God is who God is, the Son of God is what God is like. He is the visible image of the invisible God.[20] God revealed in the flesh and seen by man in the physical dimension and, God expressed in the Spirit and seen by angels in the spiritual dimension.[21]

JESUS CHRIST THE MAN

Jesus Christ, as a man in time by the foreknowledge of God,[22] was not the Word of God nor the Spirit of God but the Son of God who encapsulated the Word and Spirit of God within his body. It was the Father by his divine nature as the Word of God who was clothed with a human body that became the Son of God.[23] It was not the Word of God that dwelled in the man on earth that was called the Son of

God, but the man in whom the Word of God resided.[24] And as much as the Word of God dwelled in the Son of God in time so the Son of God abides in the Word of God in eternity and the two are one life. Although Christ (as a man) was the image of God, he is (as the life-giving Spirit) the very nature of God.[25] He is and always has been God (the Father) manifest in the flesh (the Son).[26]

CHRIST THE LIFE-GIVING SPIRIT

Only in heaven is Christ, as the life giving Spirit[27] called the Word of God[28] and not Christ as the man on earth by the foreknowledge of God.[29] While the Son of God was yet on earth as a man in human form called Jesus, he was also simultaneously in heaven in Spirit form called the Word of God.[30] In order to understand this one must keep in mind that eternity is not something that happens in the past or sometime in the distant future it is something that continuously exists in the eternal present.[31]

TIME ONLY A FORESHADOW OF ETERNITY

Time, as we currently know it, merely foreshadows eternity and is not concurrent therewith, for time is the explanation of eternity. In other words you and I would never had understood how we got to the throne of God where we are in spirit[32] and have always been had it not been for time. Had it not been for the experience of time, you and I would have thought that we were God[33] in eternity!

One of the fundamental principles of the kingdom of God provides that the physical or natural body must exist before the spiritual.[34] This is also the reason why the physical creation is experienced in the mind of God before the spiritual creation can be expressed, for once the spiritual is consciously realized, knowledge of its existence will be had through the experience of time. Once time as we know it passes by, eternity will be experienced as though time never existed but by the foreknowledge of God.[35] For such is time, the imagination of God experienced as the reality of man, for God's thoughts are not our thoughts and our ways are not his ways.[36]

SCRIPTURE OFTEN CONFUSING

Scripture is often confusing and foolish to the mind of man; [37] for God speaks of things that are not as though they are[38] because in God, the things that do not exist at the end with man in time, exists in the beginning with God in eternity.[39] What man experiences in time as reality, is merely God's imagination in eternity. It is no wonder that God laughs at man's foolishness.[40]

It is only after the physical heaven and earth have passed away[41] that the spiritual heaven and earth can be experienced[42] although both exists together in the mind of God; for all things that will exist with him in the eternal future, already existed with him in the eternal past.[43] There is no yesterday or tomorrow with God, only today.[44] He is not the 'I.WAS' (the eternal past) nor the 'I WILL BE' (the eternal future) but the almighty 'I AM'[45] (the eternal present).

OUT OF THE ONE, THE OTHER EXISTS

It is out of the natural that God brings forth the spiritual. It is out of corruption that God brings forth the incorruptible. It is out of dishonor that God brings forth glory and it is out of weakness that

God brings forth power.[46] It was out of darkness that God brought forth the light.[47] It is out of the first Adam that God brings forth the second Adam.[48] It is out of death that God brings forth life[49] and it is out of the old that God brings forth the new.[50] Man begins with the new wine first and when he has well drunk then brings out the old, but God begins first with the old wine and when men have well drunk then brings out the new.[51]

TIME IS GOD'S BEGINNING

God does not begin with eternity and end with time but with time and end with eternity.[52] God begins with the flesh and ends with the spirit. Adam, Israel, Cain, Ishmael, Esau, Manasseh, and the first born of David from Bathsheba all represented the flesh which was ultimately rejected by God while on the other hand, Jesus, the Church, Seth, Isaac, Jacob, Ephraim, and Solomon all represent the spirit which inherit the promises of God. The order of God is that the younger shall rule over the elder. The spirit will rule over the flesh.

This is also true when it comes to the Old and New Testaments of the Bible. The Old Testament and the things thereof represents the 'letter that kills' whilst the New Testament and the things thereof represents the 'spirit that gives life'. The one is representative of the flesh; the other of the spirit, giving expression to the principle of the kingdom of God which determines that that which is first shall be last and that which is last shall be first. This is a deep mystery and may prove to be difficult for you to understand at this point but through the sincere searching of the scriptures and working of God by his Holy Spirit as you continue with this study, he will reveal this deep and mysterious truth to you.[53]

CHRIST THE GLORIFIED MAN

It was only after Jesus, as the man, was resurrected in time that he returned to the Father to be gloriously united with his original state as the Word of God[54] in eternity. And as a glorified man, became so one with the nature of God[55] that the man Jesus Christ is now rightfully referred to as such.[56]

It is now a glorified man that now occupies the throne of God as both Spirit and body, Lord and Christ.[57] Both Word of God and Spirit of God,[58] and both Alpha and Omega.[59] And having received all authority both in heaven as well as on earth [60] has now become the very embodiment of God's divine nature dwelling in you and I. Christ in us, the hope of glory.[61] It is now the Word of God clothed with a glorified man[62] in heaven that occupies the throne of God[63] and we in him.[64] Such has always been his position in eternity and time merely exists as the explanation thereof.

TIME THE EXPLANATION OF ETERNITY

What you therefore think is only going to take place in the eternal future has already taken place in the eternal past and is now currently taking place in the eternal present in the mind of God.[65] Time is merely the explanation and expression of eternity and not the reality thereof. For we look not at the things that are seen but the things that are not seen, for the things that are seen are temporal but the things that are not seen are eternal.[66] And as he is in heaven in eternity so are we here on earth in time.[67] It is only time as we currently know it that passes away, eternity remains forever the same and never passes away.

THE FULNESS OF THE GODHEAD

In Christ alone dwells and, has always dwelled, the fullness of the Godhead bodily.[68] The Father (the Spirit) and the Son (the body) are now indeed (in time and have always so been in eternity) one in nature.[69] Jesus said "The Father in me and I in the Father".[70] Jesus Christ as a man in time, has always has been God in eternity;[71] for God (the Spirit), his God, made him (the man) God.[72] And what is true of him is also true of his body the church, for the Father has never seen Jesus apart from his church. The sons of God are God over all the works of God's hands for it is only God that sits on the throne of God. In eternity they have always so been and will always so be. Jesus Christ yesterday, today and forever the same[73] and time merely explains how it all is and came to be in eternity.

THE BODY FOR THE WORD OF GOD

It was God the Father who in time prepared, by his Spirit, a body for his own Word[74] and called it the Son of God and the Word became flesh.[75] And as much as the Word of God became flesh, so also in every sense, the Spirit of God, for the two are one life.[76] You cannot separate the two for they are both attributes of God's one divine nature.

While it was the Father as the Word of God in Christ that spoke the words that he spoke, it was the same Father as the Holy Spirit in him that did the work that he did.[77] In fact it was the Father, through the operation of his Holy Spirit that birthed the body of Jesus in Mary.[78] Jesus said that he spoke and did nothing save he first heard and saw the Father saying and doing for the saying and doing was not him but the Father in and through him.[79]

The Word of God does not perform save the Spirit of God is active and the Spirit of God does not speak save the Word of God is vocal. For the Father says nothing unless he says it through his Word[80] and does nothing save he does it by his Spirit.[81]

GOD IN CHRIST

When Jesus spoke it was the Father as the Word of God in him that was speaking and when Jesus performed it was the Father as the Spirit of God that was performing in him.[82] It was the Father himself, through the operation of his own nature, the Word and Spirit, that was clothed in human form that we know as Jesus Christ. It was God in Christ that was reconciling the world unto himself.[83] The fullness, (the Spirit and Word of God) of the Godhead (the Father), dwells bodily in Jesus Christ the Son of God.[84]

REJECTING THE SON IS REJECTING THE FATHER

Those who do not accept Christ to be as such have rejected what God has ordained from all eternity and those who reject the Son, reject the Father.[85] All who refuse to worship the Son: refuse to worship the Father.[86] The Father is only glorified in and through the Son,[87] because the Father by His divine nature, dwells forever and from all eternity in the Son.[88]

CHRIST THE ONLY WAY

Although Jesus taught us to pray to the Father in his name; in other words by his authority,[89] it would nevertheless be he, himself, that would answer that prayer so that the Father in the Son may be glorified.[90] We are never to direct our prayers to the Word or Spirit of God but to the Father through the Son.[91] Therefore, when we address the Father we are in fact first addressing the Son; for no man can come to the Father save he comes through the Son.[92]

There is therefore no going over the head (authority) of the Son of God to the Father but through the Son to the Father.[93] For the Son of God, our Lord and Savior Jesus Christ, is and always has been the only authority and true manifestation of God.[94] Has always so been and will always so be and time only exists in order to teach us what, how and why all things are and came to be in eternity.

THE MARK OF CAIN

Here now is a revelation of a deep mystery that many men and women have speculated upon throughout the centuries of time but now, in these last days, is being revealed to the manifest sons of God.

In order for one to truly appreciate and understand what is to follow with regards to the revelation concerning the mark of Cain, one must firstly understand that the Bible, in its entirety, concerns itself only with Christ and his church. Everything therefore which is recorded in scripture refers, in one or another, only to the manifest Sons of God.

The story of Cain and Able is a very deep spiritual story about Christ and his church. It is a story that has been misunderstood by many because God had chosen to have it remain hidden until the end of time to be revealed now within the pages of this book.

Many have rightly understood and accepted that the lives of Cain and Able spiritually reflected the lives of those (Able), which come to God by way of the blood of the Lamb of God, (Jesus Christ) while others (Cain) by way of the fruits of their own hands; of those who are saved by grace of the Spirit and those seek salvation through the works of flesh. However when it comes to appreciating what the Mark of Cain is all about they fail to understand because God had hidden[95] it from the eyes (understanding) of the worldly wise but now, in these last days, reveals it unto babes (spiritually humble) in Christ.

To fully understand this deep spiritual truth, we must start by understanding why Cain decided to kill Abel his brother. In Genesis 4:3-5 we read the following:

And in process of time it came to pass, that Cain brought of the fruit of the ground an offering unto the LORD. And Abel, he also brought of the firstlings of his flock and of the fat thereof. And the LORD had respect unto Abel and to his offering: But unto Cain and to his offering he had not respect. And Cain was very wroth, and his countenance fell.

The above scripture clearly indicates that Cain killed his brother because he was jealous of him because God accepted Abel's offering and rejected his. This was also the case in the story of Joseph and his brothers when they decided to sell him as a slave into Egypt.[96] They were jealous of him. And furthermore the case in the parable of the son and the husbandmen of the vineyard.[97] They were jealous of him. So also in the case of Lucifer's rebellion, it was again jealously that moved him to deceive Eve into eating of the forbidden tree. He could not stand the fact that God had chosen a mere man to rule over all the works of his hands instead of him. He wanted to be like the Most High.[98]

It was jealously in every case that moved the various roll players to take action against those that they were jealous of. They all resented God's grace upon those he chose to accept and bless. Such is the way of the flesh towards the spirit. It seeks at all times to usurp authority because it is jealous of the spirit's position and authority with God. The flesh cannot stand the spirit having the authority to rule over it.[99]

Such also is the case of those who see others being blessed of God while they should be the ones to receive the blessings that they are worthy of. Why in the world should God pass over them and bless those far less worthy than are, they think. Little realizing that God will choose whom he will[100] and often chooses those who are nothing [101] to bring to nothing those who think they are something. The stone that the builders cast away is often used by God to make of it the cornerstone of the building.[102] Such is the prerogative and order of God. The older (flesh) shall be ruled over by the younger[103] (spirit). The first shall be last and the last first.[104]

WHERE IS THY BROTHER?

After Cain killed Abel, God asked him where his brother was. The answer that Cain gave to God was pertinent to the mark (or seal) that God in turn placed upon Cain. And Cain said "Am I my brother's keeper?" Here we see the flesh in action once again. Am I (the flesh) the caretaker and ruler over my brother (the spirit)? Have I been given authority over him that I should know his whereabouts? This is the arrogance of the flesh. Notwithstanding its dastardly deeds, it forever seeks to cover up it own evil ways. God never asked Cain where his brother was as though the Lord sought Abel's whereabouts because he knew not of it but rather to remind Cain what evil deed he had done to his brother for his brother's blood was crying out of the ground to God for vengeance.[105]

THE COVER-UP

Notice however that Cain never once admitted to taking the life of his brother even after God informed him that he knew of his murderous deed but rather focused upon his own demise. "My punishment is more than I can bear". Never mind my poor brother, what about me. People are going to kill me when they see me! Yes, such is the flesh; always me, me, me. In answer to what Cain asked God with regards to being his brother's keeper, God placed a mark upon him that would forever serve as the answer for all generations to come. And, in effect, said "Nay, thou art not thy brother's keeper for the mark I place upon thee this day shall forever remind thee and all, that it is he, thy brother, who keepeth thee!"

THE FORGIVENESS OF GOD

Notwithstanding Cain's murderous deed and his subsequent arrogance in trying to hide it, God was still prepared to forgive him and to provide protection for his miserable life. However, before God could forgive Cain, he had to ensure that the broken law, that demanded a life for a life, would be satisfied. And although God's written law was only handed down to man a few hundred years after the death of Abel, his unwritten and immutable law was in existence before the beginning of time. For if it were not so then the killing of Abel could hardly be murder; for the law that said "Though shalt do not kill" only came many years after Cain killed able and scripture declares that where there is no law there can be no transgression. No, the law existed indeed, albeit in unwritten form.

But how then would God ensure that on the one hand his law would be satisfied while on the other hand still protect Cain from its demand for a life? For the law to be satisfied, Cain had to pay with his life. And if he had to pay with his life how then would God be able to protect him from being killed? The only way God could do this was to provide a life that would satisfy his broken law.

THE BLOOD OF THE LAMB

God then did the only other thing that would be just to the law while at the same time, be merciful to Cain. He provided a substitute for Cain and that substitute was "the Lamb slain from before the foundation of the world" represented by the blood of his own brother, Abel. The blood that Cain spilled upon the earth, through his murderous deed, became the same blood that God used, as a symbol of the blood of the Lamb of God, to protected him. Such is the mercy and righteousness of God. That while we were sinners, Christ died for us. The life we took at Calvary, because of our sin, is the same life that now protects us. And although the blood (life) of Abel spoke of good things (for Cain), the blood (life) of Christ speaks of better things for us.[106]

WHEN I SEE THE BLOOD

The only way therefore that God could forgive Cain and protect him from those who would slay him while at the same time satisfy his law that demanded a life for a life, was to place upon him the blood of his own brother that would forever serve as a sign for all to see that without the shedding of blood there can be no remission of sin. And as long as Cain placed his faith in the protective value of the blood that was placed upon him, he would be forgiven of his sin and protected from destruction. It was the blood that God would see as he passed over Cain and in turn not suffer the destroyer to slay him. Nothing else could protect Cain. No outward sign or mark would suffice. God was not concerned with the physical but with the spiritual. How in any case could men have known what Cain had done for only God knew of his evil deed? And while it was the flesh that wanted to know whether or not it was the spirit's keeper, it was God who answered that it was the spirit (the spiritual) who would keep (or rule over) the flesh (the physical).

THE MARK NOT PHYSICAL

Foolish therefore are those who speculate the Mark of Cain to be some outward physical sign that protects from the wrath of man while failing to understand that it was not so much that Cain was to be afraid of man but of God! What can man do but kill the body? It is God alone who can destroy both body and soul in hell.[107] God was not protecting Cain from the wrath of man, when he placed a mark upon him, but from the wrath of God. "And when I see the blood I will pass over you"[108] God's provision for sin has always and will always be the blood; for without the shedding of blood there can be no remission of sin and protection from the wrath of God.[109] And the only blood that was available for Cain's protection from the wrath of God was that of his own righteous brother Abel; which in truth, pointed as foreshadow, to the blood of Jesus Christ.

WE WERE GUILTY

And as with Cain, so also is it with us. For was it not we who shouted, "Crucify him"? Was it not we who killed our own brother because of our jealously and then tried to hide own dastardly deeds by seeking justification by the works of the flesh? And was he (our brother) not wounded for our transgression and bruised for our iniquities?[110] And was it not God who took of the blood of the one we killed (because of our sin) and marked us with it so that the destroyer might not slay us; for his blood speaks of better things than that of Abel?

THE MARK OF GOD

Yay indeed! The Mark of Cain (Nay, in truth, not of Cain, but of God) speaks of none but the blood of the Lamb, slain from before the foundation of the world; for it is only his blood that can truly satisfy the vengeance of God and protect us from the wrath of him who sees and knows all because he alone is the only true manifestation of God.

CHAPTER THREE

"THE THIRD THUNDER SOUND"

THE TREE OF THE KNOWLEDGE
OF GOOD AND EVIL

INTRODUCTION

At this stage of our study we are introduced, in Genesis 2:9, to a very special type of tree that stood in the center of the Garden of Eden called the Tree of the Knowledge of Good and Evil and which clearly represented something other than just being an ordinary tree. Let us now take a closer look at this tree to find out just what or who it represented and why.

Notice first of all that this was not the tree of good and evil but the Tree of the Knowledge of Good and Evil. In other words, it was the tree of Knowledge. Furthermore this was not a tree in the literal sense of the word but rather a tree that symbolically represented something or someone.[1] We must also bear in mind that this tree was not bad or evil in itself as some would have us believe, for God made all things good[2] and beautiful[3] in the day that he created them.

A REMARKABLE TREE

In considering this tree more closely we notice some remarkable things about it. In the first place we notice that it stands in the center of the garden alongside the tree of Life having the same prominent place of importance.[4] Secondly we notice that this tree was pleasant looking and its fruit was good for food and that the eating thereof could make one wise.[5] Furthermore, we notice that this tree was the only tree in the garden that was not to be eaten of by Adam and Eve.[6]

At this point I would like to point out the fact that although it was the eating of the fruit of this tree in direct disobedience to God's word not to eat there from that brought about the death of Adam and Eve, the fruit thereof was not bad or poisonous in it self. Nothing in the tree itself was poisonous or bad. It was merely the timing that was all wrong.[7] It was not the right time for Adam and Eve to eat there from. God never intended that Adam would never eat from this tree. He just never wanted them to eat from it at that stage because there was another tree that he wanted them to eat from first and there was a very good reason for this which we will discover as we proceed. The tree of the Knowledge of Good and Evil was good and nothing in scripture in any way indicates that this tree was ever removed from the garden or was held responsible for the fall of man.

A KNOWING TREE

And finally, this tree knew something that only God knew and that was that Adam and Eve was naked.[8] Adam and Eve never knew it and neither did the serpent know it. Only God and this tree had this knowledge. This was the only tree that knew the deep things of God! Not even the tree of Life had this knowledge for the tree of Life could only provide eternal life[9] and not the knowledge or understanding of the deep secrets of God. In light of the above we see that the tree of the Knowledge of Good and Evil was a very special tree indeed!

THE TREE NOT EVIL

There are many who have different views on the exact nature of this tree and especially with regards to its purpose in the great plan of God for mankind. There are those who believe that this tree represents the devil and the eating thereof by Eve was in fact she having a sexual relationship with the serpent and hence the "serpent's seed" spoken of in Genesis 3:15. Others believe that the tree represents the cannabis plant (dagga tree if you like) that somehow provides a certain knowledge of things good and evil as spoken of in Genesis 3:5.

Others simply believe that the tree was a evil tree planted by God to test the obedience of Adam and Eve as to whether or not they would chose good over evil; in other words, God's will over their own. However, be that as it may, the various different views are in any case to numerous to consider separately and apart and would indeed take a book in its own right to expound on each and every one.

The simple truth of the matter is that none of them are correct when one considers the fact that scripture, in its entirety, concerns itself only with Christ and his Church; the Spirit of God and the Word of God. When Jesus said that the scriptures are "they which testify of me".[10] He included the church in that statement for the "me" is both male and female and the two shall be one as much as the word "Adam" included Eve. It was Adam who later called his wife Eve.[11]

What God has therefore joined together, can no man pull apart[12] and God joined the church to Christ in eternity not only in time.[13] It was out of Christ that God brought forth the church in as much as he brought Eve out of Adam. Eve was always in Adam just as much as the church was always in Christ. The two have always been and shall always be one!

THE LETTER KILLS

In order to properly understand what or who this tree represented we need to allow scripture itself to provide the interpretation thereof for it is only the Word of God, when made alive by the Spirit of God, which can reveal the truth about God. For without the Spirit of God the written word of God is only the dead letter that kills.[14]

John 16:13 declares that when the Spirit of Truth comes, he will guide us in all truth because he will not speak of himself but whatever he hears, that shall he speak; and again in 1 Corinthians 2:9-11 it says—"the eye has not seen, nor the ear heard, neither has it entered into the mind of man, the things that God has prepared for them that love him. But God has revealed them to us by his Spirit: for the Spirit searches all things, even the deep things of God. For what man knows the deep things of a man save the spirit of man which is in him. So also no man knows the deep things of God but the Spirit of God".

ONLY THE SPIRIT KNOWS

These verses of scripture tell us a very important thing regarding one of the primary functions of the Spirit of God and that is to reveal the deep things of God to his creation in a way that no one else can. Only the Spirit of God can guide a person in *all truth* because only the Spirit of God is able to search the deep hidden things of God.

Only the Spirit of God knows the things that no one else knows and only he can reveal those things to God's creation. Is it any wonder that God asked Adam "who told you that you were naked?" Notice that God did not ask him *what* told him but *who* told him. It was only then that God asked Adam whether he ate of the tree of the Knowledge of Good and Evil. It is very important to understand that God already knew the answer to the question he asked Adam for God knows all things, always. God never asks a question that he does not already know the answer thereof.

THE NAKEDNESS OF ADAM

Once Adam and Eve partook of sin by disobeying God's word, the Spirit of God immediately convicted them and revealed their nakedness before the Lord. Nakedness, that went far beyond just being void of covering (clothing) for their bodies and went to the nakedness of their spirits. The truth of the matter was that man was never really naked in the true sense of the word as far as his body was concerned, because his body was in itself a covering for something far greater—his spirit. Jesus once said in Matthew 6:25 that the body was more than clothing and it was to this truth that he was referring to.

THE BODY DESTROYED

God never created man naked, in so far as he needed physical clothing, but clothed with spiritual clothing. When scripture says that man was naked yet without shame[15] it simply means that man was created without a covering for his body and not that he needed a covering for his body. Man was much more than just a body he was also spirit. Was he not so, he would not have been able to communicate with God in the way that he as he did. Because those who worship God must worship God in spirit and in truth for God is a Spirit[16] and it was the spirit that was eventually found naked[17] before the Lord because the body was destroyed by unrighteousness when Adam disobeyed God.[18]

37

THE BLOOD IS THE TRUE COVERING

Man thought that by sewing fig leaves together he could provide a covering for his physical nakedness little realizing that his nakedness went beyond his physical body all the way to his spiritual being.

It was for this reason that God provided his own covering for man. The covering that God provided for man was not so much the skin that he took from an animal[19] but the blood that soaked that skin. For without the shedding of blood there can be no remission for sin.[20] Man felt naked before God because the body that God had once provided for his covering was now dead to God[21] and in this sense man was found to be naked.[22]

It was only the Spirit of God who knew that man was naked; for man's nakedness went beyond his physical being. Beyond that which could be seen and all the way to that which could not be seen.[23] Man was in fact never created to wear physical clothing. Clothing was only the result of man's sin. God's plan was always that man's body would serve as a covering for his spirit and not as a thing that would need to be covered with physical cloth.

It was never God's intention that man would need cloth to cover his body for God created all things with their own specific body[24] and with its own specific covering.[25] The trees with bark, birds with feathers, fish with scales, animals with hair and, man, who is in reality a spirit as far as God is concerned,[26] with a body.[27] Cloth was never a part of God's plan to serve in anyway at all as a covering for man's body.

THE LUCIFERIAN REBELLION

What, in any case, was Eve's motivation in blatantly disobeying God and eating from the tree that God had clearly forbidden her to eat? Was it because she was hungry and the fruit of the tree looked too good to resist? Or was it merely because she wanted to have more wisdom than what she already had in order to know things between good and evil?

It was neither. Eve did not eat of the tree because she was hungry nor did she eat because she wanted to become wiser just for the sake of knowing good and evil. She ate of the tree of the Knowledge of Good and Evil because she wanted to be equal to God. For at that point in time the serpent's desire[28] became her own desire. She did not want to be dependant on God anymore. She wanted to be like him. She wanted to be a god herself.[29] Eve wanted the power that enabled God to be God. And that power was the Spirit of God. For it is not by might nor by power but by the Spirit of God that God is God.[30]

THE GOD OF POWER

The only time man wants to have the power of God (the Spirit of God) without the life of God (the Word of God) is when man wants to be a god without God. And that is what motivated Eve to eat of the tree of the Knowledge of Good and Evil. She wanted to be God! And not only did Eve desire to be God but so did Lucifer and the only way he could ascend the throne of God was to do so in and through the body of man. Because it was a man that God had chosen to rule from his throne.

39

THE REBELLION IN THE GARDEN

It is flawed thinking to believe that the Luciferian rebellion took place before the existence of man in the Garden of Eden based upon one single scripture which declares that the earth was void and without form in the day that it was created (see Genesis 1:2). Some believe that Lucifer previously lived and ruled on a pre-existent earth and because of his rebellion against God, the earth became void and without form and thereafter entered the Garden of Eden as Satan the devil disguised as a serpent in order to deceive Eve. This is not the truth of what happened.

The Luciferian rebellion did not take place *before* the Garden of Eden; it took place *in* the Garden of Eden. Lucifer did not enter the Garden as the devil; he existed in the Garden as the anointed cherub.[31] He existed as Adam and Eve's own personal guardian angel in fellowship with them and after deceiving Eve through the beguiling nature of a serpent, he fell from his lofty position[32] and thereafter became the devil. It was only after the fall of man that a curse was place on Lucifer (the 'serpent') and a division brought about between him and the woman[33] (the church). Before the fall of Adam there was no curse or division.

THE FALL FROM HEAVEN

Lucifer also did not fall from heaven, the fourth dimension, also called the heaven of heavens (which is explained more fully in chapter four), but from heaven, the third dimension (the Garden of Eden) the paradise of God. Had he been in heaven (the fourth dimension) in the first place he would not have said in his heart "I will ascend into heaven". One does not desire to ascend to a place that you are already in but from a place that is below that which you seek to ascend to. Scripture says that Lucifer was in Eden, the Garden of God, and not in the heaven of heavens.

THE SERPENT TALKS

Eve also did not communicate with a serpent as a physical beast of the field in the day that she was deceived. She communicated with Lucifer as the archangel in the Garden of Eden who symbolically represented a serpent. She knew very well who he was because she had fellowship with him. How long that fellowship existed before the fall, is not known at this stage, but what is known is the reason for that fall.

The problem arose when Lucifer heard God say that man was to have dominion (rulership over all the earth or physical dimension). It was then that evil thoughts, motivated by jealousy, arose within the heart of Lucifer. He was not happy that God had chosen a mere man to rule over all the work of his hands in the natural world. He wanted that position and the only way that he thought that he could get that position was if he could get man, through deception, to relinquish that authority to him.

THE PHYSICAL FIRST

What Lucifer did not know however was that it was not primarily the first Man (Adam and Eve) that God ultimately had in mind when he said "let us make man and let them have dominion" but the second

Man (Christ and his Church). Lucifer did not understand that the principles of the Kingdom of God necessitated that the physical body must exist before the spiritual body because the physical is the shadow of the spiritual in as much as the spiritual is the foundation (or the reality) of the physical. The important thing to keep in mind though is that Lucifer needed a body in order to rule as God for it would only be then that he would be able to rule both in heaven (the spiritual dimension) as well as on earth (the physical dimension) for God, in all his perfection, rules in both the spiritual as well as the physical dimension and that is why Lucifer deceived Eve into eating of the tree.

A BODY NEEDED

Lucifer needed to occupy the body of Eve in order to gain access to the throne of God. What he did not know however was that it was not the first Eve (the physical body) that occupied the throne of God but the second Eve (the church—the spiritual body).

However, in deceiving Eve, he in actual fact, by proxy, brought about the fall of the body (the church) in the physical dimension and it was this that Jesus Christ came to restore when he said that he came to save that which was lost. He came to restore his body (the church) to its original glory. It was therefore his own physical body that he lived in on earth in time that he provided for his church in eternity.

Once Christ was resurrected from the dead with a glorified body, which is pure unadulterated spiritual light, (as signified by the sun clothed woman of Revelation 12), he returned to the spiritual dimension and clothed his bride with that body. It was only the church (Eve) that took part in the Luciferian rebellion and not Adam (Christ) and that is why scripture declares that Eve was the transgressor and not Adam. What Adam did he did out of love for Eve thereby symbolizing the sin-made Christ on behalf of his church and not because he was in rebellion towards God (see 2Corinthians 5: 21).

THE MISSION OF CHRIST

Christ never came to earth for any one else but his church (the Elect). He stated very clearly that he was sent to no one else but to the lost sheep of the house of Israel[34] (the church comprised of both Jew and Gentile). When he sent his disciples out to preach the gospel of the kingdom he strictly forbade them to go in the way of the gentiles at that time and instructed them to go only to the lost sheep of the house of Israel.[35] It was only after Christ's resurrection that Paul received the revelation that the gentiles would also form part of the body.[36]

The reason why the gentiles were included only after the resurrection of Jesus Christ was because Israel, as a nation, had not yet fulfilled (by their rejection of the Messiah) its role under the Old Covenant as the shadow of the bride of Christ.[37] The gentiles were always part of God's plan in the formation of the body of Christ under the New Covenant.[38] It was always God's intention from before the foundation of the world that the two, Gentile and Jew, would become one new spiritual man.[39] The grafting of the gentiles into the house of natural Israel also typified the restoration of the fallen church back into union with her husband, the Christ, and the establishment of the true spiritual Israel.[40]

LIMITED POWER

The church is not only now indwelled with the Christ on earth but also clothed with him in heaven. Once Christ had achieved his goal in restoring his body, he received all authority and power both in heaven as well as on earth. Before his incarnation on earth, his authority was limited to heaven because he had lost his body (the medium to rule in and over the physical dimension) through the fall of Eve and could therefore only do such miracles as was permitted by the Father. But now that the church (Eve) is restored, God's plan is perfected and Jesus Christ is now both Lord and Christ having unrestricted authority both in heaven as well as on earth.

GOD'S INTENTION

It will be seen as we move along that it was never God's intention that man would never be equal[41] to him or be like him but that man would never be equal to him without first having God's life within him. Without the life of God[42] (the Living Word of God) man cannot have the power of God[43] (the Holy Spirit of God). God wanted man to partake of his Life first before he would allow man to experience his Power.

It was always God's intention that man would eventually be allowed to eat of the tree of the Knowledge of Good and Evil but not before he first ate of the tree of Life. Knowledge only puffs[44] up and makes one arrogant when one has it without the life of God.

However, because man chose to eat first of the tree of the Knowledge of Good and Evil (to partake of God's power by his Spirit) before eating of the tree of Life (to partake of God's life through his Word) God prohibited him from having his life and subjected him to death which was the inevitable result of having God's power without first having his life. The life of God is the container that encapsulates the power of God. Without it, man is inevitably doomed to die.

Simon also thought that he could have the power of God without first experiencing the life of God. And instead of receiving God's power, through the offering of money, he received a curse upon him that eventually led to his destruction. He also did not want this power to give to others as he said but rather that he may be powerful in himself; to be a god unto himself and to be like the Most High.[45] (see Acts 8:18; 19)

THE LIFE OF GOD

Once man eventually partook of the life of God through faith in Jesus Christ, God allowed man to partake of his power through His Holy Spirit[46] and man became equal to God in the sense that he has the same nature as God.[47] The power that God gives to man is not something that God has, but something that God is.[48] Man has so partaken of the nature of God in Christ that he now qualifies to ascend and to be seated on the very throne of God![49]

The only reason God prohibited man from eating of the tree of the Knowledge of Good and Evil before first eating from the tree of Life was because God knew that partaking of his power before partaking of his life could only lead to man's death. There is no creature in all of God's creation that has the capacity to contain the power of God without first having the life of God to contain it in.

THE NEW WINE

Jesus once said that if one poured new wine (the Spirit) into old bottles (unregenerate natural man) it would burst the bottles. He said that one could only pour new wine into new bottles[50] (regenerate spiritual man). Filling an unregenerate man with the Spirit of God is like trying to operate an electrical appliance that usually works with 240 volts of electricity, with 240 billion volts of electricity. Unregenerate man just does not have the capacity to contain that much power. Such a man cannot even look at God[51] without being destroyed let alone contain his power!

God was not playing games or being selfish or devious when he told Adam not to eat of the tree of the Knowledge of Good and Evil, he was protecting him! In effect God was saying to Adam, "Don't attempt to partake of my power without first parking of my life". Without eternal life you can never contain eternal power. God was not testing man in order to see whether or not he would obey, but was merely preparing to show man in a practical way that he was incapable of properly exercising, by the power of God, the dominion that was given to him[52] without first having the life of God in him by obeying his Word.

Adam was not created with the eternal life of God inherently in him. The breath of life that God initially breathed into Adam was only sufficient to animate his physical body until such time that he, through obedience to God's word, would partake of the tree of Life and live forever.[53] Adam had to choose to have the eternal life of God in him by first eating of the tree of Life. It was not automatically given to him when he was created. God set before Adam life and death in the day that he was created[54] and would that he chose life over death knowing full well that man would chose death over life. Death is the absence of life; the Spirit of God without the Word of God. That is also why the Spirit of God never resided in the prophets of the Old Testament or in those of the New Testament prior to the cross of Christ. He merely came upon[55] them and dwelled with them but never in them.[56]

THE SPIRIT AND LIFE

The Spirit of God, without the Word of God, does not give life as much as the Word of God without the Spirit of God does not impart knowledge. This does not mean however that the Spirit of God cannot give life but that this function is left to the Son of God who is the

Word of God clothed with a man. It was God the Father (as the Spirit of God) that initially gave life to the Son[57] (Jesus Christ the man) but as the Word of God,[58] Jesus Christ as the life-giving Spirit, gave life to every other creature that he had created prior to his incarnation in time as the Son of God.

It was God, the Father himself as the Word of God who was clothed with flesh and became known as Jesus Christ the Son of God[59] and who in actual fact was the one that is the creator of all things for the Son does nothing save he first sees the Father doing it.[60] It was the Father himself that was manifest in the flesh in Jesus Christ reconciling the world unto himself.[61] It is the Father in the beginning and it is the Father in the end and nothing exists unless it begins and ends with the Father.[62]

THE MYSTERY OF GODLINESS

Great is the mystery of godliness: It was God (the Father) that was manifest in the flesh (as the Son of God), justified in the Spirit (as the Holy Spirit of God), seen of angels (in the spiritual dimension), preached unto the Gentiles (in the physical dimension), believed on in the world (in time) and received up into glory (in eternity).[63]

As much as the tree of the Knowledge of Good and Evil represented the Spirit of God, so the tree of Life represents the Word of God. These two are forever together and cannot be separated. For the two shall be one. And what God has joined together let no man pull apart[64] for they are one Spirit;[65] these two are the only ones who truly witness to the existence and nature of God.[66]

And as much as the tree of the Knowledge of Good and Evil and the tree of Life represented the Spirit of God and the Word of God so they also represent Christ and his church for Christ is the Spirit of the Body[67] (the church) in as much as the Word of God is the body (the temple) of the Spirit of God.

The tree of Life only produces eternal life and that life is only found in the Word of God clothed with a body called Jesus Christ, the Son of God. It is only in Jesus Christ, the Son of God that eternal life is found. He who has the Son has life.[68] Jesus said that he came into the world that we may have life,[69] not knowledge.

THE SPIRIT AND TRUTH

Jesus said however that when the Spirit of God comes then we will receive knowledge[70] (the truth). The Spirit of God does not produce life save but through the Word of God and the Word of God does not impart knowledge save but through the Spirit of God and that is why Eve had knowledge after eating from the Tree of the Knowledge of Good and Evil but had no life. The Spirit of God without the Word of God only leads to death.[71] The Tree of the Knowledge of Good and Evil therefore represented none other than the Spirit of God and not some or other evil thing or devious scheme of God.

CHAPTER FOUR

"THE FOURTH THUNDER SOUND"

THE FOUR DIMENSIONS IN GOD

INTRODUCTION

The apostle Paul once indicated that his desire was that Christ may dwell in the hearts of men by faith and they being rooted and grounded in love, may be able to comprehend with all the saints what is the breath, and length, and depth, and height in God.[1] So also is it my desire that such understanding wil be had as we enter this portion of our study of God's word in discovering the four dimensions in God.

HAVING A SPIRITUAL MIND

Bear in mind however that in order to understand spiritual truths one must approach the word of God with a spiritual mind as spiritual truths cannot be appreciated with the natural or carnal mind[2] for they are foolishness[3] to it no matter how much Hebrew and Greek education you may think you have; "For the Jews (religious man) require a sign, and the Greeks (philosophical man) seek after wisdom" because the preaching of the crucified Christ is to "the Jews a stumbling block, and unto the Greeks foolishness"[4]

Scripture clearly instructs us not to look at the things that can be seen but at the things that cannot be seen[5] and the only way that we are able to do this is if we are born again (resurrected from spiritual death);[6] For unless one is born again one cannot see (or understand) the things of the kingdom of God.[7] Once a person is born again by accepting, by faith, the Lord Jesus Christ as his own personal Lord and Savior he will receive the mind of Christ[8] which will then enable him to eventually understand the deep spiritual things of God by the Spirit of God.[9]

HAVING THE MIND OF CHRIST

We can only understand the things of God with the mind of Christ and not with our own natural mind. The natural mind does not appreciate the things of God nor indeed can it for it is bound in a dimension that is far below the dimension in which spiritual truths can be understood and in this regard the carnal is like an animal that cannot understand the things that a man can.[10] Man cannot understand the things of God unless the Spirit of God reveals it to him for it is only the Spirit of God that knows the deep things of God.[11]

THINGS NOT SEEN

There are things that the natural eye has never seen nor the natural ear has ever heard nor has it ever entered into the natural mind of man that God has prepared for those who love him but God has revealed these things to us by his Spirit. Revelation of spiritual truths is of such intensity that both the apostles Paul and John had to be taken into a higher dimension in order to receive and understand the revelations that were given to them. Paul said that the dimension that he was taken up into was called the "third heaven"[12] (Paradise) while John identified that dimension as being in the "Spirit".[13]

It is only once a person's mind has been transformed by the Word of God[14] that one is truly able to appreciate the things of the Spirit; so enter this portion of the study cautiously and prayerfully for you stand on holy ground.

We will now consider each of these four dimensions and, by revelation of God's Spirit, see and understand how they fit into the great plan of God for his creation and why.

THE FOURTH DIMENSION—EDEN
(THE THRONE OF GOD)

This portion of our study begins with the second chapter of Genesis.[15] Here we are introduced to Eden with a very special garden in it. It is very important at the start of things not to confuse Eden with the garden that was in it as they represent two distinctly different things all together. The Garden of Eden was exactly just that, the Garden *of* Eden. In other words the garden that was in Eden or the spiritual dimension we will come to know as the fourth dimension.

THE RIVER OF GOD

At this point we are also introduced to a river that flowed out of Eden to water the garden[16] which spiritually represents the Spirit of God[17] that flows from the throne of God.[18] And, as much as the river has spiritual significance, so also the four heads into which the river flows, for they spiritually represent the four dimensions (or heavens) in God.[19]

EDEN SYNONYMOUS WITH HEAVEN

Eden and all the various things found in and around it all have spiritual significance and, by comparing scripture with scripture, we will come to understand just what those things are and represent.

Eden, first of all, spiritually represents heaven and the throne of God[20] and is the place where Christ in God alone rules from and is the highest spiritual realm which is also referred to in scripture as the heaven of heavens.[21] Christ alone directly inhabits this realm which is infinite for he is our God who alone inhabits eternity and which is the fourth dimension. Nowhere in Genesis do we find a specific description of Eden as such but only of the garden that was in Eden. However, in the book of Revelation, John gives us a glimpse into what that dimension looks like from the dimension that he was taken up into.

ONLY CHRIST INHABITS THE FOURTH DIMENSION

No angel or man, with the exception of Jesus Christ, has ever or will ever directly ascend to this dimension for it is the Father's throne. Only Christ, along with his church in him, has the right to sit down with the Father on his throne[22] for it is the throne that belongs to God and the Lamb alone[23] and it is therefore only Christ as the God-Man who directly resides in the fourth dimension with the Father.

Although the church of Jesus Christ also occupies the throne of Christ[24] and shares the same authority that he has with the Father, she only does so in and through him.[25] The church remains subject to Christ as he remains subject to the Father.[26] It is therefore only in and through Christ that we as the church may indirectly inhabit and experience the fourth dimension in as much as it was only in and the through the Garden of Eden that Adam could inhabit and experience Eden.[27] And it is only in and through Jesus Christ that we, as the church, have access to the Father for such is the Fourth Dimension, the Father.

THE THIRD DIMENSION—THE GARDEN (THE CHRIST OF GOD)

The Garden of Eden was a place that was especially provided by God for Adam and the angels to dwell in[28] and which comprised of a combination of both the spiritual as well as the physical dimensions also referred to in scripture as the third heaven[29] or third dimension and thereafter placed in Eden. The third dimension is also called the paradise of God and exists in Eden.[30] When Jesus said to the thief on the cross that he would be with him in paradise,[31] he was in effect saying "Take heart for today you will walk with me in the Garden of Eden".

NO MAN COMETH TO THE FATHER

Man and angel can only go as far as the third dimension. The fourth dimension is reserved exclusively for Christ alone and it is in and through the third dimension that we have a relationship with the Father who alone occupies the fourth dimension which is an infinite dimension also known as eternity. Jesus said that no man comes to the Father but through him.[32] Lucifer also once thought in his heart that he could ascend to Eden but soon found out that it was not possible for him to do so and found himself falling from the Garden of Eden[33] down to the earth[34] and eventually descended into hell.[35]

PAUL CAUGHT UP

The Apostle Paul was only "caught up" to the third heaven. He could go no further than that. He could go as far as the garden in Eden but not out of the garden into Eden. For Eden represents the very throne of God the Father[36] upon which only Christ alone may ascend. They that ascend the throne of God do so in and through him. It is for this reason that Christ said that those who overcome will be granted to sit with him on his throne even as he overcame and sat down with the Father on his throne.[37] For he who seeks to ascend the throne of God without being in Christ shall be consumed with everlasting fire for our God is a consuming fire.[38] No finite being can ever experience the infinite save he experiences it in and through him who alone is infinite. Our Lord Jesus Christ alone is both infinite and finite, both God and man; both Lord and Christ; both Alpha and Omega, both the spiritual and physical dimension. He is God almighty.[39]

THE THRONE OF GOD

And as much as the fourth dimension is said to represent the throne of God so the third dimension represents the place before and around the throne of God.[40] For as much as the garden was in Eden so the third dimension (Christ as the glorified man) exists within the fourth dimension (Christ as the life giving Spirit) and it is out of the third dimension that man and angels communicate with the everlasting Father.[41]

CHRIST THE FACE OF THE FATHER

All beings both in heaven and on earth who communicate with the Father do so in and through Christ.[42] When Jesus said that the angels behold the face of the Father[43] he was in effect saying that they look upon his face for he who sees him, sees the Father[44] for he alone is the face of God[45] and the express image of his glory.[46] Was so, is so and will always be so.

WHERE ADAM WALKED

It is in this dimension that God placed Adam in the day that he was created[47] and it was also in this dimension that God walked and talked with Adam.[48] Adam did not walk and talk with God in Eden as such, but in the Garden that was in Eden.

It was a garden that was made up of a special combination of both spiritual and physical dimensions for both spiritual (angels) as well physical (man, beast and plant) elements were found therein.[49] It is important to keep in mind that although the church of Christ exists with angels[50] in the third dimension she is by far more superior than the angels and have great authority and rulership over them[51] because she is the only one who partakes, by ascending the throne of God, of the forth dimension in Christ. And as much as the third dimension represents Christ, it also represents his church, for the two are one spirit.[52] The Garden of Eden in Genesis also refers to the New Jerusalem in the book of Revelation.[53]

Furthermore, it was a garden that God planted *in* Eden. In other words after God expressed himself as the spiritual dimension, Eden, he planted a very special place called the Garden of Eden in it and then placed the physical man, Adam in it. Adam could not dwell in Eden without dwelling in a place that was especially provided for him to dwell in.

THE NEW JERUSALEM

The reason why the New Jerusalem of Revelation 21:2 is said to be the Garden of Eden of Genesis 2:8 is because the same river that flowed through the garden in Genesis 2:10, also flows through the New Jerusalem in Revelation 22:1 and the same tree of life that stood in the midst of the garden in Genesis 2:9 is also the same tree of life that stands on either side of the river of the New Jerusalem in Revelation 22:2; 14. And the reason why Eden is said to represent the throne of God is because the same river that flowed out of Eden in Genesis 2:10 is also the same river that flows out of the throne of God in Revelation 22:1. The book Genesis is therefore, in truth, the shadow of the book of Revelation.

REVELATION THE EXPLANATION OF GENESIS

Revelation is in effect the explanation of Genesis in as much as the end is the explanation of the beginning and time the explanation of eternity. Man starts everything at the beginning and ends up at the end. God starts everything at the end and ends up at the beginning. Man's end is God's beginning. Man starts with life and ends with death. God starts with death and ends with life.[54] The experience of time comes before the experience of eternity in as much as the physical body must exist before the spiritual.[55] The old earth and heaven must exist and be experienced before the new, for the old is the fore-shadow[56] of the new. Man drinks first of the new wine before the old but with God he must first drink of the old wine before he can drink of the new.[57]

THE LADDER OF GOD AND THE GREAT DIVIDE

Now back to the garden. This special place speaks of Christ as the God-Man. He is the only one who is the connection between the spiritual and the physical dimensions for he alone is the combination of both dimensions as God and man. He alone is the mediator between God and man and the "ladder" upon which the angels of God descend and ascend between the spiritual and physical dimensions.[58] Christ alone is the gulf that divides the spiritual from the physical[59] and only he alone is the door[60] through which all must pass from one dimension into the next and it is therefore that he has all authority in both realms.[61]

CHRIST THE THIRD DIMENSION

Christ Jesus (as the God-Man) represents the third dimension which exists within the fourth dimension and the church within him. This is brought out by what Jesus once said when he claimed that he is in the Father and we, as the church, were him.[62] As much therefore as the garden was in Eden (the Father), so man (the church) was in the garden (Christ). Christ, as the third dimension, is also referred to in scripture as the secret place and shadow of the Almighty[63] because it is only in and through him that we can communicate with God and God with us.[64]

THE GARDEN WAS NOT "CREATED"

It is important to note that scripture does not say that God *created* a garden and placed it in Eden but that he simply *planted* or placed a garden in Eden.[65] The reason for this so being is because the garden is representative of Christ and Christ had no beginning and also has no end.[66] Jesus Christ as the life-giving Spirit is not a created being. He exists from all eternity to all eternity. Only his physical body on earth had a beginning and an end. As the life giving Spirit he is God forevermore!

What is also important to note is that Adam was not created from the ground of the garden but of the ground that existed outside of the garden[67] (a part of the physical dimension that God had not included in the make-up of the garden). It was also not the ground of the garden that was cursed for Adam's sake but the ground of the earth that existed outside of Eden from which he was taken in the day that he was created.

Death therefore does not exist in the paradise of God. This represents a deep spiritual truth and speaks of the translation of the church from the power of darkness, represented by the physical dimension under the influence of the devil, into the kingdom of God's dear Son.[68] We as the church of Jesus Christ were translated from death into life in as much as Adam was taken from the ground of the earth and placed in the garden of Eden.[69]

WATERED BY THE SPIRIT

Furthermore, it was only the garden that was watered by the river that flowed out of Eden[70] and not the earth out of which Adam was taken in the day that he was created; for such was watered by a mist (condensation of water by the sun) that rose up from the earth.[71] The river that flowed out of Eden and watered the garden was spiritual and speaks of the Spirit of God that flows from the throne of God and quickens the Word of God. In other words, it is Christ, as the life-giving Spirit, who emanates from the throne of God, and empowers his body, the church.

And although the garden speaks of Christ as the third dimension it also refers to the church of Christ for the two are one Life. Whatever therefore is true of him is also true of his church. We need only to discern, by the revelation of the Holy Spirit, when and where the types are to be applied to Christ and his church and to what extent.

THE GARDEN IN THE BEGINNING AND THE END

And as the garden was in the beginning so is it in the end. For out of Eden, God again brings forth the garden (the Bride of Christ clothed with the Christ)[72] and plants it this time on the new earth with "Adam and Eve" (the Spirit and the Bride)[73] still the keepers thereof. This is so that the physical dimension may once again be made alive by the spiritual dimension for without the spirit, the body is dead.[74]

In Genesis, God placed the garden in Eden[75] but now in Revelation he takes it out of Eden.[76] In the beginning when God created Adam he created him with Eve inside of him but then came a day when

God took Eve out of Adam and brought her to the man[77] and the two became one flesh.[78] Each endowed with his and her own personality and consciousness yet indivisibly one.[79]

So also in the day when God birthed his Son Jesus (the second Adam) in the flesh he did so with the church within him[80] yet in the day that he died (put to sleep), God brought forth the church (the second Eve) out of him and on the day the he was resurrected (awakened) he presented her to him without spot or wrinkle[81] and the two became one Spirit[82] and placed them both on the throne of God far above all principalities and power.[83] Each endowed with his and her own personality and consciousness yet indivisibly one.

THE DOMINION OF MAN

In the beginning God gave to the first Adam, both male and female, dominion over the earth[84] but in the end God gives to the second Adam, Christ and his church, dominion over both the spiritual dimension (heaven) as well as the physical dimension (earth).[85]

And as it is in time so has it always been in eternity. This, among others, is a deep mystery that was hidden in God before the foundation of the world but now in these last days is being revealed by the manifest sons of God[86] to the principalities and powers of the unseen world.[87]

Scripture abounds with types and anti-types of Christ and his church but always includes Christ and his church. Christ in his church and his church in him. God not only joined the church to Christ in time but also in eternity and what God has joined together no man can pull apart.[88] Always bear in mind that everything in scripture points to Christ and his church (the Spirit and the Word of God) for the two are one! To have the one without the other is the same as having clouds without water.[89] Neglecting to understand and apply this vital principle of God's kingdom, is to fail to rightly divide the word of Truth.[90]

THE CHURCH NOT AN AFTER-THOUGHT

The church is not an after-thought of God but a fore-thought.[91] It is the church who represents the Word of God and Jesus Christ, the Spirit of God; for there is one body (the church born out of the living word of God)[92] and one spirit (Jesus Christ, the life of the church). And the two shall be one! God has only got one Son that is made up of multiple trillions of men and women of all nations, tribes and tongues from the beginning of time and before who, through faith in the cross of Christ, has come to the knowledge of salvation. And only one Spirit that is one with the Word of God that became flesh and dwelled among us.

Jesus Christ was not the arch angel Michael in eternity as some would have us believe. For God has never at any time called any of his angels his son[93] nor was he such in time for he did not take on the nature of angels but that of man.[94] However, the arch angel Michael is nevertheless a type of Christ,[95] although not Christ himself. It was the Word of God that took on flesh,[96] not an angel of God.

CHRIST THE LIFE OF THE BODY

Jesus Christ is the head of the body[97] and not the arch angel Michael. The arch angel Michael, although a mighty and majestic angel above all God's angels, remains but a ministering spirit unto the heirs of salvation and subject to the church of Jesus Christ.[98]

Jesus Christ was not only man[99] but also God.[100] He was Emmanuel, God with us. The physical human body that the Spirit

63

indwelled, he no more occupies[101] for he has a new body, the church. Christ is therefore still on earth in physical form while at the same time on the throne of God in heaven in Spirit form. And likewise the church; she is not only on earth in physical form but also in heaven in spirit form.[102] Christ and his church, while physically on earth, are both spiritually in heaven. Christ dwells on earth in his physical body while the church dwells in heaven in her spiritual body.[103] The only difference between the two is the consciousness thereof.

When Jesus told his disciples that he would return to them again[104] he did not mean that he would only return to them at the end of the world but that he would also return to them in his true form and being as the Holy Spirit of God and be with them even to the end of the world[105] for that is who he really is. He is the life giving Spirit and the living Word of God[106] that was clothed with flesh and called Jesus Christ the Son of the God.[107] It was God the Father himself who was manifest in the flesh as the Son of God called Jesus Christ!

THE SPIRIT IS NOT THE SON

It was not the Spirit that was in Jesus that was called the Son of God but the body that encapsulated the Spirit.[108] The word "Christ" was also not the surname of Jesus but rather his status in God. He was anointed.[109] That is what the word "Christ" really means; the anointed of God. And that is what the church is, the anointed of God. In reality you are George, Peter, Mary, Michael the Christ! As much as our elder brother was Jesus, the Christ of God, I am John, the Christ (anointed) of God for in me also dwells the Holy Spirit.[110] Christ in me, the hope glory![111]

Bear in mind that only Jesus Christ as a man was the Son of God not Jesus Christ as the Spirit, for Jesus Christ as the life giving Spirit is the Word of God. Jesus once said that while he was yet on earth, he was at the same time in heaven.[112] Jesus Christ did not only exist in heaven as the Word of God, but on earth as the Son of God[113] and while he is such in heaven, his church is also so on earth.[114] The church is now the Son of God on earth with Christ being the Spirit of God within her. He is the head of the church. He is the Spirit of the Body and the two are one Life.

The Word of God is not clothed anymore with flesh save in the church of Christ. She is now the embodiment of the Spirit of God. The body which Jesus had when he walked on earth exist no more in that form for it was the seed that was sown and died and raised again incorruptible. It was sown a physical body and raised a spiritual body.[115] It was sown as flesh but raised as Spirit. Although glorified, Jesus Christ is now a man who is also God. Christ, the God—Man. God (the Father—the Spirit) made Jesus Christ (the Son—the Body—the Church), God.[116] In other words, God (Jesus Christ as the life giving Spirit), made his own body, (Jesus Christ the man), God. Great is the mystery of godliness!

THE BODY IS THE SON

While on earth Jesus occupied the office of the Son but now in heaven, as the Word of God, he is the High Priest after the order of Melchisedec existing to intercede on our behalf for evermore.[117] It is now the church who occupies the office of the Son of God on earth. It is for this reason that the whole creation waits eagerly for the revelation of the sons of God.[118] For their revelation is Christ's appearing.[119] The Word of God is still clothed with flesh; your flesh and mine. We are now the Son of God with Christ, our head in us, the Spirit of God. And the two are one Spirit. God has only got one Son—Christ and his church (the third dimension, the Lord Jesus Christ).

THE SECOND DIMENSION—EARTH
(THE SONS OF GOD)

The word "earth" has multiple meanings in scripture and its respective meanings must be understood within the context thereof. While the word earth primarily refers in scripture to the planet we live on,[120] in certain instances it refers only to the dry land[121] of the planet as opposed to the sea while in other instances it refers to the whole physical dimension[122] in which all the planetary systems exists.

When it is said therefore in the first verse of Genesis that in the beginning God created the heavens and the earth we are not to understand that the earth spoken of at that stage only comprised of the planet that we know as earth but rather the physical dimension in which the planet earth along with all other planetary systems would exist.

THE SPIRITUAL DIMENSION

In other words what Genesis 1:1 is really saying is that in the beginning God created the spiritual and the physical dimensions first; all things visible and invisible.[123] It was only after God had prepared a dimension in which physical elements could exist that he began to fill that dimension with those physical elements. God first laid the foundations of the earth[124] before he brought it into existence.

In fact Genesis 1:1-13 has really nothing to do with the creation of the material world as we know it at all, but everything to do with the spiritual world and the words used to describe that part of creation are only used metaphorically. The first, second and third days of creation are entirely spiritual and not physical. These words are describing the creation of heaven that included thrones, dominions, principalities, and powers[125] using earthly terminology to describe heavenly things.

THE PHYSICAL DIMENSION

I have no doubt that the physical dimension or world as we know it also literally included some of the things as described on the first, second and third day of creation in one way or another, but the description given of these first three days of creation are not pointing to the creation of physical things as such, but to the creation of spiritual things.

It is quite understandable that your immediate reaction to this deep revelation of God's word would be to reject it out of hand but, remember that scripture says it is foolishness to a man to reject a matter before he understands it.[126] Once you consider more closely what was done by God on these days of creation you will begin to understand that before God started to build the house he first laid the foundations thereof, for the spirit is the life of the body[127] in as much as the spiritual dimension is the life of the physical dimension and heaven, the life of the earth.

Although it is generally believed that God created both heaven and earth yet nowhere in scripture does it say just what and when God specifically did in the day that he created heaven other than the fact that God, in general, created heaven which included thrones, dominions, principalities and powers.[128] All you have is a specific description of what and when he seems to have done on the days that he created the earth. Also keep in mind that nowhere in scripture does it say that God only created the earth in six days and on the seventh day he rested. It says that God created the *heaven* and the *earth* in six days and rested on the seventh day.[129]

NOT ONLY THE EARTH

Creation therefore did not only include the earth but also heaven. In understanding this truth one eventually comes to realize that in reality God only took three days (or divisions of time) to create the material world and three days to create the immaterial world and that the spiritual dimension was brought into existence before the physical dimension. It is very interesting to note further that scripture makes mention that the Lord shall be "perfected" on the third day.[130] This is most likely referring to the resurrection of our Lord Jesus Christ on the third day. However, be that as it may, the number three in biblical numerics often refers to a period of perfection.

This spiritual truth is also brought out when Jesus said that he would build the "temple" within three days of it being destroyed. Although the three days mentioned here again more specifically refers to the fact that the holy one of God would not see corruption in not being more than three days in the tomb, it may also refer to the fact that God perfected the physical world in three days or divisions of time.

THE DIVISION OF DIMENSIONS

The division of day and night that established the first three days of creation was not determined by the revolution of the earth around its own axis in relation to the sun, moon and stars, but by the Spirit of God that "moved upon the face of the waters"[131]

If one takes everything that was created from day one to day six literally then the description of creation as described in Genesis makes no sense at all. No wonder there are so many scientist that do not believe in the literal six days of creation. The creation account in Genesis could not possibly only consist of the physical world but also the spiritual for the "furniture" of God consists of both a throne (heaven) as well a footstool (earth) for it is from the spiritual dimension that God rules in the physical dimension. It is from heaven that God rules on earth.

THE SUN ON THE FOURTH DAY

The first day of creation could not have been the creation of the material world as there were as yet no material elements in the universe to determine the division of light and darkness of that day. It was only on the fourth day that such elements were created and only from thereon could the division of light and darkness be determined in order to make one day. Most Bible commentators also agree that God, in terms of the Genesis account of creation, only created the sun on the fourth day. And furthermore if one is to accept that the earth existed as a physical entity on the first day while the sun was only created on the fourth day then one must logically believe, seen from a natural perspective, that the earth was at that time one ball of solid ice and where the fluid waters came from at that time only God alone knows. It is true that with God all things are possible[132] but God is nevertheless not the author of confusion but of peace![133] We must not always conveniently ascribe the things that we cannot understand and that are sometimes confusing to us to the omnipotence of God merely to avoid our responsibility to search the scripture for understanding.[134]

A MERE CONVENIENCE

There are many who often conveniently misuse the scripture that says we only know in part now but then in full forgetting that the "then" that Paul was speaking about was not so much about the life hereafter but when that which was "perfect" would come and the perfect[135] which he was referring to was not so much about heaven as it was about love! Paul was in effect saying that if we had the God kind of love (Agape) towards one another we would no longer have prophesy and knowledge in part but in full because the pure unconditional love of God would enable us to know as we are known and to comprehend what is the breadth, and length, and depth, and height.[136] To accept anything less would render 1Corinthians 2:9-16 meaningless.[137]

PREPARATION FIRST

It is furthermore a scientific fact that the earth could not possibly have sustained any form of life without the existence of the sun or any form of light. Yet on the third day God created vegetable life. It would seem to me, with the greatest of respect at this point, that God had his priorities back to front. For no one plants a tree first and then digs a hole to put it in. Not even God, although he could do so if he wanted to. Jesus once said that he was going away to prepare a place for us[138] and once it was prepared he would then come and take us to it. Not first take us to the place and then prepare it!

LUDICROUS THINKING

It would be ludicrous to believe that God would first build a house and then after a few days dig a hole to lay the foundations for it.[139] Yet we readily believe that God would first create the earth with clouds and vegetable life on and then only think of putting the sun in the sky to sustain it. Keeping in mind that clouds were actually created through the process of condensation of water by the sun and hence the mist that rose from the earth[140] to water the whole earth. No wonder there are so many who find the Genesis account of creation so hard to swallow. For in terms of the creation account of Genesis, the earth existed long before the sun was created and, not only that, but that it existed without the need for any life to be sustained by the sun.

It is furthermore erroneous thinking to believe that the creation of the heavenly bodies that were created on the fourth day is the same heaven that scripture is referring to in Genesis 1:1. The heaven referred to in this verse is referring to the spiritual dimension wherein spiritual beings dwell and not the heaven that is referred to in Genesis 1:14.

THE TWO FIRMAMENTS

The firmament of the heaven referred to in Genesis 1:14 is the expanse or physical dimension of heaven wherein the planetary systems exist and not heaven itself wherein angelic beings exist as indicated in Genesis 1:8. In Genesis 1:8 the firmament itself is called heaven and from thereon everything material existed within the firmament of that heaven. In other words we are dealing with two firmaments; one which is called heaven and the other which exists within heaven.

To put it a simpler way, the firmament of Genesis 1:6-8 is said to be the space[141] between the waters (clouds) and the waters (seas) yet in Genesis 1:14-19 the firmament here is said to be the space wherein all the planetary systems (sun, moon and stars) dwell.[142] So if you put the two scripture verses to together you will discover that the sun, moon and stars are in actual fact not very far away from the earth, because in terms of Genesis 1:8;14 they exist in the sky between the earth and the clouds. Absolute nonsense you may say. Well, that's exactly my point. Glad you could see it!

DAY WITH A CAPITAL "D"

The foundation of the physical dimension is the spiritual dimension. God created heaven long before he created earth. The spirit is the life of the body. Adam was created before Eve. It was also out of Adam that God brought forth Eve. Adam was also not created before there was a spirit of life that God could blow into his nostrils that enabled him to become a living soul. The spirit therefore existed before the body was created yet came to exist within the body that was created.

In order to better understand what creation is all about we need to take a closer look at the first day of creation and what was brought into existence on that day. Scripture tells us that the first thing that God created (or brought into existence) was light, also called the Day with a capital "D". Genesis 1:3; 4 says "and God said let there be light . . . and God called the light Day"

TRADITIONAL THINKING

It has always been the traditional way of thinking and teaching of some that the light that was brought into existence on that day was the light that we now know as the sun, moon and stars. For it is only by the revolution of the earth around its own axis, in relation to these heavenly bodies, that we have the division of day and night. However, it was only on the fourth day, in terms of Genesis 1:14-19, that God created these heavenly bodies called the sun, moon and stars and if this be so, by what means then did God determine the "evening" and the "morning" that brought about the first, second and third days. And what light was in actual fact brought into existence on the first day of creation if it was not the sun?

For the answers to these questions one must go back to the written word of God. For it is only when we compare scripture with scripture and spiritual things with spiritual things that we are able to understand the deep things of God as they are revealed to us by the Spirit of God.

CHRIST THE FIRST DAY

There are three very specific places in scripture that clearly indicate to us what it is that was "in the beginning" of the creation of God. In John 1:1 it says that "in the beginning was the word" and in 1John 1 it says "that which was in the beginning" was "the word of life" and again in Revelation 3:14 it specifically says that Jesus was the "beginning of the creation of God" If this then is indeed so then somewhere else in scripture Jesus must also be referred to as the "light" and the "day". In John 8:12 Jesus said that he was the light of the world and 1 Thessalonians 5:5 it says that we (the church of Jesus Christ) are the children of the light and of the day. Also in 2 Peter 1:19 and speaking of Jesus, scripture calls him the day and day star. So in terms of the above scriptures we are told that in the beginning of God's creation of all things Christ was the light that was first brought into existence out of darkness and called the Day.[143]

Christ was indeed the first day of creation. In fact he was not only the first day but also the second and third day. He was the days that did not need the earth to revolve around its own axis in relation to other heavenly bodies in order to determine the division between light and darkness to make a day. It was the Word of God by the Spirit of God that brought about the division of light and darkness that established the existence of the first, second and third days of creation; for the Word of God, which is sharper than any two edged sword, is the Sword of the Spirit of God, and it is this which brings about division of all things in the spiritual dimension.[144]

THE EXPRESSION OF GOD

God the Father, through the expression of his own Word and Spirit, was the determining factor that divided the light from the darkness that brought about the establishment of the first, second and third days of creation. The words used at this point of creation were only used metaphorically in order to instruct us in the deep things of God.[145]

Now, if Christ was the light that was brought into existence on the first day, who then was the darkness out of which that light shone? In order for us to properly understand who this darkness was out of which the light shone, we need to understand firstly that darkness in the true sense of the word is not to be understood to be only a bad or sinful thing in its self although such word is also used in scripture to indicate bad and sinful things and, it is in this regard, that it is said that God is light and in him there is no darkness at all.[146]

THE DARKNESS OF GOD

For one to hold that darkness is only a bad thing is to hold that the day which God made and, which comprised of both the light and darkness, is a bad thing. Notwithstanding the fact that God said it was a good thing. You see, God intended that a day should always comprise of both the light and darkness for therewith could he show us that without the body (light) the spirit (darkness) had no expression and without the darkness the light had no meaning. For how would you know that light was light if you had no darkness with which to compare it?

There are many places in scripture where darkness is said to be something that God holds to be good and not bad yet in the same breath the word "darkness" is often used in scripture to be something that is bad and must be avoided. When darkness represents the bad it represents unrighteousness, evil, ignorance, sin and the devil. But when it represents the good it represents deep mysteries, profound truths, secret places, and God. It is however only through the leading of God's Holy Spirit that we are able to discern when and where the word "darkness" represents the good and when and where it represents the bad; for such is the tree of knowledge, it is the knowledge of both good and bad.

In 1 Kings 8:12 we find that God said that he will dwell in thick darkness. In Psalm 18:11 it says that God made darkness his secret place. David again says in Psalm 97:2 that God covers himself with darkness. In Isaiah 45:7 it says that God creates darkness. Yet in 1John 1:5 it says that God is light and in him is no darkness at all. Again in 2Corinthians 6:14 it says that light has no communion with darkness. When one therefore considers these scriptures then it is clear that the word "darkness" does not only denote things bad, but also things good.

DARKNESS IS ETERNAL

Darkness existed long before there was any light. In fact darkness existed before there was anything in creation but God. Darkness has always existed with God and will always exist with God. Darkness is the mantle of God wherein he dwells as the light forever. And when scripture says that God divided the light from the darkness it simply means that out of darkness God brought forth the light and gave each its own individual existence apart from each other yet forever one with each other.

The day will always consist of both light and darkness. Equal in length and strength and both glorifying the handy work of God for the two are one; Day and Night, the Spirit and the bride, Christ and his church, the Spirit and the body, the spiritual dimension and the physical dimension, heaven and earth, the Spirit of God and the Word of God, Life and Death . . . God!

THE FIRST THREE DAYS OF CREATION

This then was the first day of creation; the manifestation of the Christ (the sons of God) out of God. God revealing himself as the Word, darkness clothed with light. The Spirit clothed with a Body and Death encapsulated with Life.

The second day of creation speaks equally of the first day. For here God creates the firmament that would serve as the divide between the waters and the waters. And as the light represented Christ on the first day, so also on second day the firmament represents Christ who is the great divide between the waters (third dimension) wherein dwell spiritual beings and the waters (second dimension), wherein dwell physical beings.

And finally on the third day God turns his attention specifically to Christ and his church by separating the waters (Christ the Spirit—the third dimension) and the dry land (Christ the Body—the second dimension) and giving to the dry land the blessing of fruitfulness to bring forth life in abundance that all who may dwell upon her and within her presence, may enjoy the blessings of God. For although Eve (the church) came from Adam (Christ), all life thereafter came out of Eve.

All three days of creation therefore speak only of Christ and his church using metaphorical concepts and deep secret meanings in order to reveal the light that was hidden in the darkness before the foundation of the world. And as the first three days of creation speak of Christ and his church so also do the whole of scripture from Genesis through to Revelation. It was Jesus Christ himself who said that what he tells us in darkness[147] (in secret) we are to tell others in the light (openly).

SCRIPTURE ONLY ABOUT CHRIST

And it was also our Lord who once said that the whole of scripture speak of him[148] (including his church for the two are one) but men refused to come to him. This is so because men have rejected the truth for the lie and have worshiped the creature more than the creator.[149] You may also decide to reject this truth of the first three days of creation as nonsense yet you will remain unable to plausibly explain what the light was that was brought into existence on the first day and how the first, second and third days were determined to be days consisting of day and night when the sun, moon and stars were only created on the fourth day or how it is possible that the sun, moon and stars are said to exist in the sky between the clouds and the earth. And remember, it is foolishness and a shame for a man to judge a matter to be right or wrong before he fully understands it.[150] Such is the second dimension. Earth (the body)—the Sons of God—the Church.

THE FIRST DIMENSION—HELL
(THE VENGEANCE OF GOD)

Of all the dimensions in God, this dimension, which is also said to be under the earth[151] (or below the second dimension), must surely be the one that is least understood for it is in this dimension that God, as the End, is shown to be who he really is as the Omega. It is in this dimension that God is revealed to be that which we have always been taught to reject as not being a part of God in any way at all.

The reason for this is because this part of God has been veiled in time past until now but in these last days is being revealed to the manifest sons of God in order that they may truly come to understand that he alone is the Lord of all. He alone is both the Alpha and Omega, the Beginning and the End of all things. We have always only known God as the Beginning but now in the first dimension in the last days of time we are introduced to God as the End. For I sincerely believe that it is now the time to reveal what the seven thunders had uttered.[152]

GOD NOT ONLY LIGHT

It has always been the understanding of some that God is only light and not darkness only life and not death for we are taught that the devil is death and God is life as though God is the beginning and the devil is the end.

There is really no basis in scripture that sustains this kind of doctrine for it is God alone who is the beginning and end of all things. When scripture says that in him there is no darkness (see 1John 1:5) it really means that in God's nature there is no unrighteousness, ignorance or sin and not that there is no darkness as a creature in him. For all things are from him, through him and back to him.[153] All things have their being and existence in the omnipresence of God for God knows everything, can do anything and is everywhere all at the same time!

WHERE GOD BEGINS

The beginning of God is not light but darkness not life but death for it is out of darkness (himself) that God expressed himself as the light[154] and it is out of death that he expresses himself as life.[155] Out of destruction he brings restoration.[156] It is out of that which is lost that God has that which is found.[157] Man begins with that which is good and ends up with that which is bad. But God begins with that which is bad and ends up with that which is good! When your situation is bad it is then that God makes all things work together for your good![158] God begins with the physical and ends with the spiritual.[159] Man begins with the new wine and ends with the old but God begins with the old wine and ends with the new.[160] Out of corruption God brings the incorruptible.[161] Out of the Old Testament he brings forth the New.[162]

The seed must first die before it can live! From God's perspective, everything began with that which was lost by his foreknowledge of time. But in the end, in his reality of eternity, everything is found. Everything was corrupt but now everything is incorruptible. Everything was dark but now everything is light. The prodigal son was first lost then found, first dead and then made alive. The night is the first part of the day. There was evening first then there was morning the first day. The physical (flesh, death, darkness, the letter that kills, the first Adam, Old Testament, Adam and Eve, the old Israel the old earth and heaven) is first and then comes the spiritual (spirit, life, light, the spirit that gives life, the second Adam, New Testament, Christ and his church, the new Israel, the new earth and heaven).

God is not only the first source of all life he is also the first source of all death. He is the first source of all the physical dying and also the first source of all the spiritual dying. God is the second death (the lake of fire) spoken of in scripture. No one but God is the one who gives all life and is also the one alone who takes all life. It is he alone who kills and makes alive again.[163] Vengeance belongs to no one else but God alone.[164] He alone is the Life of life and the Death of death.

THE DEVIL IS NOT DEATH

Scripture does not say that the devil is death but the destroyer.[165] Not death, but one having the power of death[166] and only so much power as God permits.[167] Not the power of spiritual death, but of physical death. And it is this death that will be cast in to the lake of fire[168] which, in scripture, is also called the second death and it is in this regard that God is the Death of death.

Physical death is temporal and is the separation of all physical beings from temporal physical life which is the first death and is also called in scripture, the last enemy of Christ,[169] and it will be this death that will placed under his feet. For all things in the physical dimension is the footstool of the great King![170] Physical death only kills the body but spiritual death obliterates the soul[171] and returns the spirit back to God who gave it[172] and where it remains eternally void of any knowledge or memory of previous existence;[173] for the soul exists no more because the two vital parts that make up the soul are separated. The spirit and body have no memory, will or emotion of their own, they both have one memory, will and emotion and that resides as the soul. Not in the soul, but as the soul. Without it, the soul does not exist anymore for they are the soul.[174]

Spiritual death (the lake of fire) is eternal[175] (everlasting) as only God is eternal[176] and is the separation of all spiritual beings from eternal spiritual life, which is the second death and is the nature of God for he alone gives and takes life, physical and spiritual.[177] It is only God who is the power that can separate any creature eternally from the memory of its own previous existence[178] by separating his spirit from his body.

ERRONEOUS THINKING

It is erroneous thinking to believe that the devil is the one who punishes those in hell. Vengeance does not belong to the devil but to God.[179] It is God himself who is the lake of fire, the second death for only our God alone is a consuming fire wherein all things are consumed, the devil included.[180] It is only God that after killing the body has the power to cast the soul into hell (another word symbolizing the lake of fire or second death) and, keep it there . . . eternally.[181] Keep in mind that the word "hell" has various different meanings in scripture and has to be understood in the context thereof in order for one to rightly divide the word of truth.[182]

THE FIRE THAT CONSUMES

Those who are cast into the lake of fire (the final end of those currently existing in the first dimension in the mind of God) do not exist eternally therein as though they have eternal life spent in anguish but rather that they are eternally consumed therein and the memory of their existence eternally blotted out of God's book of remembrance.[183] For although fire oftentimes refines and purges,[184] its primary nature is to burn up. Leaving nothing behind, neither root nor branches, but ashes.[185]

THE PROCESS OF DEATH

It will only be the process of that dying that will bring eternal anguish (in quality and not in quantity) and not the end thereof. The lake of fire is not a place wherein the wicked will live forever but where their worm (the cause of their pain) will never die and the fire (the source of their destruction) will never be quenched.[186] It is therefore not so much the length of the dying but the strength thereof that makes the difference and it is for this reason that man is no so much afraid of death as he is of dying.

To die by fire is said to be the most excruciating process of death in the physical dimension and, as it is in the physical, so is it in the spiritual. It is also for this reason that many have said that they would like to die in their sleep rather than go through any excruciating pain before death. There is no man on earth that truly believes that the dead rest in pain but rather in peace and it is therefore that the letters R.I.P on tombstones do not mean "Rest in Pain" but rather "Rest in Peace".

There is no pain in death after dying for the dead know nothing.[187] There is no pain in death, only in dying. For dying is the journey and death is the destination and once the destination has been reached the journey ends. It is therefore the process of death and not death itself, that will be painfully experienced by those who are cast into the lake of fire.[188] For God that process will be but a fleeting moment but for all those who go through it, it will be experienced as though it is an eternity.[189]

It is truly a fearful thing to fall into the hands of the Almighty God.[190] But as much as he is a God of vengeance he is also a God of mercy. And it is therefore that he invites all and sundry to come now and drink of the water of life while there is yet time.[191] Those who come, do show thereby that they are indeed the called in Christ before the foundation of the world. For no man can come, in time, unless he was given to Christ, in eternity.[192] It is also for this reason that Jesus Christ gave his life, so that all who believe in him (by the foreknowledge of God) should not die but have everlasting life.[193]

THE PASSING OVER OF DIMENSIONS

Those in the first dimension (hell) cannot pass over into the third dimension (paradise—also called "Abraham's bosom") for there is a gulf that divides all dimensions from each other and Jesus Christ alone is that divide.[194] He alone is the door through which all must pass from one dimension into the next.[195]

It was into this first dimension (hell) that Jesus descended[196] from the second dimension (earth) to set free the dead (through the preaching of the gospel) that where held captive therein and from whence he ascended into the third dimension[197] (the paradise of God, the garden of Eden).

Once he delivered the spirits of the dead to the third dimension he returned to the second dimension in order to show himself to his disciples.[198] And after having spoken to his disciples he then ascended past the third dimension into the fourth dimension[199] to the Father[200] from where, with his bride (the church), he now forever rules as God almighty.[201] Such is the First Dimension, hell . . . the place of the dead . . . the devil.

CHAPTER FIVE

"THE FIFTH THUNDER SOUND"

THE MYSTERY OF TIME

INTRODUCTION

The following may at first leave you feeling as though you are spiraling through a worm hole in space without any sense of direction of what is up and what is down but don't worry, you will soon come to realize as we proceed, what is up and what is down, what is fiction and what is real, what is temporal and what is eternal.

LOSS OF MEMORY

To begin with, scripture says that there is no remembrance (or awareness) of former things; neither shall there be any remembrance of things that are to come with those that shall come after.[1] In other words, we who exist on earth lack remembrance of the things that have taken place in heaven and those in hell will lack remembrance of things done on earth.

The time has however arrived for the church to begin understanding her true existence and not only her past experience in time concerning this life, but of her existence concerning eternity.[2] Once the church becomes aware of who, where, and why she is in eternity, in relation to the Christ, there will be no more need for time for then she will have reached her full stature in Christ, being no more feeble and tossed about by every wind of doctrine.[3]

FIRST THINGS FIRST

Time only exists in the mind of God in order that the church may understand the consequences of her rebellion. Rebellion that had not, in God's reality, taken place; for Christ is the lamb slain before the foundation of the world and therefore the church is also saved before the foundation of the world. In other words, before the consequences of rebellion could exist in time God provided the remedy in eternity.

It is therefore that God can speak of the church as being something in eternity before she even existed in time. For she is said not only to be foreknown by God in eternity, but also predestined to be conformed to the image of his Son in time by already being called, justified and glorified.[4] God did not call, justify and glorify the church of Jesus Christ only in time, but in eternity; long before she could rebel in time. God has, is and will always be first in all things.[5]

NOTHING LOST IN ETERNITY

Jesus came into the world to save that which was lost,[6] in time, but not in eternity. In eternity (God's reality) nothing was lost.[7] In other words, things are only lost by God's foreknowledge of time (man's reality) and not lost in eternity (God's reality). That which was done in eternity eventually played out in time. When the right time came[8] God sent his son, by his foreknowledge, into the world to perform, in the physical dimension, that which had already taken place in the spiritual dimension and although scripture speaks of this yet very few really understand or any have any knowledge of it.[9]

NOTHING CHANGES

The death of Jesus Christ really did historically take place in time (in man's reality) but not before it first took place in eternity (in God's reality). And it was that which took place in eternity that will never pass away although it passes away in time. In eternity it stands unchanged forever.[10] Jesus will therefore always be remembered as the Lamb slain before the foundation of the world and not as one slain during the existence of the world. For our reality is not God's fact. It is his fact that will eventually become our reality.

This is a great mystery, but in God's reality, Christ died in eternity before the church could ever rebel in time. The rebellion of the church only took place in God's foreknowledge of time and not in God's reality of eternity. In God's reality the church has always and will always remain untainted by sin because he provided the solution in eternity before the church fell in time.

God succeeded before man could fail because God does not have to wait for man to act so that he can re-act. God never re-acts. He is eternally pro-active. Man thinks God acts because he prays little realizing that he prays because God has acted.[11]

FAILURE BY FOREKNOWLEDGE

Man only failed by God's foreknowledge thereof. Everything Christ did and went through in time he had already done and gone through in eternity. Time is only a reflection of eternity. A foreshadow thereof, and not the reality. Time only exists in order that we may know what was already done in eternity. Nothing can change what God has done. Nothing can be added to it nor taken away from it.[12] Everything that will exist in the eternal future has already existed in the eternal past and currently exists in God's eternal present.[13]

As the church will be in the end so is she now and so has she ever been. And as the devil and his angels along with all things wicked will be in the end so are they now and so have they ever been. No one is going to hell that is not there already in the mind of God! This is God's perspective of things and with him nothing changes or passes away. Everything is eternally constant with God. Those who will be condemned and banished to an eternal hell are there already and have ever been there in God's eternity.[14]

To put it another way, a person would say that he believes that God knows everything; even the end from the beginning. Well, if that is true then God must surely know who are all in hell at the end of time, right? And if that is true then surely what God knows to be true in the end has always been true with him in the beginning because scripture says that God knows the end from the beginning. In fact God is the beginning and end!

HELL IN ETERNITY

And if that is true then all who are going be in hell in the end are already there from the beginning in the mind of God and have always been there. Eternity with God has no beginning and no end only an eternal present. What therefore is going to be has always been and what has always been, always is now. God is forever in the present and everything else along with him.

Time only serves to witness of God's righteousness[15] in taking action before any other action by man could ever take place. Make no mistake, what you and I experience now in the time is very real to us but to God it is something that only exists in his awareness by his foreknowledge in eternity of time.[16]

Time is merely the unfolding of God's thoughts[17] in eternity. This may be very hard for you to understand now but through God's Spirit all things will be revealed, for he has come to reveal all truth[18] because he searches the deep things of God[19] in order to reveal it to the church. Revelation and the mysteries of the kingdom of God only belong to Christ and his church and to no one else.[20] And through the church, God will eventually reveal his mysteries to all of his creation.[21]

JOB A TYPE OF THE CHURCH

The church's unawareness of her position in Christ is typified when God once asked Job where he was when God laid the foundations of the earth and the sons of God shouted for joy.[22] Job of course could not answer God at that time as he could not remember. God did not ask Job a question that had no answer but a question that could not be answered because Job had no awareness of his previous existence in God. If Job had memory of his eternal past he would simply have answered God by saying "I was there with you Lord shouting for joy because I was in Christ from the very beginning[23] and Christ was with you from all eternity creating all things that exist".[24]

ALWAYS ONE

There was never a time that the church was not a part of Christ. Just as it was out of Adam that God took Eve[25] even so it is that out of Christ that God has brought forth the church. Christ and his church have always been one in every way; for such is the manifestation of God from all eternity.[26] What is therefore true of Christ in eternity is also true of his church; for what exists now has always existed, and what has existed will always exist in the future. And that which shall exist in the eternal future has always existed in the eternal past and both exist in the eternal present with God.[27] Like a circle that has no beginning or end so is it with eternity in God.

WHAT CHURCH?

People often ask me to what "church" I belong to in order that they may thereby determine what specific brand of doctrine I have in thinking the way that I do. In answer to their question I simply answer that I do not belong to any specific denomination or "church" . . . I am the church! Every one of us who are in Christ are living stones build up as a holy temple (church—*ecclesia* or the called) of the Lord.[28] Jesus did not say that we are to go out and build buildings and call them churches. He said we must go out and teach all nations, making disciples [29] and calling them the sons of God.[30]

Not only are we collectively the temple (church) of God but also individually so.[31] Please don't get me wrong, I am not saying that you must get not together with your brothers and sisters in the Lord for a time of fellowship in a building of some sort. On the contrary, you aught to it all the more as you see the day of the Lord drawing near.[32] However, you must not be deceived into thinking that you are going *to the church* to do so, but rather that you are going *as the church* to do so.

THE CHURCH HAS NO OTHER NAME

There is no such thing as the Body of Christ being called the "Full Gospel Church", the "Anglican Church", or the "Roman Catholic Church" etc; for that is indeed all that they are, the church (or denomination) that belongs to the Full Gospels, the Anglicans and the Roman Catholics. They are not necessarily the church of Jesus Christ that is made up of the sons of God and called by his name.[33] In the denominational churches you will find all kinds of people, believers and unbelievers alike, but not so in the church of Jesus Christ. In the body of Christ there are no unbelievers, for light and darkness cannot dwell under the same roof and has nothing in common with each other.[34]

FROM EVERY NATION, TRIBE AND TONGUE

It is also not any specific denomination that has the name "The church of Jesus Christ" engraved on their building corner stone that is the true church of Christ, but individuals of every nation, tribe and tongue that has the cross of Christ branded within their hearts by the Holy Spirit of God and, who follow the pure unadulterated word of God wherever it goes, that are deemed to be the true church of Christ, whether they are members of a denomination or not.

But didn't Jesus say that we must go into all the world and make disciples? Yes he did. He said *go out* into all the world. Not bring all the world into you. It is only once we have made believers out of the unbelievers, that they are entitled to partake of our fellowship (in communion) as our brothers and sisters in Christ. In allowing unbelievers to form part of our assembly as members thereof is tantamount to not properly discerning the body of Christ.[35] What God says of us individually, he says of us collectively and *vice versa*. The church of Jesus Christ is the bride of the Spirit and in her must not be found anything that is defiled for she is a pure.[36]

THE DENOMINATIONAL CHURCH

The sad state of affairs that now exist within the denominational "churches" that have been created by men is the result of the fact that they were all ignorant of the word of God (were all sleeping). Jesus said that while men slept, the enemy (the devil) sowed (added) tares (his children) among the wheat (the children of the kingdom of God). He said however that we were not to try and separate the tares from the wheat (for the angels in the last day will do that) but that we as the wheat must come out from among them and be separate.

This may sound all very confusing to you but it simply means that although we are not to try and identify and separate the tares from the wheat, we are to recognize that we are the wheat by discerning the true word of God through His Holy Spirit and in so doing separate our ourselves from the tares.

If you know therefore that the word that you are receiving is false then you have a duty upon you to come out from among them. Don't accept their words merely because you want to be a man pleaser. Jesus said the day is coming and now is that men will not endure sound doctrine but having itching ears will heap unto themselves preachers that will preach to them those things that they long to hear, teaching for doctrines, the commandments of men. Come out from among them and be ye separate says the Lord.

ETERNAL SALVATION

There are many in these so-called denominational churches today who do not accept that once a person is saved he is forever saved. They have a doctrine that teaches that God has a whole lot of sons and daughters eventually ending up in hell and that the saving grace of God is often frustrated by the hell bent ways of a man. They do not teach that salvation is of the Lord but of man. Not by grace but by works (see Titus 3:5). Works have indeed a place when it comes to faith (see James 2:18) but it has nothing whatsoever to do with salvation (see Ephesians 2:8-10) One must understand that those who are saved in time are those who were already saved in eternity by the foreknowledge of God. In other words, if one was not saved in eternity one will never be saved in time. Salvation is therefore not depended upon what man does in time but upon what God has done in eternity (see Rom 9:13-16).

They often quote passages of scripture such as Hebrews 6:4-8 in order to substantiate their claims that a saved person can end up lost and in hell at the end of the day but fail to understand that God has already finished the work of salvation before the foundation of the world (see Romans 8: 28-30) and had it not been so it would indeed have been impossible for those who were once enlightened, and have tasted the heavenly gifts, and were made partakers of the Holy Spirit, to be renewed to repentance should they fall away.

The focus however must not be placed on the impossibility of being renewed again but on the impossibility of falling away to destruction (see John 10:28; 29). For if it were possible for one, being born again, to fall away to destruction after being saved then it would indeed be impossible to renew such to repentance again. But scripture emphatically teaches that it is impossible for one who is truly born again into the kingdom of God to again loose that position in Christ simply because the election was made sure in eternity and not in time (see Romans 9:11; Hebrews 10:14). It is therefore possible for a born again Christian to backslide (see Proverbs 24:16) into the world for a while (see Luke 15:11-32) but it is not possible for such a person to fall away to destruction and ultimately end up in hell (see 1John 3:9). For those who end up in hell at the end of time were those who were there, in the mind of God, before time began!

Those who are therefore saved are not saved because they chose God in time but because God chose them in eternity (see Ephesians 1:4). Salvation is therefore not of man but of God (see Revelation 19:1). Jesus said that it was not possible for the elect to be deceived! (see Mark 13:22) Those who do fall away to destruction after being enlightened, and having tasted the heavenly gifts, and were made partakers of the Holy Spirit are those who were not really part of the body of Christ to begin with. (see Acts 1:16-20) They are those who were only called, in time, but not chosen in eternity; for many are called but only a few are chosen (see Matthew 22:14). Those who eventually fall away to destruction are in actual fact the "tares" that were sown among the "wheat" (see Matthew 13:24-40). They are burned in the end as tares because they were tares to begin with!

GOD'S BEGINNING AND END

God's end has and always will be his beginning and *vice versa*. If one wants to know what the beginning was like one needs only to read in scripture what the end is going to be like and the scripture says that in the end everything is going to be perfect without any death or pain.

And if in the eternal future every is going to be perfect with the church on the throne of God ruling over all the nations with a rod of iron[37] then so was it in the beginning and, so is it now. Nothing has changed and nothing can change that.[38] Change from one event to another and from one day to the other only takes place in time and not in eternity. In eternity everything has, will, and always shall remain the same.[39]

Time and the things that take place in it is merely a projection of God's foreknowledge of things he knew would take place had he not intervened in eternity. What man currently thinks is reality is merely his conscious experience of God's imagination.

TIME A FRACTION OF ETERNITY

Time is only a fraction of eternity. It is one insignificant blip on a line that has no beginning and no end and which only exists in the conscious mind (awareness) of God and the physical experience of the church; soon to vanish away without any trace of ever having existed other than in the mind of man and the foreknowledge of God. In reality you are, if you are part of the church through the saving grace God in Christ Jesus, currently sitting on the throne of God without any realization of the fact that what you think is real, on earth, is merely a conscious experience of God's foreknowledge of time.

What happened in time two thousand years ago already happened in eternity before the beginning of time. The reason that it took place in the mind of God before time commenced is so that God could pre-empt the consequences of the Luciferian rebellion he saw before it could happen in eternity and yet still judge and condemn all those he foreknew would take part in that rebellion.

GOD ETERNALLY PROACTIVE

Before anything can happen, God acts. The devil (a spiritual being bound by the physical dimension) only exists in time and not in eternity. For he does not exist in the end and therefore neither did he exist in the beginning, in God's reality (eternity) because Lucifer the archangel, was judged, condemned and banished into eternal oblivion (the lake of fire, the second death) in the mind of God, even before he could think of ever rebelling against God; and with him, his angels and all those who, in time by God's foreknowledge, proved that God is justified in acting before the event.[40]

Oh nonsense, you may hasten to say. How can God take action against anyone before they've done anything wrong? Well, consider the following before you think you know what God can and cannot do.

Before Jacob and Esau was born or had done anything good or bad, God decided to reject Esau and accept Jacob, to love Jacob and to hate Esau.[41] Not based on what they did or did not do but based on election by the foreknowledge of God in order that his purpose in eternity might stand. God did not have to wait for Jacob or Esau to do anything good bad before he could act. He acted based on what he knew in eternity and not on what they did or did not do in time.

Jesus also once said that a thought is tantamount to an action.[42] God is therefore also justified to act based on the thoughts of a man's heart. God does not have to wait until a man's thoughts are expressed in an act before he can take action. He is sovereign and therefore can do all that he wills without having to explain himself to anyone.

God does not love you because you are good but because he is God. For only God is good.[43] If a man lives a good life, it is because God is the life that is good in man. There is no man on earth that does good save it is God who is doing it. No matter how bad you are, if God has chosen in eternity to love and bless you then nothing can change that. Man is saved by grace and grace alone. Not by works lest any man should boast. It is God alone who wills and works in man to do that which pleases him. It is not he who wills or he who runs but he who calls and shows mercy. The good works that man performs have all been prepared by God before time began for man to walk therein.

GOD IS SOVEREIGN

However, although God is sovereign and can do whatever he wills, he is nevertheless righteous and fair in all that he does and it is for this reason that he has set time[44] (the world as we now know it) in the hearts (minds) of men and angels that they may come to know and understand the wickedness of their ways by their own choice, in time, even before they actually lived it, in eternity.

No one is therefore going to hell without being there already in eternity based entirely on what they did in time by the foreknowledge of God. For as much as God, in eternity, called, justified and glorified the church of Jesus Christ[45] so he also rejected, judged and condemned those who are of the devil.[46]

This is a great mystery and can only be truly appreciated once the Spirit of God reveals it to your heart. Jesus also once said that there were many deep spiritual things of the kingdom of God that he would have liked to share with his disciples at that time but that he couldn't as they could not bear to hear it.[47] As I said once before, I now say again, everything that exists in the eternal future already existed in the eternal past and no one can add or take anything away from it for they are both the eternal present in God.

THE FALL IN TIME NOT IN ETERNITY

The church only fell in time by the foreknowledge of God and not in eternity. She is on the throne of God in the end and was therefore on the throne in the beginning. In the end there is no night, darkness, death, corruption, and sin in her and therefore in the beginning there was nothing of the kind in her. Nothing has changed in eternity, only in time. Before a thought arises God acts. He is preeminent in all things.

Time, in the mind of God, is not the past but the potential future. When the church regains her consciousness she will understand that time was not something that happened in the past but rather something that happened in the potential future by the foreknowledge of God.

It is then that every knee shall bow and every tongue shall confess that Jesus Christ is Lord to the glory of God the Father. How great and unsearchable are his ways! It was the Father's will to have a kingdom of peace without any rebellion with Christ and his church ruling over all the works of his hands. And his council will stand forever! However before such could consciously commence in eternity, time had to exist by conscious experience in the mind of man and angel in order to show all and sundry the consequences of the rebellion should such have been allowed to empirically exist in eternity.

SATAN BOUND BY TIME

Lucifer experiences the same dimension of time as does the church for he was cast into the physical dimension along with Adam and Eve and will also receive awareness and understanding through the church of Christ[48] that will bring enlightenment of his actions in time which was withheld in eternity and why God is justified in banishing him, his angels, and all the wicked and evil human beings that existed in time to an eternal oblivion even before their empirical existence in eternity within the mind of God.

The manifold wisdom of God[49] that was hidden from before the foundation of the world not only includes the mystery of the fellowship with regards to the gentiles being made partakers of the inheritance along with the household of Israel but also of other hidden manna[50] that is now being revealed to the sons of God.

JUDGMENT IN ETERNITY

Although judgment has already taken place in eternity, it will also be reflected in time; for Christ is to appear on earth to judge the living and the dead.[51] No one is going to heaven to be judged for such judgment has already taken place in eternity. This time the Judge is coming to earth. It is in time that the devil and his angels along with the entire ungodly wicked are to experience the anguish of eternal hell fire in the physical dimension. For it is only in time that they exist and not in eternity. In eternity they have already been judged and obliterated even before they could experientially exist within God's perfect world.

By the foreknowledge of God, Christ was slain before the foundation of the world. Jesus Christ not only suffered the punishment due to his church, in time, but also in eternity and through this, God pre-empted the actions of the church. For it was while we yet sinners (in time) that Christ died for us in eternity.

There is no creature in all of God's creation of time (other than those to whom the Spirit of God now reveals it to) that currently knows that time exists only in the mind of God as a potential future and not as a regretted past. Nothing in God will ever pass away and the remembrance of God's potential future will always be experienced as God's immeasurable grace of what could have been in eternity had he not taken action by providing a Lamb slain before the foundation of the world. These things are not for the feint hearted but for those who by faith will allow the Spirit to reveal the things of God. Yea even the deep things of God.

THINGS HIDDEN

These things have been hidden from before the world was but has now been revealed to the church for the time has come that eternity, as God has always intended it, must consciously begin. For the mysteries of God's kingdom is not given to everyone to understand.

Nothing will ever be lost in eternity because nothing has ever been lost (save in the mind of God by his foreknowledge of time). God was never taken by surprise when Lucifer rebelled or when Adam and Eve decided to disobey. For what they did way back in the beginning of time, is only God's imagination in eternity. He who knows all things at all times already did in the eternal past what we think he is only going to do in the eternal future; not realizing that the eternal past and future are both the eternal present with God.

How foolish are the ways of man. Thinking that they are wise they will soon discover that in reality they were fools. For he will catch the wise in their own craftiness when they eventually realize that they really did not know as they thought they knew. Then shall they know as they are known. For all that is done is done by the foreknowledge of God and nothing will ever be done save God has foreknown it to be done.

THE LAMB OF GOD

Christ is not only the Lamb slain from before the foundation of the world but is also the Lamb resurrected and seated in heavenly places far above all principalities and powers before the foundation of the world. And who do you think was in him when all this took place in the mind of God in eternity? Yes of course, you and I . . . the church. This not only happened in time (by the foreknowledge of God) but also in eternity (the reality of God). And what happens in eternity is more of a reality than what happens in time. For what happens in time passes away (is temporal) but what happens in eternity never passes away (is eternal). The beginning and end is eternally and unchangeably present with God.

The nations that the church of Jesus Christ currently rules over (in God's reality) has always existed in eternity and will always be ruled over by Christ and his church (the sons of God). All things belong to Christ and his church. Have always and will always. Nothing has changed and nothing will ever change, world without end. In eternity (the mind of God) every planet in the universe exists to accommodate the nations that already inhabit them. In the mind of God such already exists. What exists in the mind of God is a reality that will never pass away. What God sees in the eternal future already exist with him in the eternal present and has always existed with him from the eternal past.

ONLY THE PRESENT EXISTS WITH GOD

There is no past, present and future with God, only the eternal present. God is not the I WAS nor the I WILL BE but the eternal I AM. The heavens and the earth that was created by God (in time) already existed (in eternity) and will always exist and be inhabited. Nothing will ever pass away and of the increase of his government there shall be no end. All things, past, present and future exists in the mind and nothing which exists, exists outside of him. For in him we all exist and have our being.[52]

The only thing that has happened is that our consciousness was projected into the physical dimension (time) prior to being placed into the spiritual dimension (eternity) by God's foreknowledge and in that way we are able to experience the devastation of sin and the wickedness of our own ways without having an impact on God's eternal plan for his creation. Such was done so that God may be justified in his sayings and have victory when he is judged (accused).

The spiritual dimension is the reality of God's mind whilst the physical dimension is a figment of his imagination. Man's reality is only God's imagination. When God says in scripture that the church is seated in heavenly places in Christ Jesus far above all principalities and power, man thinks that this is only true in a philosophical (imaginary) sense and not according to his reality.

ONLY GOD'S REALITY IS REAL

However, in God's reality this is indeed so because this is the way things have always been and will always be. This is where the church has always been. She has only moved from there in consciousness but not in God's reality. All that ever is, as far as time is concerned, will always exist in the mind of God as something that was avoided and not as something that could have been avoided.

God has no regrets for there is nothing for God to regret. He lost nothing in eternity and will never lose anything. That which we believe to be the future is in reality, the past. Man is only returning, in consciousness, to that which has always been. Man does return in being but only in consciousness. For the body returns to the earth from whence it comes and the spirit (life) returns to God who gave it. It is only the soul that houses the consciousness of the being and such consciousness can only be experienced once body and spirit are united; for it is the body in unison with the spirit that constitutes the soul. The soul is not an entity on its own without the spirit and the body but the constitution of spirit and body.

Once the spirit returns to God who gave it, it will be housed (at a time determined by the Father) in the body that awaits it eternally in the heaven. As soon as the spirit unites with its heavenly body you will be consciously aware of your surroundings as though nothing had taken place notwithstanding the fact that you may have been in the grave for a thousand years! The only difference will be is that you will have memory of time and the things that were done therein. Where and when that time existed will remain only in the hands of the Father . . . forever![53]

THE AWAKENING

Therefore awake[54] all you that sleep for that which you think is reality is but a dream created by God's foreknowledge in eternity. As real as it may seem to you now, the truth of the matter is that time only exists as God's forethought in eternity which is currently experienced by you and I as our reality. The only thing that is real is what God says is real and he says that only that which cannot be seen is real because it never passes away.

The time has come for the church to consciously take her rightful place in Christ and to rule over all the works of God's hands knowing once and for all that she is not God, the creator of heaven and earth, but rather God anointed [55] by God to rule in heaven over earth with her heavenly husband, our Lord and Savior Jesus Christ, being her head. So has it always been and so will it always be. What God says of Christ he says of the church, there is no difference; for the body is part of the head and the head part of the body, they are one in being.[56]

WHAT WILL BE, WILL BE

What God knows to be, will be, and there is nothing you or I can do to make it not to be. All that exists in the eternal foreknowledge of God will be manifest in the fullness of time and nothing will ever be able to change that. What God foreknows in eternity will take place in time whether you like it or not. You may think that you are in control of future events, little realizing that what you think must still happen, is happening right now in the mind of God and has always happened! For God knows all things from always and never changes his mind about anything. God is I AM and changes not . . . never!

Do you think for one moment that when Jesus said to Peter that before the cock crows Peter would deny knowing him, that Peter could do any thing to stop that from happening? Do really you think that Peter could do anything to change what God foreknew would happen? Much less then can you and I change what God knows, in eternity, what is going to be in time. Things don't happen because God makes it happen, but because God, by his foreknowledge, knows it is going to happen and has chosen in eternity either to prevent it from happening or to permit it to happen. Even the crucifixion of Jesus Christ only happened, in time, because God had already delivered him up, by his foreknowledge in eternity.[57] Either way, whether a thing happens or not, God foreknows!

The man who commits a crime does so because God foreknows he is going to commit a crime, and not because God makes him to do so. The choice a man makes, he makes of his own "free" will, based upon the circumstances surrounding the situation at the time. However, God knows beforehand the choice a man will make before he makes it therefore make it he will, whether he likes it or not. It is God alone who decides, in eternity, whether to permit or prevent a thing happening in time. A man's will is free only in so far as it is free within the foreknowledge and will of God.[58] Much like a train that is free to move to and fro as long as it does so within the confines of the tracks upon which it moves. So whatever a man does, he does by the foreknowledge of God while at the same time be held accountable for the things that he does. You might not like it or agree with it but it nevertheless remains a fact.

God does not act in time but in eternity. In other words there is nothing that God is doing now that he hasn't already done, by his foreknowledge, in eternity. God does not therefore answer your prayer now because you have prayed (in time), you pray in time because God has answered your prayer in eternity. God does not act because you pray, you pray because God has acted![59]

Jesus did not wait on purpose for four days before attending to Lazarus because he wanted to boast about the power he had to raise the dead (even after four days) or because he wanted Martha and Mary to suffer a little longer before he did anything to help them. He waited because he had seen what and when the Father had done in eternity and, only what the Father had done in eternity could be manifest in time. Jesus as a man only did, in time, what he, as the life-giving Spirit, had already done in eternity. Jesus, as Man, (the body) said and did nothing unless he first heard and saw Jesus, as God, (the Spirit) saying and doing it.[60]

Man therefore does nothing in time what God hasn't already foreknown and done in eternity. Man is, in reality, only living out the thoughts which God had of him before the beginning of time. A man may of course think that he is in control of his own life only to discover that it is the Life of God that is in control of him! Whatever a man therefore does, think or say, he does, think and say because God foreknows from all eternity what he is going to do, think and say. Many are the thoughts and plans of a man's heart but God directs them all; for it is his counsel alone that will stand, unchanged forever; like it or not!

Although this is a deep mystery and may be very difficult for you to understand, it however remains a fact. God loves you, not because you are good, but because he is God. God does not love you less today because of the bad things he knows you are going to do tomorrow. He has chosen to love or hate you from all eternity to all eternity and nothing will ever change that. The gifts and calling of God are irrevocable.[61]

MAN'S REALITY IS GOD'S IMAGINATION

Man's experienced past is only God's imagined future. What man thinks is in the eternal past is really in God's eternal future and what he thinks is his eternal future is really God's eternal past and both exists within God's eternal present.

Angel, man and beast have not moved one millimeter from God's eternal present. All things past, present and future are eternally present with God. The day that you were born is as present with God as the day that you will die. In fact the day that Adam was created is as present with God as the day that you and I will die.

What you may therefore hope to experience one day in heaven you are living right now in the mind of God. As a born again saint in Christ you may hope to one day ascend the throne of God. Little realizing that in the mind of God, you have never ever descended it! You have always been there and you will always be there and nothing will ever change that. You just know it. Scripture talks about it but you don't understand and believe it because you are not conscious of it. But it remains the truth. Heaven and earth will pass away but God's word remains forever true in the mystery of time.

CHAPTER SIX

"THE SIXTH THUNDER SOUND"

THE SONS OF GOD

INTRODUCTION

What you are about to read may be a little difficult to understand at first but please don't stop reading for you will come to know the truth and the truth will set you free.[1] Free from the bondage of man's doctrines[2] and long list of rules and regulations[3] that produce no life at all for it only leads to the letter that kills.[4]

In order for one to rightly divide the word of God as revealed by God's Holy Spirit properly,[5] one must first understand the relationship that exists between Christ and his church; the manifest sons of God.[6] As scripture is not only about Jesus Christ but also about his church.

This is a very important truth to understand if one is to have proper insight into the overall plan of God concerning man. Christ without the church is the Spirit without a body and the church without Christ is the body without the Spirit. For there is one body and one spirit and the two are one Spirit (Life).

As Adam and Eve were one flesh[7] so Christ and his church are one spirit.[8] Notice that the scripture does not say *"one in the flesh"* or *"one in the spirit"* but *"one flesh"* and *"one spirit"*. The two are one being or life in every sense of the word as far as God is concerned.

EVERYTHING IS ABOUT CHRIST AND THE CHURCH

Everything in the scripture revolves wholly around Christ and his church; from the very beginning in Genesis[9] to the very end in Revelation.[10] What therefore is true of Christ (the Spirit of God) in scripture is also true of His church (the Word of God). They are joint-heirs of God.[11]

There are many terms used symbolically in scripture that refer to Christ and his church but all of them refer only to Christ and his church as one being and to nothing else. Understanding this will open one's mind to understanding God's eternal purpose and plan for all of creation. The church does not consist of a particular denomination or specific group of believers but of all those of every nation, tribe and language who through faith, have accepted the offering God provided (in eternity and time) on the cross in Jesus Christ.[12]

At this point you may be wondering why it is that I couple the words "Word of God" with that of the church and the "Spirit of God" with that of Christ. Well, because that is exactly who the church of Christ represents: the Word of God, the body in which Jesus the Christ (the Spirit of God) dwells. And the two are one Spirit or Life.

The church represents the Logos (written or spoken—past tense) Word of God (the body) while Jesus Christ represents the Rhema (living or speaking—present tense) Word of God (the Spirit). Without the Spirit, the body has no life and without the body the Spirit has no expression. Without the Spirit the written word is the letter that kills[13] and without the body the living word is a light without a lamp.[14]

THE ATTRIBUTES OF GOD

The Word and Spirit of God are the divine attributes (or nature) of God the Father that is expressed through the sons of God (Christ and his church). These concepts are interchangeable and applicable as the Spirit of God reveals. Failing to keep this in mind can create confusion and a lack of rightly dividing the word of truth.

To see Jesus (the man) as a single entity is failing to rightly divide the word of truth. Jesus Christ, although one man, represented two beings in himself; the Spirit and the bride,[15] the body and the Spirit,[16] the Christ and his church,[17] the lamp and the light,[18] the Word of God and the Spirit of God.[19] These two are one and always have been one and will always be one. Jesus knew and referred to this when he spoke to Nicodemus. When Jesus addressed Nicodemus with regards to the things of heaven he referred to himself as "we" and not as "I". Plural and not singular;[20] He was not only making reference to the Father that was in him[21] but also to the church that was in him from before the foundation of the world[22] who through John the Baptist and all the other Old Testament prophets, witnessed and testified of the things that they saw and experienced.[23] What God has therefore joined together can no man pull apart . . . ever![24]

When God the Father by his foreknowledge delivered up his Son, Jesus Christ, to be sacrificed on the cross of Calvary for our sin,[25] he gave everything that he is; Spirit and body, Christ and church, the Word of God and the Spirit of God—everything! The Father was not only in heaven on the throne watching the Son die here on earth, he was in the Son on the cross reconciling the world unto to himself.[26] It was the Father (the Spirit) himself, who through the Son (the Word) that was the ransom for our sin.

WHAT GOD HAS JOINED

To separate the two is to undo what God has done in eternity and no man can unto what God has done. It stands forever and nothing can be added to it and nothing can be taken away from it.[27] Christ is the Lamb slain before the foundation of the world[28] and the church was right there in him.[29] She was never apart from him and wil never be apart from him. The two are one Spirit.[30] From eternity past to eternity future, forever![31]

The church of Jesus Christ did not only begin her existence here on earth in time. She has always existed in Christ in eternity[32] by the foreknowledge of God. The church has always been the body wherein the Spirit dwells.[33] The church of Christ is not only something that was formed in time but also in eternity for what is to be in the end after time, has always existed in the beginning before time and currently exists now in time, world without end.[34] Jesus Christ and his church have always been and will always be the manifest sons of God.

The body that clothed the Spirit of God and called Jesus the Son of God represented the Word of God that became flesh. And that flesh represented the church of Jesus Christ. She is the body that houses the Spirit and it was this body that was to bear the reproach (but not to be the ransom price) for the sin that came into the world through her rebellion.

THE PHYSICAL BODY

It was not the physical body of our Lord Jesus Christ as such that was the Word of God but the Spirit that indwelled that body. When scripture says that the Word became flesh it really means that the Word of God was manifested (or revealed) in the flesh. The Word of God did not change form but rather took on form. The Spirit was clothed with a physical body and that body represented the church of Christ with him being the Spirit within it, the hope of glory.[35]

It was the church (Eve) that God foreknew (in eternity) that took part in the Luciferian rebellion against him in paradise and it was Christ (Adam) that had to pay the price. It was God (the Father, the eternal Holy Spirit) in Jesus Christ (the man) on the cross reconciling the world unto himself. It was the Spirit in the body that was the ultimate price. Great is the mystery of godliness, God was manifest in the flesh!

It was not so much the body but the Spirit that indwelled that body that was the ransom price. For it was not so much the physical flesh of that body but the blood (spirit-life) that flowed from that body that was pleasing to God. For without the shedding of blood there can be no covering for sin.[36] Although Jesus said that his body was to be sacrificed as an offering, only his blood was to be shed for the remission of sins.[37]

THE TRUE PRICE

The body only housed the true price that was to be paid. And the true price that was paid was *"Christ in you the hope of glory"* (the life of God that flowed in the blood of man). In the Old Testament it was only the blood that was offered upon the horns of the alter for sin that was pleasing to God because the life of the animal was found in its blood and only it could atone for sin[38] and not in the flesh of the animal, and without the shedding of blood there can be no remission of sin.

The law demanded a life for a life[39] and only the blood[40] (wherein existed the life of the creature) could suffice. Only it was brought into the sanctuary by the high priest for sin while the bodies of the beasts were burned outside the camp.[41] After the blood was offered upon the horns of the altar, the flesh was burn outside the tabernacle by the priest.[42] And although the flesh of the animal was sacrificed as a burnt offering that was pleasing to the Lord, it could not atone for sin. Only the blood (wherein the life of the animal existed) could do that. It was only after Jesus shed his blood for the remission of our sins that he suffered the reproach outside the camp where we are also said to go to him in order to bear this same reproach.[43] The blood of the Lamb was not only shed on the cross but also before the cross; for most of his blood was poured out for us while he was being scourged before going to the cross.[44]

Although it was the body of our Lord Jesus Christ that bore the reproach for our sin, it was his blood that paid the ransom for our righteousness. It was the church—Eve (the body) that rebelled but it was the Christ—Adam (the Spirit) in that body that paid the price and felt every stitch of pain that was brought to bear upon that body; for it was Eve (the church) that rebelled against God and not Adam (Christ).

ADAM NEVER SINNED

Scripture clearly says that it was not Adam that sinned but Eve who was in the transgression.[45] Adam was not deceived. What Adam did, he did out of love for Eve and not because he was motivated to rebel against God. Adam represented Jesus Christ who was made sin for our sake in order that we may be made the righteous of God in him.[46] When scripture declares that by one man, (Adam) sin came into the world,[47] the Spirit is more specifically referring to Eve (the church—the natural element of man) and not to Adam (Christ—the spiritual element of man) for the two were one flesh and both called Adam and it is to this 'Adam' that Paul refers to in (Romans 5: 14) when he says *"Nevertheless death reigned from Adam to Moses, even over them that had not sinned after the similitude of Adam's transgression, who is the figure of him that was to come"*.

The *"him that was to come"* is not referring so specifically to Jesus (Adam) as such but to his Church (Eve) and should therefore correctly be rendered as *'her that was to come"* for the transgressing "Adam" that Paul is referring to in (Romans 5:14) is not Adam the man but Adam the woman! Paul was therefore not contradicting himself when he said in Romans 5:14 that Adam was the transgressor yet in 1Timothy 2:14 he categorically denies that very thing when he says *And Adam was not deceived, but the woman being deceived was in the transgression* (or was the transgressor).

One must always keep in mind that although it was Paul that was writing, it was nevertheless the Spirit of God that was speaking for it is only the Spirit of God who alone knows and reveals the whole truth of the matter!

The body without the spirit[48] (the head) does not feel pain, for without the spirit the body is dead.[49] The body cannot experience any sensation unless the head (the brain) through the nervous system, communicates that sensation to the body. The head must first experience the pain and thereafter the body. Although the body is the first receptor of the wound, it is the head that is the first receptor of the pain. If the brain is dead the body feels no pain. Once Christ finally gave up his spirit on the cross his body felt no more pain.

THE SPIRIT IS THE PRICE

It was the spirit of the body that felt the full wrath of the law first and thereafter the body. And as the blood (Christ) of the beast was offered for the atonement of sin, so also the body (the church) was sacrificed as a sin and peace offering to the Lord.[50] Christ did not only die *for* his church, he died *with* his church. She drank of the same cup that he drank of and was baptized with the same baptism that he was baptized with.[51] Before she could be buried and resurrected with him, she first had to die with him[52] and this all took place already before the foundation of the world.[53] The blood (the spirit) provided the way back into fellowship (right standing) with God while the body (the church) only provides the joy experienced by that fellowship.[54] Without the one you cannot have the other but you must have the one before the other.

Jesus told his disciples that they would indeed drink of the same cup (experience God's wrath for sin) that he was about to drink and be baptized with the baptism that he was about to be baptized and hence the great tribulation that the church has gone through since its inception on earth.[55] But he had to drink (experience) it first. The church cannot experience the glory of Christ unless it also first experiences his suffering.[56]

Although Jesus said that his body would be given as a sacrifice to be broken for our transgression, it would be his blood that would be shed for the remission of our sin, for our resurrection. What Christ suffered in his body on the cross was the reproach for our sin (our death) what he shed from his body (his blood) was the ransom price for our salvation to purge us from sin (our life).

THE GOD OF LAW

His body (temporal life) only satisfied the law of God. His blood (eternal life) satisfied the God of law. His body enabled us to die but his blood enables us to live! Without his body we could not die but without his blood we could not live. In giving his body he suffered our death, but in shedding his blood he paid for our life.

Jesus Christ not only suffered for us in his body but also died for us in his spirit. It is not so much that his spirit died, for spirit cannot die but that his body was separated from his spirit. This was the only time that his spirit and body were apart from each other.[57] For his blood (spirit—life) was drained from the body till the last drops in as much as all the blood of the bullock in the Old Testament had to be poured out.[58]

Jesus laid down his precious life for us; not only his physical, temporal life, but also his spiritual, eternal life. Nothing less could satisfy God. The law declared that the wages of sin is death[59] and therefore demanded a life for a life[60] and only eternal life could deliver from eternal death.

GOD THE FATHER WAS THE RANSOM PRICE

God the Father, in Christ, bore the pain and suffered the full penalty of his own law for our sin. It was his life—Spirit (the blood that flowed from the physical body of our Lord Jesus), that was given as a ransom[61] and not so much the physical body. The physical body was merely the earthen vessel that contained the glory that paid the price.[62] Without the

Spirit the body could not experience the pain and without the body, the Spirit could not be the ransom. The Father was not sitting on a throne somewhere in heaven watching his Son die on a cross. He was in him taking upon himself the full wrath of his own law. God the Father was in Christ reconciling the world unto himself.[63] Once the ransom price was paid, the whole creation set about to wait eagerly for the manifestation of the purchased sons of God.[64]

It is important to note at this time though; that while the whole creation waits for the manifestation of the collective sons of God (Christ *through* his church) the "church" is waiting for the manifestation of the individual Son of God (Christ *to* his church). Not realizing that their hope of glory is not in the sky but in them. Christ the hope of glory in you and I.[65]

THE RETURN OF CHRIST

Christ is not coming to be glorified and admired in the sky. He comes to be glorified and admired in and through his saints![66] When Jesus said that he was coming on the clouds, he was not speaking literally but metaphorically. Not meaning that those clouds would be made up of millions and trillions of little water droplets upon which he would make his glorious appearance but of millions and trillions of little saints, each accompanied by his own angel. They are not clouds of water but clouds of glory and the glory is not in the sky, but in you! The church is the "cloud of glory" upon which the Christ appears for she is his glory as much as the woman is the glory of the man.[67] It is for this very reason that we are to meet him in the air[68] (translated into the spiritual dimension) in order that we may be the 'cloud' upon which the glorified Christ returns to the earth (physical dimension).

Jesus often spoke metaphorically and in parables so that the mysteries of the Kingdom of God would be hidden from them for who it was not intended.[69] For it was not right for him to give the bread (the oracles, mysteries and blessings of God) that belonged to the children (saints—the church), to dogs[70] (the children of the devil). That is why scripture says that we 'speak the wisdom of God in a mystery, even the hidden wisdom, which God ordained before the world unto our glory.[71]

THE IGNORANCE OF THE CARNAL CHURCH

The reason why the institutionalized or carnal church is, by and large, ignorant of this truth is because she is fast asleep![72] And while she slept she became infested with "foolish virgins" (man made institutions called churches), "tares"[73] (children of the wicked one) and the "leaven of the Pharisees and of the Sadducees"[74] (doctrines of devils).

NO HEAVENLY GOOD

She (the worldly denominational church) has become so earth bound with the god of this world, that she is no heavenly good with the Word of God. She has become rich with worldly goods but poor of heavenly treasure[75] and has become known in scripture as "Mystery Babylon" and is become the habitation of devils, and the hold of every foul spirit, and a cage of every unclean and hateful bird"[76] She is the "church" in which the true church of Jesus Christ currently finds herself. She is the outer shell of the inner spirit. The church of Jesus Christ literally finds her self as a church within a "church". This is a mystery indeed but nevertheless a fact.

THE CURSE OF MALACHI

There is a very good reason why the institutionalized church of today is so rich in worldly goods. It is because her shepherds have for many years held the saints of God under bondage to her threats of curses. They have threatened the saints with the curse of Malachi[77] if they did not bring their tithes and offering of money to their (the shepherds) so-called house of God so that there may be "meat" in his house.

FLEECING THE SHEEP

And instead of feeding the sheep as Christ commanded, their shepherds have fleeced the sheep for all they were worth. It is true that scripture says that the labourer is worthy of his hire[78] and that those who tend the flock have a right to drink of the milk from the flock.[79] But some of these unscrupulous shepherds not only drink of the milk of the flock for their daily survival, they "kill"[80] the poor sheep in order that they may obtain mansions for their luxurious living but they do not feed the sheep. They drive in the most expensive cars and dine at the most exotic places while their sheep go hungry and have to walk miles on bare foot to their worldly temples of filthy lucre.

LUXURIOUS LIVES

But woe to the sheep if they do not pay their tithes and offerings! For then a curse of mammoth proportions will descend upon them from heaven and consume their livelihood because they robbed God by failing to bring into his storehouse the money that rightly belongs to him. These shepherds have no conscience when they knowingly under-trample[81] the sheep and leave them broken and ravished of their daily living so that the latest BMW or Mercedes may be added to their stable of luxury cars. Some of these shepherds even have their own private jets!

MISQUOTED SCRIPTURE

They feverish hammer away every week at how important it is for the sheep to pay their tithes and offerings using Malachi as their accomplice with a curse while all the time not having one stitch of New Testament scripture to support their insatiable lust for money. One of their favorite New Testament scripture (misquoted) to support their endeavor to be rich is 1Corinthians 16 where Paul encourages the congregation of Corinth to ensure that the collection is done on the first day of the week so that there won't be any collecting done when he eventually arrives.[82]

CHEERFUL GIVERS

What these shepherds don't tell the sheep though is that Paul said that the collection that was to be taken on the first day of the week was for the *saints* and not for the *shepherds!* If this was done today then perhaps the sheep would also be able to live in big mansions and drive luxury cars like their illustrious shepherds. Tithing (the giving of money to the ministry under compulsion by law) is not a New Testament ordinance. Never was and never will be. It is the bountiful and cheerful giving, without necessity, by grace, which is the true giving of the New Testament that is well pleasing to the Lord, for God loves a cheerful giver.[83]

There are many shepherds that know this truth of God's word but have nevertheless allowed themselves to be bullied by the spirit of mammon and have . . .

"gone in the way of Cain, and ran greedily after the error of Balaam for reward, and perished in the gainsaying of Core". (Jude 1:11)

VEILED FACES

Those who teach and practice tithing have failed to rightly divide the word of truth and do not understand what tithing was all about in the Old Testament and what it represents in the New Testament. They cannot see the glory of the new because they are still bound to the old and it is of them that it is written that a veil covers their faces[84] so that they are unable to see that Christ is the end of the law[85] to those that have been chosen and called. Shame on them that threaten the bride of Christ each week with a curse in order to force her to give money to the "work of God", so that they, (the shepherds), can live luxurious lives. Shame on them!

BUILDING MANSIONS

Of everything that was left in the Old Testament, only tithing has been brought over by these shepherds so that they could build for themselves mansions on earth, being rich and having need of nothing, not knowing that it is they who are poor, wretched and blind. They fight and fuss among themselves over various issues such at to the form and way that people must be baptized, whether or not the Spirit of God is a person or a substance, whether Jesus was the word of God manifest in the flesh as the Son of God or the angel Michael, whether Jesus died on a cross or a stake, whether Sunday or Saturday is the true Sabbath day, whether Jesus is coming back on a cloud or not. Whether or not Catholicism, Protestantism or Pentecostalism is the true way of worship . . . Etc, etc, etc., *ad infinitum.* There are so many different issues that they are divided on, except one. Tithes and Offerings! They all hold to that one thing for it is one that thing that ensures their kingdoms on earth.

Show me just one "Christian Church" today that still practices the art of circumcision or the sacrificing of a lamb for the remission of sins and I will show you a "church" that is, in truth, the synagogue of Satan. These shepherds do away with other Old Testament forms of outward worship but hold on for dear life to the paying of tithes. They have no faith in God to provide their needs for the ministry and therefore feel that they must threaten the children of the Most High with curses to force them to give them money in order to build their shrines of self importance and grandeur. Shame on them!

THE FLESH PROFITS NOTHING

All things of the Old Testament were foreshadows pointing to the Christ (Jesus and his church) in the New Testament. Nothing can be brought over from the old into the new; for the head of him, John the Baptist, who was the link between the Old and the New Testaments, was cut off thereby ensuring that nothing could be brought over. Paul also once said that they who would practice the old (justified by law)[86] in the new had fallen from grace for the letter kills and only the spirit gives life. The flesh profits nothing at all.

POINTING THE WAY

Everything in the Old Testament has its counterpart in the New and all of them (without exception) point to Jesus Christ and his church. The lamb of the old points to Jesus Christ, the Lamb of God in the new; The Israel of the old points to the church of Jesus Christ in the new; The temple (and the tent tabernacle) of the old points to the body (the church) of Jesus Christ in the new; The Ark of the Covent of the old points to the hearts of those (the church) who are born again in the new; The circumcision of the foreskin of the old points to the circumcision of the hearts (the church) from the evil works of the flesh (satanic nature) of those who are washed and cleansed by the blood of the Lamb in the new;

The crossing of the red sea on dry ground by Israel in the old, points to the baptism of those (the church) who identify with the death, burial and resurrection of Jesus Christ in the new; The water that flowed from the rock in the old points to the spirit (Jesus Christ) that flows from the word (the church) in the new; The rending of the outer garments of the old points to the rending of the hearts of those (the church) that humble themselves under the mighty hand of God in the new; The fast from food declared in the old, points to the fasting from the works that feed the flesh (satanic nature) of those (the church) who have been translated from the power of darkness into the kingdom of God's dear Son in the new.

The manna that fell from heaven in the desert of the old points to Jesus Christ, the true bread of life of the new; The seventh day Sabbath rest (Saturday) of the old points to Jesus Christ, as the life giving Spirit, the true rest of God from the works of the flesh in the new; The tithe of the old points to that part (Jesus Christ and his church) which belongs to God in the new. Everything points to Jesus Christ and his church and to them alone for it is the Spirit and the Bride which say come! "He that hath an ear; let him hear what the Spirit is saying to the churches"

THE CHILDREN ARE FREE

Jesus said that the children are free! Who then are those who oblige the sons of God to pay tithes when all things belong to them? Who are they that lay a heavy burden upon the backs of the chosen of God to give money under threat of a curse when it is they who are the heirs of all the works of their Father's hand? Woe to them, for they are the pastors that:

"destroy and scatter the sheep of my pasture! saith the Lord" (Jeremiah 23:1)

Therefore, O ye shepherds, hear the word of the LORD:

"Thus saith the Lord GOD; Behold, I am against the shepherds; and I will require my flock at their hand, and cause them to cease from feeding the flock; neither shall the shepherds feed themselves any more; for I will deliver my flock from their mouth, that they may not be meat for them". (Ezekiel 34:9, 10)

THE TRUE SABBATH

The question of the Sabbath day has been a bone of contention among many in the Christian faith as well as across the board between various religions. Each have determined unto themselves a Sabbath day which is kept holy in one way or another to what each has identified and accepted to be their God.

Although there may be two specific days in the week, such as Saturday and Sunday, that has been identified to be the Sabbath days for the different sections of the Christian faith, as well as in the Jewish religion, there is however a third day, Friday, which is also identified by Muslims to be their Sabbath day. All three of these days are the "Sabbath" of each of those who have so identified their Sabbath day to be, but none of these days are the true Sabbath day of the Lord.

In the Old Testament the seventh day, being the Saturday, was set aside to be the Sabbath day on which the Jews would refrain from all kinds of labour (Exodus 20:10) and keep that day holy unto their God in terms of the Ten Commandments given to Moses on mount Sinai and handed down to the people of Israel. The keeping of this Sabbath day was a strict ordinance and the breaking thereof was met with stern punishment which would lead to death (Exodus 31:14).

This Sabbath day was also given to Israel as a covenant sign (see Exodus 31:16;17) between God and the nation and which sign would also testify to all and sundry, forever, that is was the God of Israel that was the true God who created heaven and earth.

However, as with all things natural in the Old Testament, the Sabbath day thereof also only existed, at that time, as a shadow of the true Sabbath day that would eventually come to exist in the New

Testament (see Colossians 2:17). And no, the Old Testament *Saturday* Sabbath did not become the New Testament *Sunday* Sabbath as so many in the Christian faith would have us believe. The New Testament Sabbath day is far more than just another natural day of the week. In fact it is not a day at all, it is a person!

We are introduced for the first time to the true Sabbath day of the Lord in the book of Hebrews (see Hebrews 4:1 1-11) which can only be entered into (or kept) by those who truly believe in and accept Jesus Christ as their personal Lord and Savior. No unbelievers may enter or keep this day holy as in the case of those who go to church on Saturday or Sunday and still remain unbelieving of the saving grace of God in the cross of Jesus Christ. This Sabbath day is a very special day created especially for those who are born again by the Spirit of God and who are in truth the true sons of God.

This Sabbath day is not called Saturday or Sunday but Today. It is also not the natural seventh or first day of the week but the spiritual 'eighth' day of the week! It is a day that has neither time, (hours, minutes and seconds), nor matter (sun, moon and stars) but kingdom principles, (righteousness, peace, and joy in the Holy Ghost) (see Romans 14:17) that determines its length and strength. It is a day that does not depend upon the revolution of planetary systems and bodies in relation to each other to determine the night and day thereof but upon the Word and Spirit of God.

It is not a day upon which men cease from their daily chores of the body that includes hammers and nails but a day upon which men cease from the works of the flesh (see Galatians 5:19) that includes hatred and unforgiveness towards one another. It is a day of rest that revitalizes the spirit and sets the tone for the worship of God that never ends (see 1Thessalonians 5:15-18). It's an eternal day that never ends and whose peace (see Matthew 11:28) is not as this world gives, but as the Son of God has provided (see John 14:27). This day is not known as Friday, Saturday or Sunday (or any other natural day for that matter) but as Jesus Christ, the life giving Spirit who lives and abides forever in the hearts of those who are born again into the kingdom of God. He alone is the true Sabbath day of God.

There is of course nothing wrong with men keeping their own respective Sabbath days such as Friday, Saturday and Sunday (or any other day for that matter) holy *unto* the Lord (see Colossians 2:15 and 16) but there is only one day that is the true Sabbath day *of* the Lord and he is called . . . Today, Jesus Christ, the Son of God!

THE GREAT WHORE

It is not so much those dear individual Roman Catholics, Protestants, Seventh Day Adventists, Jehovah Witnesses, Mormons, Quakers, Pentecostals, or Charismatics who are called, in scripture, the "great whore". It is all of their man made institutions called "churches" collectively that are called such. It is the institutionalized church— "Mystery Babylon" the first Church of Rome who is the Mother of harlots that has many daughters.[87] She is the one that went whoring away from the truth of God's pure and unadulterated word and spawned countless daughters after her own kind. It is the carnal church (with the exception of an elect few that are found to be in her) that has become lukewarm and of no good to the Master and is in reality the true Antichrist. For instead of feeding the sheep as Christ commanded, her shepherds fleece the sheep[88] teaching for doctrines the commandments of men.[89]

THE LAODICEAN CHURCH

The message to the angel of the Laodicean church was not only for a certain denomination of the church but to the institutionalized church as a whole. It is noteworthy that Christ had something against all the church ages from Ephesus to Laodicea that was wrong, with the exception of Philadelphia. The reason for this is because it is only the church age of Philadelphia that represents the remnant "who have not bowed the knee to the image of Baal"[90]. The rest all went "in the way of Cain, and ran greedily after the error of Balaam for reward, and perished in the gainsaying of Core"[91]. And this is all so because when Jesus told his church to go out into the world and make disciples they invited the world to come into the church and defile the disciples, introducing to them, amongst other things, the celebration of pagan festivals such a Easter and Christmas filled with Easter bunnies, eggs and phallic symbols such as Christmas trees[92] while glorifying a mystical man called Santa Claus (Saint Nicolas) a.k.a. Father Christmas and whose so called name (Santa) may very well be a diabolical manipulation of the alphabetical letters for the word Satan![93]

It is for this reason that God, in these last days, is calling his chosen ones out of this morass of wheat and tares, believers and unbelievers, righteous and unrighteous, light and darkness, of idols and temple of God, and of Christ and Belial;[94] for it is out of darkness that God brings forth the light and out of death he brings forth life. It is out of the "mountain" that he took a "stone". And it is out of "Egypt" that God calls forth his son.[95]

THE UNIVERSAL BODY OF CHRIST IS THE TRUE CHURCH

It is not all those beautiful buildings adorned with glorified crosses on them with sophisticated theological names engraved in shinny brass plates, having their own Greek and Hebrew scholars come to explain in the original languages what God really means in his word that God sees as the true church of Christ but all those precious men and woman inside of them that have the cross of Christ branded within their hearts by the blood of the Lamb and who have the Holy Spirit as the only one who comes to explain and reveal the truth of God's word to them; those who follow the Lamb (the pure unadulterated word of God) wherever he goes and knows his voice.

It is those elect few that have not "defiled their garments" (contaminated the word of God with the doctrine of devils) that God is saying "come out from among them, and be ye separate, saith the Lord, and touch not the unclean thing; and I will receive you".[96]

Christ is currently in the process of sending out his "angels" (messengers with the pure and unadulterated word of God) all around the world in order to gather together his elect out of all these man made institutions called "churches" by feeding them with true knowledge and understanding in preparation for the great and glorious day of our Lord and Savior Jesus Christ.[97] It will only be these who will prove to be the true Church of Christ; and it is only to these precious souls that this message is given for they are the body of Christ and his true church.

ONLY THE CHOSEN WILL UNDERSTAND

No one else other than those who God has chosen in Christ before the foundation of the world will understand[98] and accept the message disclosed within the pages of this book. For the mysteries of God are only given to them to understand[99] for it is only to them that God has given all things as their inheritance,[100] and it is only they who will rule over the nations with a rod of iron for only they are the true sons of God.[101]

CHAPTER SEVEN

"THE SEVENTH THUNDER SOUND"

THE MILLENNIAL REIGN OF CHRIST

INTRODUCTION

The reign of Christ is primarily associated with the concept of the Millennium reign (one thousand years of peace on earth) as described in the book of Revelation chapter 20 and has been explained by many different ministers of the word of God in as many different ways as there are ministers.

However, although there are many different versions which each claim to be the correct one, there can of course only be one that can be correct and that is the one that is subject to the interpretation of the scripture because only scripture can interpret itself. No scripture can be privately interpreted by anyone.[1] If scripture therefore does not itself testify of its own veracity then the interpretation of anything, so privately interpreted, must be treated as being wrong. In order therefore to understand what the book of Revelation is all about one must allow the scripture to explain itself.

THE BOOK OF SYMBOLS

The whole book of Revelation consists of symbols with spiritual meaning and only a few things here and there can be taken literally and only in so far at the context allows. For instance, it can be taken literally that the Apostle John was on the Isle of Patmos for the word of God because scripture, aided by history, confirms the fact that such a person and Isle existed and furthermore that seven different church groups existed throughout literal places like Ephesus, Smyrna, Pergamos, Thyatira, Sardis, Philadelphia, and Laodicea on the continent of Asia along with a person who once existed on earth in human form called Jesus Christ.

However, besides these and other literal facts the rest of the book of Revelation is not to be taken literally for scripture itself declares that the revelation of Jesus Christ was signified (or symbolized) by the angel of the Lord to John.[2] Wherever a symbol therefore appears in the book of Revelation that is not specifically explained by that particular scripture itself, then other parts of scripture must be used to explain that particular symbol. Nothing in the book of Revelation must be taken literally unless scripture itself, in context, clearly indicates that such may be taken literally.

REVELATION 20 MOSTLY SYMBOLICAL

Almost everything in and about Revelation chapter 20 is symbolical with a deep spiritual meaning and must therefore be subject to the comparison of other scripture in order to understand the content thereof.

John begins the chapter by saying that he *saw* an angel descending from heaven.[3] Now, for John to have "seen" this angel he must have been in the spirit[4] himself as no one can see an angel in his true spiritual form unless the Lord opens such a person's spiritual eyes in order to see into the spiritual dimension.[5] Angels that were seen by men with their physical eyes were angels that appeared in human form[6] theologically called a theophany. This is the only time that man can see an angel with the natural eye.

THE KEY, CHAIN AND BOTTOMLESS PIT

The angel that John saw had a key to the bottomless pit and a great chain in his hand. Both the key and the chain that the angel had were both symbols having deep spiritual meaning and so scripture itself must be used to interpret the meaning of those symbols

THE KEY

The key is the first symbol that we will look at. In Matthew 16:19 Jesus said to Peter that he would give him the keys to the kingdom of heaven so that whatever he would bind on earth would be bound in heaven and whatever he would loose on earth would also so be loosed in heaven. It is clear, according to this scripture, that the keys spoken of here of represent authority to act with power.

Only he who has the keys of a place has the authority to enter such a place. Jesus said in Revelation 1:18 that he had the keys of hell and death and that this was so because in Matthew 28:18 he said that all power in heaven and earth was given to him. To have all authority therefore is to have all the keys.

The key therefore represents authority and the authority to act is the Word of God; for the Word of God is the only authority that anyone has to act on God's behalf. However, to have authority to act without having the power to enforce such authority is the same as a police officer of the law having a badge without a firearm. For it is the badge (authority) that authorizes the officer to act but it is only the firearm (power) that empowers the officer to enforce that authority. The key that the angel had in hand therefore represents the Word of God.

THE CHAIN

The angel not only had the key (authority) to the bottomless pit, he also had a chain (power) with which to bind the dragon. We will now take a closer look at what the chain represents that the angel had in his hand. Jesus once said that a person could not spoil a strong man's house lest he first bind the strong man.[7] In order therefore to bind a spirit being (the devil) one needs spiritual power to do so and the only spiritual power that one has in order to bind spiritual beings is the finger of God[8] which in turn represents the Spirit of God.[9]

Although Jesus once gave Peter the keys (authority) to the kingdom of God,[10] he also said that Peter must wait until he receives the Spirit of God (power) to enable him to enforce that authority.[11] The Word of God is the authority to act but it is only the Spirit of God that enforces that authority.[12] The angel that John saw not only had the key (authority) to the bottomless pit but also a chain (power) with which to bind the dragon within that bottomless pit. The angel was therefore in reality armed with both the Word of God (authority) as well as the Spirit of God (power). For without the Spirit of God the Word of God is powerless and without the Word of God the Spirit of God is void of authority. The chain therefore represents the Spirit of God.

THE BOTTOMLESS PIT

Now that we have an understanding of what the key and chain represents, let us have a look at what the bottomless pit represents. In Revelation 1:18 Jesus said that he had the keys (authority) of hell and of death and in Psalm 30:3 David prayed (prophetically of Jesus) to God and said:

"O LORD, thou hast brought up my soul from the grave: thou hast kept me alive, that I should not go down to the pit"

In Isaiah 14:15 scripture says of the devil:

"Yet thou shalt be brought down to hell, to the sides of the pit"

and again in 2Peter 2:4 and Jude 1:6 scriptures says that the angels that fell from their first position are held chained in everlasting darkness until the day of judgment.

According to these scriptures and many others like it, the bottomless pit is said to represent the place where the dead are found, a place of everlasting darkness. It is a spiritual dimension where death holds its occupants without relent. It is also to this dimension that God has banished the angels that kept not their first estate and are said to be bound with everlasting chains under darkness, reserved unto the Day of Judgment. The bottomless pit is therefore the place of the unrighteous dead and is also known, in scripture, as hell.

BINDING THE STRONG MAN

The question that remains to be answered is when were the devil and his angels taken and bound in the bottomless pit and by whom. When Jesus said that a person could only spoil a strong man's house once he was bound, he was referring to the time that he was casting out devils by the power of God and also to the time that his disciples would also receive power from on high with which to do the same.[13]

From the time of Christ up to the present day Jesus Christ and his church have been taking hold of the dragon and binding him and his angels in the bottomless pit by the Spirit of God. Jesus himself took hold of the dragon (the devil) and bound him in the bottomless pit when he was resurrected from the dead and received all power in heaven and on earth. And once the strongman was bound he told his disciples to go and spoil the strongman's house by taking hold of his angels (demons) and also caste them into the bottomless pit.

SPOILING THE STRONGMAN'S HOUSE

This is what spiritual warfare (Armageddon) is all about: It is about spoiling the strongman's house[14] until such time that that house is completely overturned and the captives that have been held therein have all been released.[15] When the full number of them that were held captive are released and the good news of the Kingdom of God has been preached to all nations then the end of the age will be upon us.[16]

THE MILLENNIAL REIGN

And as much as the key and chain of Revelation 20 has spiritual significance, so also the thousand years or Millennial Reign. The thousand years in reality represents a symbolic period of time[17] commencing with the resurrection of Christ and his ascension to the throne of God from whence he now currently reigns with his church[18] (until all things have been restored)[19] to the time when the institutionalized world church begins its final decline into deception and falling away.[20] This, in truth, is the separation of the chaff from the wheat[21] and the taking away of the little stone from the mountain spoken of in Daniel.[22]

REIGNING AS PRIESTS NOT AS KINGS

The reign of Christ with his church during the thousand years of Satan's incarceration is not on earth over men as kings[23] but over the power of sin, sickness and evil[24] on earth as priests interceding on behalf of all saints in every nation.[25] The reigning of the church at this time is not as kings of the earth but as priests of heaven on earth and it is this reign that only lasts for a "thousand years". The reign as kings to come over the earth however does not only last for a thousand years but forever.[26] It is therefore that scripture says that those who reign with Christ during the thousand years, reign with him only as priests and not as kings and priests.[27]

CHRIST THE HIGH PRIEST

Although Jesus Christ is currently the King of kings and Lord of lords, he does not now reign as such but as the High Priest after the order of Melchisedec.[28] It is only once he is revealed[29] from heaven that he will begin his reign as King of kings and as Lord of lords. For it is only once the kingdoms of this world have become the kingdoms of our Lord and his Christ (church) that they will take up their positions as the kings of the earth and start to reign for ever and ever.[30]

THE CHRIST RETAINED

Heaven must however retain the Christ until all things have been restored and the last enemy (death) has been vanquished.[31] The millennial reign is therefore not something that is going to take place sometime in the distant future but is something that is taking place right now. It is the thousand year reign of peace on earth within the true church of Christ. Not the peace which the world gives but that which Christ himself gives.[32] Not peace with the world but with one another[33] as members of the body of Christ!

ARMAGEDDON THE WARS OF WARS

The concept of the Armageddon (Har-Megiddo-n) war has also been one that has confused many as to the form, manner and time that such is going to take place. The reason why so many are confused with regards to this issue is because such is seen in the letter (literal sense) and the letter often kills.[34] To see Armageddon as a physical war of sticks and stones that break mens bones (or of guns and bombs if you like) is to fail to understand that our warfare is not against flesh and blood but against principalities and powers, against spiritual wickedness in high places.[35] Against the flesh (the satanic nature) that wars against our spirits;[36] the battle of the mind.[37]

STICKS, STONES AND MACHINE GUNS

Christ does not make war with a machine gun but with a sword.[38] Not a sword that he holds in his hand but one that protrudes from his mouth.[39] This is not a sword that kills the body but destroys the flesh[3] (the satanic nature in man) for this sword is the sword of the Spirit and is the word of God.[40] It is the word of God the Christ uses to smite the nations and it is also this sword that he referred to in Matthew 10:34 when he said "Think not that I am come to send peace on earth: I came not to send peace, but a sword".

143

ARMAGEDDON AN ENIGMA

It is interesting to note at this point that the word 'Armageddon' only appears once in the whole of scripture and that only in its symbolic meaning taken directly from the Hebrew language meaning "mountain or hill of Megiddo. Although the real meaning of the word is not truly known, many scholars of the Bible have nonetheless identified it with the valley of Megiddo, a place in Palestine where it is said that a certain king of Israel (Josiah) once fought a great battle and was wounded therein and eventually died.

However, to wait for a literal war of cataclysmic proportions called Armageddon to take place somewhere in the distant future is to fail to rightly take up your position as a solder chosen by God in the battle that has been raging for the past two thousand years! In this battle we have amour that has nothing to do with the wars of this world.

A BATTLE OF A DIFFERENT KIND

Armageddon is a battle that does not concern itself with the temporal affairs of men[41] but with the eternal affairs of God. This is the good fight of faith[42] which Paul also once claimed that he fought and finished.[43] This is the battle of the ages that is fought in the valley of *Jehoshaphat*, in the valley of decision[44] (in the mind of man)[45] between the truth and the lie; between the arch enemy of Christ (Satan) and the Christ of God (Christ and his church); between the flesh and the spirit.[46]

This war has nothing to do with the kingdoms of this world and does not include the killing machines of this temporal life but the slaying Sword of Eternal Life, the Word of God. This is the true war of Armageddon in the valley of decision; a war of spiritual worlds.

THE TWO KINGDOMS

In amongst all the physical kingdoms on earth there are two spiritual kingdoms that are continually at war with each other. They are the kingdoms of light and of darkness, also known as the kingdom of heaven (or God) and the kingdom of this world (or Satan). In the kingdom of light, Jesus Christ is the King and in the kingdom of darkness Satan rules as its king. In both kingdoms there are citizens and laws by which those citizens live by. The principles of each kingdom are contrary one to another and the applications thereof do bring about the results that those laws and principles are so designed to bring about.

No matter who applies the law of the respective kingdom the results are always the same without any respect to the person applying such law. In the kingdom of light the citizens are called saints whilst in the kingdom of darkness the citizens are called sinners. There are no saints who are citizens of the kingdom of darkness as there are no sinners who are citizens of the kingdom of light. The citizens of the kingdom of light do nevertheless sometimes apply the laws and principles applicable to the kingdom of darkness and visa versa. When such is done the results of the applied law is experienced but the citizenship of the applicator is not forfeited.

In other words when a saint foolishly decides to indulge his flesh by stealing another's property such saint will experience the wrath of the broken law by being sent to prison for theft but will nevertheless remain a saint and citizen of the kingdom of light. On the other hand should a sinner decide to apply the laws and principles of the kingdom of light by committing some act of kindness or love such sinner will experience the blessings that naturally flow from such application of law but will nevertheless remain a sinner and citizen of the kingdom of darkness. The doings of each respective individual does not therefore determine his or her status in the kingdoms that they find themselves in.

Citizenship is not obtained through the action of the individual but through the actions of the king of such kingdom. For each king has in reality given birth to the citizens of his own kingdom and hence has become the father of his own kingdom's subjects. Those who in time, have been translated from the power of darkness into the kingdom of light, have so been translated before the creation of time.

Citizens of these two kingdoms are therefore not such by their own choice or actions but by the choice and actions of another (their king). It is not true that saints are such because they chose to love God in time but because God chose to love them in eternity. Had God not decided, before the foundation of the world, to love an individual and make him a saint alive through the operation of the new birth by faith in Jesus Christ as Lord, such individual would forever remain dead in the kingdom of darkness.

The citizens of each kingdom are therefore determined before time began and so the number of citizens belonging to each kingdom will therefore not increase or diminish in anyway at all. There are forever two types of citizens in the spiritual dimension, those who are alive and those who are dead; those who are the sons of light and those who are the sons of darkness. Those who are born of the flesh and those are born of the spirit. Those who are the vessels of God's mercy prepared, before the foundation of the world, unto glory and those who are the vessels of his wrath fitted, before time began, to destruction. Nothing will ever change what God has determined in eternity to be in time.

All those whom the Father has given to the Son in eternity will come to the Son in time and nothing will ever prevent them from doing so. Nothing can or will ever thwart or hinder the plan of God that he has for each individual whether he be a citizen of the kingdom of light or of darkness. God does not have a plan 'B'. Those who are destined for the kingdom of light in time have ever been the citizens of the kingdom of light in eternity and so likewise with the citizens of the kingdom of darkness. The die was cast in eternity and nothing or no one can ever change that in time.

You may think that your choice in time will determine your status in eternity but little do you realize that it is your status in eternity that determines your choice in time. Your decision to accept or reject the Christ in time was determine by your status as a citizen of the kingdom you belong to in eternity. No one can come to Christ in time that has not been given him in eternity. You may also decide to reject this truth as being false in time but you will never be able to change the veracity thereof in eternity. Heaven and earth will pass away but God's word will remain forever. The only question that remains to be answered is . . . to what kingdom do you belong to?

THE FIRST RESURRECTION

The first resurrection is another concept that has a lot of people confused as to when such will take place and in what manner. Many believe that at the last day at the beginning of the one thousand reign of Christ on earth, certain saints will be resurrected to begin their reign with Christ and that this, in a literal sense, constitutes the first resurrection.

However, if one is to believe that the first resurrection is a literal resurrection of certain saints at the commencement of the Millennial reign then one is forced to believe that there are other saints in Christ who can be hurt by the second death (the lake of fire) for "they lived not again until the thousand years were ended". This would then be a complete contradiction of scripture which declares that all who have the Son have eternal life now. The first resurrection can therefore not be a literal resurrection of only certain saints but a spiritual resurrection of all the saints in Christ; for the church is resurrected as a whole in eternity and not only as individual members thereof in time.

Did Jesus himself not say on many occasions that those who believe in him would be resurrected by him on the last day . . . you may ask? Yes he did but what many don't understand though is that the first resurrection is not a day or an event or that the last day is not a literal period of time but a person.

Martha and Mary also once thought that their brother Lazarus would rise again on the last day, at the resurrection . . .

"Martha saith unto him, I know that he shall rise again in the resurrection at the last day". (John 11:24)

but "Jesus said unto her:

"I am the resurrection, and the life: he that believeth in me, though he were dead, yet shall he live". (John 11:25)

CHRIST THE LAST DAY

Christ himself is the last day and the first resurrection. In fact he is not only the last day of resurrection, he is also the first day of creation for he is both Alpha and Omega; the beginning and the end. Only in him do we have life. And he who has the Son now has the everlasting life now.[47]

Ephesians 2:4-7 clearly describes the first resurrection in the following words:

"But God, who is rich in mercy, for his great love wherewith he loved us, Even when we were dead in sins, hath quickened us together with Christ, (by grace ye are saved; And hath raised us up together, and made us sit together in heavenly places in Christ Jesus: That in the ages to come he might shew the exceeding riches of his grace in his kindness toward us through Christ Jesus".

Paul furthermore says in Colossians 2:12-13 that we were:

"Buried with him in baptism, wherein also ye are risen with him through the faith of the operation of God, who hath raised him from the dead. And you, being dead in your sins and the uncircumcision of your flesh, hath he quickened together with him, having forgiven you all trespasses"

THE NOW RESURRECTION

Nothing could be more plainer to me than the fact that we who believe in Jesus Christ as Lord have already been resurrected from the dead and that the resurrection that many believe is still going to take place is in reality the second resurrection of the unrighteous dead[48] which is still to come in the not to distant future. Christ said himself that the hour of hearing his voice unto resurrection was not only in the distant future but also currently with him in the present time.[49]

THE SECOND RESURRECTION

Paul was referring more specifically to the second resurrection of the physical body[50] of the dead at the end of the age when he said in (2Timothy 2:18) that there were some:

"who concerning the truth have erred, saying that the resurrection is past already; and overthrow the faith of some"

Hymenaeus and Philetus had no insight whatsoever into the deep spiritual truth of the first resurrection and could therefore not have been speaking of it when they, among others, were saying that the resurrection was already past.

They are merely as brute beasts knowing nothing of spiritual things at all,[51] and could therefore not have known that there is no passing through the waters (death) over the Jordan for those who are in Christ because they have already passed over[52] on dry ground![53]

CROSSING JORDAN

Our High Priest (Jesus) also stands in the midst of the Jordan (the passing over from one life to the next) on dry ground (resurrected life) and waits there until all of Israel (the church) have passed over. The saints do not die (experience death and the horrors thereof) when their bodies dissolve and return to the earth from whence it came, they merely pass over as though they went to sleep one moment and awoke the next to a new dawn without consciously experiencing the night they went through. Paul put such in these words:

> For we know that if our earthly house of this tabernacle were dissolved, we have a building of God, an house not made with hands, eternal in the heavens. For in this we groan, earnestly desiring to be clothed upon with our house which is from heaven: If so be that being clothed we shall not be found naked. For we that are in this tabernacle do groan, being burdened: not for that we would be unclothed, but clothed upon, that mortality might be swallowed up of life. Now he that hath wrought us for the selfsame thing is God, who also hath given unto us the earnest of the Spirit. Therefore we are always confident, knowing that, whilst we are at home in the body, we are absent from the Lord: (For we walk by faith, not by sight:) We are confident, I say, and willing rather to be absent from the body, and to be present with the Lord. (2Corinthians 5:1-6)

RESURRECTION AND THE WRITINGS OF PAUL

The teachings of Paul on the resurrection were in many instances confusing (even for the disciples themselves)[54] for the revelation that Paul received on various issues was progressive[55] and hence the ambiguity that seems to exist between his writings concerning the teachings of the resurrection to the Ephesians, Colossians and Galatians with that to the Thessalonians and others.

ETERNAL LIFE NOW

Nevertheless, be that as it may, those who take part of the first resurrection have eternal life already for he who has the Son has eternal life and it is therefore that the second death (lake of fire) has no power over them. The first resurrection is not just a nice philosophical idea but a spiritual reality. Those who die in Christ do not have to wait for the resurrection at the end of the age before they are raised from the dead for they have already been resurrected. All that happens at that stage is the reawakening of the soul or the return of consciousness to the saints that lie "sleeping" under the altar of God.

At the death of the righteous dead their physical mortal bodies return to the earth from whence it comes and their spirits return to God who gave it to be united with their new resurrected spiritual immortal bodies that await them eternally in heaven and their souls (conscious individual personality) wait in silent and peaceful sleep under the altar (in the secret place of the Most High) to be awakened at the return of our Lord at the end of the age. There is no resurrection of the physical body once belonging to those who die in Christ for their physical body (Jesus Christ) has already died and been gloriously resurrected on their behalf. Jesus Christ did not only die with and for his church, he was also resurrected with and for her!

CHRIST OUR BODY

It is Christ himself that houses the righteous dead at their passing over. It is the body that he once lived in on earth that was raised and glorified that now awaits his bride. As much as he now dwells on earth in his physical body (the church) so she dwells in heaven in her spiritual body (the Christ).

Jesus said that those who overcome will be made pillars in the temple of his God. In reality this means that those who are saved by grace in him will be the new occupants of the body that is now the glorified temple of God. For in him alone dwells the fulness (the sons of God) of the Godhead bodily. The church is in every sense of the word the body of Christ, both on earth as well as in heaven. She has and always will house the eternal Spirit of God for the two are one being. Always was, always is and always will be.

THE RAPTURE

Here now is one of Christianity's favorite disputations that has the church of Jesus Christ up in arms with each other for as long as the church itself exists on earth. There are as many versions of the subject of the rapture as there are different denominations of the church and each are purportedly supported by scripture. However there can of course only be one version that is the truth. But what is really the truth concerning the rapture or taking away of the saints at the return of Jesus Christ? Is there really going to be rapture? And if so how will it occur; silently or with a loud noise? And when will it occur, before or after the "Great Tribulation? And if not, what then is to happen? Well, in order to get the answers to these questions one is forced to return to the scriptures for it is only there that we can truly receive insight into what Christianity has treated as one of its most treasured topics.

The fundamental teaching on the concept of the rapture is taken primarily from 1 Thessalonians 4:13-17 which reads as follows:-

> But I would not have you to be ignorant, brethren, concerning them which are asleep, that ye sorrow not, even as others which have no hope. For if we believe that Jesus died and rose again, even so them also which sleep in Jesus will God bring with him. For this we say unto you by the word of the Lord, that we which are alive and remain unto the coming of the Lord shall not prevent them which are asleep. For the Lord himself shall descend from heaven with a shout, with the voice of the archangel, and with the trump of God: and the dead in Christ shall rise first: Then we which are alive and remain shall be caught up together with them in the clouds, to meet the Lord in the air: and so shall we ever be with the Lord. Wherefore comfort one another with these words.

In order to properly understand what Paul was taking about we need to see it in the light of the following words, *"For this we say unto you by the word of the Lord."* In other words what Paul was really saying is that his teaching, concerning the subject at hand, was in line and subject to what Jesus taught concerning the matter. So in order to properly understand what Paul was saying, we need to investigate what Jesus said in this regard. Failing to do this will inevitably cause one to end up confused and disappointed in the long run concerning the rapture.

The first time we find Jesus teaching on the end time and his return to earth is in the gospel according to Matthew chapter 24 as follows:

> And Jesus went out, and departed from the temple: and his disciples came to him for to shew him the buildings of the temple. And Jesus said unto them, See ye not all these things? verily I say unto you,

There shall not be left here one stone upon another, that shall not be thrown down. And as he sat upon the mount of Olives, the disciples came unto him privately, saying, Tell us, when shall these things be? and what shall be the sign of thy coming, and of the end of the world? (Matthew 24:1-3)

Notice that after Jesus told his disciples about the destruction of the temple, his disciples asked him three specific questions relating to what he said. They were:-

☞ "when shall these things be?" and

☞ "what shall be the sign of thy coming?" and

☞ "what shall be the sign of the end of the world?"

There are many teachers of the Bible today who teach that Jesus answered the questions above in the consecutive order that they were asked. However when one has regard to the fact that Jesus once said that which is first shall be last and that which is last shall be first, then one can easily come to understand in which order he answered those questions. Many are confused today because they do not really understand the principles of God's kingdom and the reasons why the mysteries of the kingdom were often explained in such a way that many could not (and still do not) understand them.

The first answer that Jesus gave did not relate to the first question asked but to the last question. In other words, to the question "what will be the sign of the end of the world?" Jesus gave the following answer:

And Jesus answered and said unto them, Take heed that no man deceive you. For many shall come in my name, saying, I am Christ; and shall deceive many. And ye shall hear of wars and rumours of wars: see that ye be not troubled: for all these things must come to pass, **but the end is not yet**. For nation shall rise against nation, and kingdom against kingdom: and there shall be famines, and pestilences, and earthquakes, in divers places. All these are the beginning of sorrows. Then shall they deliver you up to be afflicted, and shall kill you: and ye shall be hated of all nations for my name's sake. And then shall many be offended, and shall betray one another, and shall hate one another. And many false prophets shall rise, and shall deceive many. And because iniquity shall abound, the love of many shall wax cold. But he that shall endure unto the end, the same shall be saved. And this gospel of the kingdom shall be preached in all the world for a witness unto all nations; and **then shall the end come**. (Matthew 24:4-14)

Jesus told his disciples firstly about all the things i.e. false prophets, wars and rumors of war, famines, pestilence, hatred, and betrayal that will take place before the end of the world and then clearly told them what will be the sign that will usher in the end of the world. Remember that the question was, "what will be *sign* of the end of the world?" In other words what will be the one thing that will tell us that the end of the world is eminent or at the door? And Jesus answered, "And this gospel of the kingdom shall be preached in all the world for a witness unto all nations; and then shall the end come. There is the sign; the preaching of the gospel (or good message) of the kingdom of God to all nations for a witness. Every nation on earth has already heard the good message (gospel) of the kingdom of God in one way or another, with the exception of one.[56]

Yes indeed! Believe or not, the church of Jesus Christ. She has been so busy preaching the gospel to other nations these past two thousand years that she herself, as a "holy nation", has not properly heard it; for if she had, she would not be in the sorry state of affairs that she currently finds herself in.[57] Confused, infiltrated, and divided as she is. It is for this reason that his book is written, so that the Church of Jesus Christ may hear the gospel of the kingdom of God and in hearing and understanding it may usher in the return of her Lord and Savior. The church has been preaching the gospel to everyone around her for years and now the time has arrived that she is "preached" to; for judgment must begin at the house of God.

The second answer that Christ gave was in relation to the second question asked. "What will be sign of thy coming?" Here we have the issue that deals specifically with what so many in Christianity call the rapture. In answer to this, the Lord said:-

When ye therefore shall see the abomination of desolation, spoken of by Daniel the prophet, stand in the holy place, (whoso readeth, let him understand:) Then let them which be in Judaea flee into the mountains: Let him which is on the housetop not come down to take any thing out of his house: Neither let him which is in the field return back to take his clothes. And woe unto them that are with child, and to them that give suck in those days! But pray ye that your flight be not in the winter, neither on the sabbath day: For then shall be great tribulation, such as was not since the beginning of the world to this time, no, nor ever shall be. And except those days should be shortened, there should no flesh be saved: but for the elect's sake those days shall be shortened. Then if any man shall say unto you, Lo, here is Christ, or there; believe it not. For there shall arise false Christs, and false prophets, and shall shew great signs and wonders; insomuch that, if it were possible, they shall deceive the very elect. Behold, I have told you before. Wherefore if they shall say unto you, Behold, he is in the desert; go not forth: behold, he is in the secret chambers; believe it not. For as the lightning cometh out of the east, and shineth even unto the west; so shall also the coming of the Son of man be. For wheresoever the carcase is, there will the eagles be gathered together. Immediately after the tribulation of those days shall the sun be darkened, and the moon shall not give her light, and the stars shall fall from heaven, and the powers of the heavens shall be shaken: And **then shall appear the sign of the Son of man in heaven**: and then shall all the tribes of the earth mourn, and they shall see the Son of man coming in the clouds of heaven with power and great glory. And he shall send his angels with a great sound of a trumpet, and they shall gather together his elect from the four winds, from one end of heaven to the other. Now learn a parable of the fig tree; When his branch is yet tender, and putteth forth leaves, ye know that summer is nigh: So likewise ye, when ye shall see all these things, know that it is near, even at the doors. Verily I say unto you, This generation shall not pass, till all these things be fulfilled. Heaven and earth shall pass away, but my words shall not pass away. But of that day and hour knoweth no man, no, not the angels of heaven, but my Father only. But as the days of Noe were, so shall also the coming of the Son of man be. For as in the days that were before the flood they were eating and drinking, marrying and giving in marriage, until the day that Noe entered into the ark, And knew not until the flood came, **and took them all away**; so shall also the coming of the Son of man be. Then shall two be in the field; the one shall be taken, and the other left. Two women shall be grinding at the mill; **the one shall be taken, and the other left**. (Matthew 24:15-41)

Here we have the answer to the second question "the one shall be taken and the other left". The sign of the Son of man before his return to the earth as King of kings and Lord of lords is the taking away of the wicked from the earth. And although the "abomination that maketh desolation" speaks, in the natural, of Antiochus Epiphanes, who is said to have done certain vile things, especially with regards to the Jews and their holy place as well as to the destruction of the temple by the Romans in 70 AD, it more specifically refers spiritually to the spirit of the anti-christ, which shall arise and manifest itself in the last days before the revealing of the Christ from heaven and the destruction of the apostate church.[58]

Before the Christ is revealed from heaven, dramatic and cataclysmic events shall come upon the earth as never before and "take them all away" Not those who are saved (as so many are prone to believe) but those who are "eating and drinking, marrying and giving in marriage"; people who are doing normal everyday things but who do not know the God of Israel nor have accepted his Son, Jesus Christ, as their Lord and personal Savior and who live ungodly wicked lives.

Who can truly deny that the things we are witnessing in our day, such as the earthquakes, volcanic eruptions, tsunamis, (such as that which recently took place in Japan and previously elsewhere) pandemic outbreaks of diseases, the ever increasing rise of crime, etc, etc, is not out of the ordinary and getting worse with each new event?

Perhaps some will say that I am being harsh in saying that these things are primarily happening to those nations who are not saved and who are living ungodly lives not having the seal of God in their foreheads. However, let me hasten to remind you that it is not I who says it, but the word of God.[59]

We will now deal with the answer to the first question before returning again to the second in our study of the rapture. "When will these things be" Notice that this question is somewhat different than the other two, for it deals with "when" and not "what". Christ's answer to questions relating to "when" has always been the same.

"And he said unto them, It is not for you to know the times or the seasons, which the Father hath put in his own power". (Acts 1:7)

And, true to the way that the Lord has always answered questions relating to "when", he answered the first question as follows:

Watch therefore: **for ye know not what hour your Lord doth come**. But know this, that if the goodman of the house had known in what watch the thief would come, he would have watched, and **would not have suffered his house to be broken up**. Therefore be ye also ready: for in such an hour as ye think not the Son of man cometh. Who then is a faithful and wise servant, whom his lord hath made ruler over his household, to give them meat in due season? Blessed is that servant, whom his lord when he cometh shall find so doing. Verily I say unto you, That he shall make him ruler over all his goods. But and if that evil servant shall say in his heart, My lord delayeth his coming; And shall begin to smite his fellowservants, and to eat and drink with the drunken; The lord of that servant shall come in a day when he looketh not for him, and in an hour that he is not aware of, And shall cut him asunder, and appoint him his portion with the hypocrites: there shall be weeping and gnashing of teeth. (Matthew 24:42-51)

Notice that in each answer the Lord gave, there are key words that give us some clue as to what question that answer relates. For example:

Question 1, which related to the destruction of the temple building (or house) and answered last, Christ said "But know this, that **if the goodman of the house had known** in what watch the thief would come, he would have watched, and **would not have suffered his house to be broken up**"

Question 2, which concerns itself with the sign of the coming of Christ and answered second, the Lord said "**then shall appear the sign of the Son of man in heaven** . . . For as in the days that were before the flood they were eating and drinking, marrying and giving in marriage, until the day that Noe entered into the ark, And knew not until the flood came, and took them all away; so shall also the coming of the Son of man be. Then shall two be in the field; the one shall be taken, and the other left. Two women shall be grinding at the mill; **the one shall be taken, and the other left**".

And question 3, which related to the sign of the end of the world and answered first, Jesus said, "**And this gospel of the kingdom shall**

be preached in all the world for a witness unto all nations; and **then shall the end come"**.

Setting the questions side by side we find that they fit together like a hand in a glove as follows:-

☞ "when shall these things be?"—"watch therefore, for ye know not what hour your Lord doth come"

☞ "what shall be the sign of thy coming?"—"the one shall be taken and the other left"

☞ "what shall be the sign of the end of the world?"—"this gospel of the kingdom shall be preached to all nations"

Now that we have dealt with the sequence of the questions and their answers let us return to the question of the rapture.

It is generally taught that before the end of the world as we now know it, Christ will secretly return to the earth, like a thief in the night, and take his church away and then there will be a seven year period commonly known as the great tribulation, which all who "missed" the rapture and left behind, will have to go through before the Lord returns to earth for the third time in order to judge the living and the dead. However appealing this all may sound, this is not what Jesus taught and neither did Paul. Yes indeed! The church is going to be "raptured" but not in the manner and at the time that many believe.

Jesus clearly taught that those who are going to be taken away are not those who are saved but those who are ungodly. Not taken to heaven but to destruction! The above verses of scripture dealing with "the sign of the Son of man" before his return to earth, clearly indicates that those who are "taken away" were taken away with a flood and not with a "chariot of fire" as the prophet Elijah was. The two in the field, where the one shall be taken and the other left and, the two women grinding at the mill, where the one shall be taken and the other left, must be seen in the context of the preceding verse that deals with the taking away of the ungodly with the flood.

Those who are left behind are not the ungodly wicked who have to go through a so-called seven year period of tribulation in order to refine them and bring them to the knowledge and understanding of salvation in Jesus Christ, but the sons of the kingdom. God is going to take the ungodly away from the earth first before Christ is revealed from heaven to take (rapture) his church unto himself. This is confirmed by the following scripture.

Another parable put he forth unto them, saying, The kingdom of heaven is likened unto a man which sowed good seed in his field: But while men slept, his enemy came and sowed tares among the wheat, and went his way. But when the blade was sprung up, and brought forth fruit, then appeared the tares also. So the servants of the householder came and said unto him, Sir, didst not thou sow good seed in thy field? from whence then hath it tares? He said unto them, An enemy hath done this. The servants said unto him, Wilt thou then that we go and gather them up? But he said, Nay; lest while ye gather up the tares, ye root up also the wheat with them. Let both grow together until the harvest: and in the time of harvest I will say to the reapers, Gather ye together first the tares, and bind them in bundles to burn them: but gather the wheat into my barn. (Matthew 13:24-30)

Then Jesus sent the multitude away, and went into the house: and his disciples came unto him, saying, Declare unto us the parable of the tares of the field. He answered and said unto them, He that soweth the good seed is the Son of man; The field is the world; the good seed are the children of the kingdom; but the tares are the children of the wicked one; The enemy that sowed them is the devil; the harvest is the end of the world; and the reapers are the angels. As therefore the tares are gathered and burned in the fire; so shall it be in the end of this world. The Son of man shall send forth his angels, and they shall gather out of his kingdom all things that offend, and them which do iniquity; And shall cast them into a furnace of fire: there shall be wailing and gnashing of teeth. Then shall the righteous shine forth as the sun in the kingdom of their Father. Who hath ears to hear, let him hear. (Matthew 13:36-43)

Again, the kingdom of heaven is like unto a net, that was cast into the sea, and gathered of every kind: Which, when it was full, they drew to shore, and sat down, and gathered the good into vessels, but cast the bad away. So shall it be at the end of the world: the angels shall come forth, and sever the wicked from among the just, And shall cast them into the furnace of fire: there shall be wailing and gnashing of teeth. (Matthew 13: 47-50)

It is abundantly clear that Christ taught that the wicked are to be gathered together (taken out) first and burned and then the righteous shall be gathered together (taken out) into his "barn". The wicked are to be severed (violent torn) from among the just and not the other way around. Paul also taught this when he said:

"Then we which are alive and remain shall be caught up together with them in the clouds, to meet the Lord in the air: and so shall we ever be with the Lord. Wherefore comfort one another with these words.

Notice that Paul said "Then we which are alive and remain" Not only alive but also remaining. Remaining until when? Until the coming of the Lord! It is only after the wicked are taken away that we remain until the coming of the Lord to be "raptured" into the air and so shall we ever be with him. The sign of the Son of man is the taking away of the wicked from among the just.

Some will however say that the church must first be taken out of the way (raptured) before God rains judgment on the wicked as Lot was first taken out of Sodom before God judged the ungodly wicked.[60]

What these dear saints don't understand though is that this particular verse is not referring so much to the church being raptured from the earth before God destroys the wicked, but to the coming out of the saints from Mystery Babylon.[61] The separation of the saints out of the end day apostate church.

Awake my dear brothers and sisters and understand what is really happening upon the face of the earth at the present time. "And when they shall say peace and safety then sudden destruction shall befall them". But fear not dear saint, for though a "thousand shall fall at thy side, and ten thousand at thy right hand; but it shall not come nigh thee. Only with thine eyes shalt thou behold and see the reward of the wicked. Because thou hast made the LORD, which is my refuge, even the most High, thy habitation; There shall no evil befall thee, neither shall any plague come nigh thy dwelling. For he shall give his angels charge over thee, to keep thee in all thy ways". (Psalm 91:7-11)

The return of the Lord is indeed at hand! After the ungodly wicked have been taken away from the earth then shall the sons of the kingdom (the true church of Jesus Christ) remain behind and only then shall they be taken away (changed in a twinkling of an eye) to meet their Lord and Savior in the air (spiritual realm). Herein lays the truth about the rapture of the church. This may prove to be a great mystery to many but I speak of Christ and his church; the manifest sons of God and partakers of the first resurrection during the Millennial Reign of Christ and awaiting the Rapture that is soon to take place.

A SPECIAL MESSAGE TO CHRISTIAN HUSBANDS AND WIVES

THE MYSTERY OF THE HAIR MINISTRY

Scripture says that the woman bears upon her head (her long hair) the authority (or power) of her husband[1] thereby signifying to the angels that she under the authority of her husband thereby representing the authority that Christ has over the church.[2] There are many who do not understand why Paul dealt with the importance of a woman having long hair and also why a man should not have long hair. Because of the lack of understanding there are some woman in the church today who have beautifully long hair yet still cover it with a hat or veil when they pray or worship God in the church building failing to understand the mystery of the ministry to angels.

They do this because they do not understand at all what it is really about for a woman to have long hair. They do not understand that their long hair has been given to them as a covering[3] to signify to the angels that the church stands under the covering (authority) of Jesus Christ. A woman's long hair represents the covering that Christ provided for his church and that covering was his blood shed for the remission of her sins.[4] And his blood in turn represents the Spirit of God that was in Christ reconciling the world unto himself.[5] For the life (spirit) of the being is in the blood of the being.[6]

When a born again Christian woman (in a marriage relationship with her husband) prays without her covering (short or shaven hair) she dishonors him[7] as much as the church dishonors Christ when she goes about claiming salvation by good works of the law and not by the grace of God through the blood of Jesus Christ. She seeks to justify herself by the works of her own hands while refusing to walk in the good works that God has ordained that she should walk in.[8] Her short hair is her testimony to the fact that she refuses to be subject to the rulership of her husband over her as God had ordained from the beginning.[9] It is a shame for a woman to pray without her covering because she neglects to witness to the angels of the fact that the church of Jesus Christ stands covered before God because of the blood of Christ and so stands clothed with the Spirit of God[10] and is under his authority and rulership.

REBELLIOUS WIVES

Is it any wonder that so many women stand in rebellion towards their husbands? They no longer want to submit to their husbands as the church submits to Christ for they believe that they have the right to do whatever their husbands do, little realizing that Christ is the husband's head and that he (Christ) will deal with him (the husband) accordingly. It is not for the wife to rebel against her husband because of his failures. She is to remain obedient to God by honoring her husband and by her gentle and submissive spirit convince him of the error of his ways.[11] She has no right to take it upon herself to avenge herself by doing the same things her husband does. She is his glory (crown of rulership and authority) as he is the glory of God[12] and must submit to her husband in everything as unto the Lord.[13] This is a deep spiritual truth and concerns itself with the ministry that the husband and wife stand in towards the angels.[14]

BLUNDERING HUSBANDS

This does not mean however that the husbands have the right to ill treat their wives as they deem fit. They are to love their wives as Christ loved the church and gave his life for it.[15] However should a husband blunder in some or other area of his life it still does not give the wife the right to rebel against him but to remain obedient to the Lord by honoring her husband in a spirit of meekness and submission and in so doing allow the Spirit of God to deal with the husband to the correction of his ways.[16] The woman has no other head but her husband and the man has no other head but Christ.[17] It is not God's order of things that the woman should usurp authority over the man nor the man over Christ by becoming rebellious.[18] God will not tolerate such behavior, no matter what excuse the woman or man may have. Both man and woman have the responsibility to function within the given order of God.

It is because of this sad state of spiritual rebellion that men and women often find themselves in today that they fail to understand the deep spiritual things of God as they stand in disobedience towards God's word. For women either cut their hair short to look like men or have a hat or veil over it and men grow their hair to look like women and even wear earrings in their ears to go with it. This is a complete perversion of God's order.[19] Keep in mind though that salvation is not based on whether or not men and women have long or short hair for God saves the church based not on what she does or does not do but based on grace and faith in Jesus Christ as Lord.

It is therefore not about the hair at all but about that which the hair represents and the attitude of the heart. God desires that a husband and his wife (in their marriage relationship towards each other) will stand in ministry towards the angels[20] testifying to the authority that Christ has over his church. For all must know, through the ministry of the church,[21] that Jesus Christ is Lord and that his bride is subject to his authority as God determined in the day that he told Eve that Adam would rule over her.[22] The Ministry to angels have nothing at all to do with the preaching of salvation to men but of the witnessing to angels of the rulership of Christ over his church.

There is therefore no real miracle working power or any legalism attached to a woman having long hair other than it being symbolic of a deep spiritual truth that the Spirit (Christ) is the head of the body (the church) and that the authority that she stands under is the blood of the Lamb, the Spirit of God.

This ministry was also typified by Samson in his day. For while his hair remained long the Spirit of God was with him but no sooner had his hair been cut than the Spirit of God left him and he was left to the mercy of the Philistines.[23] If the long hair (of Samson, as a

Nazarite under covenant with God) signified a deep spiritual truth that the Spirit of God was the head (husband) of the Israel in the Old Testament,[24] how much more so does it do in the New Testament?[25]

A woman covering her long hair with her own covering when praying or worshipping God is tantamount to saying to the angels that the blood of Christ was not sufficient alone to provide for the remission of sins[26] and that good works of the law need to be added to complete God's plan of salvation.[27] Such is the condition of the Babylonian church today. She is rich in worldly goods but very poor in God's word.[28] Whether she has long or short hair she still insists on wearing her own covering as Adam and Eve did in the day that they felt naked before God[29] and in this the scripture rings true. She has gone in the way of Cain,[30] bringing to the altar an offering of the finest fruits (good works) of her own hands thinking that the word of God says that *salvation* (redemption by grace) without works is dead when in reality it says that *faith* (belief in God's word) without works is dead.[31]

On the other hand we have born again Christian men who go about with long hair like pretty woman on their way to a fashion parade little realizing that they are dishonoring their head, Jesus Christ.[32] For when a man goes about with long hair, he is in effect saying to the angels that Christ, his head, was also in need of a covering for sin. One might say, but what is long and what is short? Well, let nature be the judge of that. For the scripture says that nature itself tells us that it is a shame for a man to have long hair. When one can't tell the difference anymore between a man and a women from behind then nature itself shouts out aloud, perversion. Oh, but Jesus had long hair, I hear someone saying. Yes, perhaps he did, but he also walked on water!

Although Christ was tempted in every way as we are, he remained without sin and without any need for a covering.[33] Men and woman in the Laodicean church today have indeed fallen far short of being true witnesses of Christ and his church.[34]

The word of God is not just full of nice stories of historical figures and events, nor was it written willy-nilly because God needed to fill up space in the Bible so that it could eventually be a compilation of

66 books comprising of the Old and New Testaments. Everything that is written was inspired by the Spirit of God[35] and is written for our learning and instruction[36] in order that we may come to understand that the entire scripture concerns itself with Christ and his church,[37] the Spirit and the bride,[38] the Word of God and the Spirit of God,[39] the manifest sons of God,[40] God almighty[41] and to nothing else.

Today's carnal church thinks that she pleases God with her many great gifts of praise and worship, tithes and offerings, boasting of the fact that she neither eats, drinks, swears nor smokes and carries a huge Bible to church every Sunday while neglecting to be obedient to the Spirit in the little things[42] that please God. God is not looking for sacrifice but obedience.[43] And if sacrifice then a sacrifice of a broken spirit and a contrite heart.[44] King Saul also once thought that he could please God by keeping a little sheep and oxen alive to sacrifice to God but soon found out that God is indeed a God of his word and means every word he says. May God grant that there may still be men and women brave enough in this last day that will dare to stand up and be counted for the word of God and the testimony of our Lord and Savor Jesus Christ.[45]

REBEL SPIRITS

The following matter does not concern itself with the hair of a man or woman but with the rebellious spirit and ungodly behavior of a man towards Christ and a woman towards her husband. No disciplinary measures are called for in scripture when it comes to the ministry to angels through the hair of the husband and wife. Such contentious issues remain to be resolved on a personal level by the Spirit of God alone.

THE WAYWARD HUSBAND

In the event that a man, who confesses to be born again, is rebellious and refuses to submit to Christ as his head he then must be admonished by the corporate body (the church who in this case stands in the place of Christ as the head of man) to repent of his ways.[46] In this regard a woman has the right to approach any sister in the church to accompany her to the Pastor (in the event that the Pastor is male) of the church, as the head of her wayward husband, in order there to take up the matter.[47] It is then for the Pastor to approach the husband on the matter and deal with it according to the scripture. Should her husband continue to be wayward, he is to be excommunicated from the fellowship and treated as an unbeliever. Should the man continue to live in such a way as to bring ill repute on the name of Christ, the church has the power to hand such a person over to Satan for the destruction of the flesh in order that his spirit may be saved in the day of the Lord Jesus Christ.

THE CHURCH'S RESTRICTED AUTHORITY

The church does not have the authority to deal with a woman, who stands in a marriage relationship with her Christian husband, in this way. Pastors also do not have the right or authority to advise wives in their congregation to loose themselves from their wayward Christian husbands and, should the Pastors do so they are out of order, and acting contrary to the order that God has set in the church of Jesus Christ. It is the husband's right and duty to deal with his wife as it is the church's right to deal with her husband. Paul was quite clear when he wrote that wives should consult their own husbands if they wanted to know anything regarding the word of God and not their Pastors. It is not the Pastor who is the head of the wife but the husband.

THE WAYWARD WIFE

On the other hand should a woman refuse to submit to her husband as her head and become rebellious in her ways towards him, he is to admonish her in love in a sincere attempt to restore her to himself. It is not for the husband to take the matter of his wayward wife to the church but to deal with it himself. The church has no authority over the woman in this regard. It is the husband that rules over his wife and not the church. Should she continue with her rebellion, he then has the right to treat her as an unbeliever and consequently hold that she no longer seeks to remain with him in which case he is quite entitled to distance himself from her. In such case the man is no longer bound (spiritually in the Lord) to the woman but may seek to loose himself (legally by the law of man) from her and to marry another in the Lord. Every effort must however be made by the man, in the spirit of love and forgiveness, to restore his wife to himself before taking drastic measures to loose himself from her. God has called us to peace in the body of Christ and in this matter I also have the Spirit of God.

"He which testifieth these things saith, Surely I
come quickly. Amen.
Even so, come, Lord Jesus".

(Revelation 22:20)

SCRIPTURE INDEX

CHAPTER ONE

[1] Be still, and know that I am God: I will be exalted among the heathen, I will be exalted in the earth. (Psalm 46:10)

[2] And I, brethren, could not speak unto you as unto spiritual, but as unto carnal, even as unto babes in Christ. I have fed you with milk, and not with meat: for hitherto ye were not able to bear it, neither yet now are ye able. For ye are yet carnal: for whereas there is among you envying, and strife, and divisions, are ye not carnal, and walk as men? For while one saith, I am of Paul; and another, I am of Apollos; are ye not carnal? (1Crinthians 3:1-4)

[3] Go ye therefore, and teach all nations, baptizing them in the name of the Father, and of the Son, and of the Holy Ghost: (Matthew 28:19)

[4] All things are delivered to me of my Father: and no man knoweth who the Son is, but the Father; and who the Father is, but the Son, and he to whom the Son will reveal him. (Luke 10:22)

[5] But to us there is but one God, the Father, of whom are all things, and we in him; and one Lord Jesus Christ, by whom are all things, and we by him. (1Corinthians 8:6)

[6] For all the law is fulfilled in one word, even in this; Thou shalt love thy neighbour as thyself. But if ye bite and devour one another, take heed that ye be not consumed one of another. (Galatians 5:14; 15)

[7] God is not a man, that he should lie; neither the son of man, that he should repent: hath he said, and shall he not do it? or hath he spoken, and shall he not make it good? (Numbers 23:19)

[8] Because that, when they knew God, they glorified him not as God, neither were thankful; but became vain in their imaginations, and their foolish heart was darkened. Professing themselves to be wise, they became fools, And changed the glory of the uncorruptible God into an image made like to corruptible man, and to birds, and fourfooted beasts, and creeping things. (Romans 1:21-23)

[9] And the LORD appeared unto him (Abraham) in the plains of Mamre: and he sat in the tent door in the heat of the day; And he lift up his eyes and looked, and, lo, three men stood by him: and when he saw them, he ran to meet them from the tent door, and bowed himself toward the ground; (Genesis 18:1)

[10] For our God is a consuming fire. (Hebrews 12:29)

[11] God is a Spirit: and they that worship him must worship him in spirit and in truth. (John 4:24)

[12] And God said unto Moses, I AM THAT I AM: and he said, Thus shalt thou say unto the children of Israel, I AM hath sent me unto you. And God said moreover unto Moses, Thus shalt thou say unto the children of Israel, The LORD God of your fathers, the God of Abraham, the God of Isaac, and the God of Jacob, hath sent me unto you: this is my name for ever, and this is my memorial unto all generations. (Exodus 3:14; 15)

[13] Jesus Christ the same yesterday, and to day, and for ever. (Hebrews 13:8)

[14] And Jesus looking upon them saith, With men it is impossible, but not with God: for with God all things are possible. (Mark 10:27)

[15] And Moses said unto God, Behold, when I come unto the children of Israel, and shall say unto them, The God of your fathers hath sent me unto you; and they shall say to me, What is his name? what shall I say unto them? And God said unto Moses, I AM THAT I AM: and he said, Thus shalt thou say unto the children of Israel, I AM hath sent me unto you. (Exodus 3:13; 14)

[16] And I will harden Pharaoh's heart, that he shall follow after them; and I will be honoured upon Pharaoh, and upon all his host; that the Egyptians may know that I am the LORD. And they did so. (Exodus 14:4)

[17] And God said, Let us make man in our image, after our likeness: and let them have dominion over the fish of the sea, and over the fowl of the air, and over the cattle, and over all the earth, and over every creeping thing that creepeth upon the earth. So God created man in

his own image, in the image of God created he him; male and female created he them. (Genesis 1:26; 27)

And John bare record, saying, I saw the Spirit descending from heaven like a dove, and it abode upon him. (John 1:32)

[18] And the angel of the LORD appeared unto him in a flame of fire out of the midst of a bush: and he looked, and, behold, the bush burned with fire, and the bush was not consumed. And Moses said, I will now turn aside, and see this great sight, why the bush is not burnt. And when the LORD saw that he turned aside to see, God called unto him out of the midst of the bush, and said, Moses, Moses. And he said, Here am I. (Exodus 3:2; 4)

[19] For our God is a consuming fire. (Hebrews 12:29)

[20] And the angel of the LORD appeared unto him in a flame of fire out of the midst of a bush: and he looked, and, behold, the bush burned with fire, and the bush was not consumed. (Exodus 3:2)

[21] Go ye therefore, and teach all nations, baptizing them in the name of the Father, and of the Son, and of the Holy Ghost: (Matthew 28:19)

[22] Jesus answered and said unto him, If a man love me, he will keep my words: and my Father will love him, and we will come unto him, and make our abode with him. (John 14:23)

[23] But to us there is but one God, the Father, of whom are all things, and we in him; and one Lord Jesus Christ, by whom are all things, and we by him. (1Corinthians 8:6)

[24] But many that are first shall be last; and the last shall be first. (Matthew 19:30)

[25] I am Alpha and Omega, the beginning and the ending, saith the Lord, which is, and which was, and which is to come, the Almighty. (Revelation 1:8)

[26] I form the light, and create darkness: I make peace, and create evil: I the LORD do all these things. (Isaiah 45:7)

[27] See now that I, even I, am he, and there is no god with me: I kill, and I make alive; I wound, and I heal: neither is there any that can deliver out of my hand. (Deuteronomy 32:39)

[28] With the pure thou wilt shew thyself pure; and with the froward thou wilt shew thyself froward. (Psalm 18:26)

[29] Then said Solomon, The LORD hath said that he would dwell in the thick darkness. (2Chronicles 6:1)

[30] In the beginning was the Word, and the Word was with God, and the Word was God. (John 1:1)

[31] And the earth was without form, and void; and darkness was upon the face of the deep. And the Spirit of God moved upon the face of the waters. (Genesis 1:2)

[32] And without controversy great is the mystery of godliness: God was manifest in the flesh, justified in the Spirit, seen of angels, preached unto the Gentiles, believed on in the world, received up into glory. (1Timothy 3:16)

[33] Believest thou not that I am in the Father, and the Father in me? the words that I speak unto you I speak not of myself: but the Father that dwelleth in me, he doeth the works. (John 14:10)

[34] But when the Comforter is come, whom I will send unto you from the Father, even the Spirit of truth, which proceedeth from the Father, he shall testify of me: (John 15:26)

[35] I will not leave you comfortless: I will come to you. (John 14:18)

[36] For in him we live, and move, and have our being; as certain also of your own poets have said, For we are also his offspring. (Acts 17:28)

That in the dispensation of the fulness of times he might gather together in one all things in Christ, both which are in heaven, and which are on earth; even in him: (Ephesians 1:10)

[37] Who being the brightness of his glory, and the express image of his person, and upholding all things by the word of his power, when

he had by himself purged our sins, sat down on the right hand of the Majesty on high; (Hebrews 1:3)

³⁸ And he said unto them, When ye pray, say, Our Father which art in heaven, Hallowed be thy name. Thy kingdom come. Thy will be done, as in heaven, so in earth. (Luke 11:2)

³⁹ For of him, and through him, and to him, are all things: to whom be glory for ever. Amen. (Romans 11:36)

⁴⁰ But will God indeed dwell on the earth? behold, the heaven and heaven of heavens cannot contain thee; how much less this house that I have builded? (1Kings 8:27)

⁴¹ And without controversy great is the mystery of godliness: God was manifest in the flesh, justified in the Spirit, seen of angels, preached unto the Gentiles, believed on in the world, received up into glory. (1Timothy 3:16)

⁴² In the beginning was the Word, and the Word was with God, and the Word was God. And the Word was made flesh, and dwelt among us, (and we beheld his glory, the glory as of the only begotten of the Father,) full of grace and truth. (John 1:1; 14)

⁴³ Go ye therefore, and teach all nations, baptizing them in the name of the Father, and of the Son, and of the Holy Ghost: (Matthew 28:19)

And whatsoever ye do in word or deed, do all in the name of the Lord Jesus, giving thanks to God and the Father by him. (Colossians 3:17)

That at the name of Jesus every knee should bow, of things in heaven, and things in earth, and things under the earth; (Philippians 2:10)

⁴⁴ I can of mine own self do nothing: as I hear, I judge: and my judgment is just; because I seek not mine own will, but the will of the Father which hath sent me. (John 5:30)

⁴⁵ Then he answered and spake unto me, saying, This is the word of the LORD unto Zerubbabel, saying, Not by might, nor by power, but by my spirit, saith the LORD of hosts. (Zechariah 4:6)

[46] So shall my word be that goeth forth out of my mouth: it shall not return unto me void, but it shall accomplish that which I please, and it shall prosper in the thing whereto I sent it. (Isaiah 55:11)

[47] For in him dwelleth all the fulness of the Godhead bodily. (Colossians 2:9)

For there are three that bear record in heaven, the Father, the Word, and the Holy Ghost: and these three are one. (1John 5:7)

[48] This then is the message which we have heard of him, and declare unto you, that God is light, and in him is no darkness at all. (1John 1:5)

[49] For of him, and through him, and to him, are all things: to whom be glory for ever. Amen. (Romans 11:36)

[50] Who only hath immortality, dwelling in the light which no man can approach unto; whom no man hath seen, nor can see: to whom be honour and power everlasting. Amen. (1Timothy 6:16)

[51] Then spake Solomon, The LORD said that he would dwell in the thick darkness. (1Kings 8:12)

[52] Yea, the darkness hideth not from thee; but the night shineth as the day: the darkness and the light are both alike to thee. (Psalm 139:12)

[53] And the earth was without form, and void; and darkness was upon the face of the deep. And the Spirit of God moved upon the face of the waters. And God said, Let there be light: and there was light. And God saw the light, that it was good: and God divided the light from the darkness. (Genesis 1:2-4)

For God, who commanded the light to shine out of darkness, hath shined in our hearts, to give the light of the knowledge of the glory of God in the face of Jesus Christ. (2Corinthians 4:6)

[54] Martha saith unto him, I know that he shall rise again in the resurrection at the last day. Jesus said unto her, I am the resurrection, and the life: he that believeth in me, though he were dead, yet shall he live: (John 11:24; 25)

Verily, verily, I say unto you, Except a corn of wheat fall into the ground and die, it abideth alone: but if it die, it bringeth forth much fruit. (John 12:24)

[55] For the LORD will pass through to smite the Egyptians; and when he seeth the blood upon the lintel, and on the two side posts, the LORD will pass over the door, and will not suffer the destroyer to come in unto your houses to smite you. (Exodus 12:23)

And they had a king over them, which is the angel of the bottomless pit, whose name in the Hebrew tongue is Abaddon, but in the Greek tongue hath his name Apollyon. (Revelation 9:11)

[56] Forasmuch then as the children are partakers of flesh and blood, he also himself likewise took part of the same; that through death he might destroy him that had the power of death, that is, the devil; (Hebrews 2:14)

[57] And death and hell were cast into the lake of fire. This is the second death. (Revelation 20:14)

[58] For he must reign, till he hath put all enemies under his feet. The last enemy that shall be destroyed is death. (1Corinthians 15:25; 26)

[59] But I say unto you, Swear not at all; neither by heaven; for it is God's throne: Nor by the earth; for it is his footstool: neither by Jerusalem; for it is the city of the great King. (Matthew 5:34; 35)

And David himself saith in the book of Psalms, The LORD said unto my Lord, Sit thou on my right hand, Till I make thine enemies thy footstool. (Luke 20:42; 43)

[60] Then shall he say also unto them on the left hand, Depart from me, ye cursed, into everlasting fire, prepared for the devil and his angels: (Matthew 25:41)

[61] Now unto the King eternal, immortal, invisible, the only wise God, be honour and glory for ever and ever. Amen. (1Timothy 1:17)

[62] See now that I, even I, am he, and there is no god with me: I kill, and I make alive; I wound, and I heal: neither is there any that can deliver out of my hand. (Deuteronomy 32:39)

[63] Dearly beloved, avenge not yourselves, but rather give place unto wrath: for it is written, Vengeance is mine; I will repay, saith the Lord. (Romans 12:19)

[64] Wherefore if thy hand or thy foot offend thee, cut them off, and cast them from thee: it is better for thee to enter into life halt or maimed, rather than having two hands or two feet to be cast into everlasting fire. (Matthew 18:8)

For our God is a consuming fire. (Hebrews 12:29)

And the devil that deceived them was cast into the lake of fire and brimstone, where the beast and the false prophet are, and shall be tormented day and night for ever and ever. (Revelation 20:10)

[65] But I will forewarn you whom ye shall fear: Fear him, which after he hath killed hath power to cast into hell; yea, I say unto you, Fear him. (Luke 12:5)

[66] For our God is a consuming fire. (Hebrews 12:29)

Then shall the dust return to the earth as it was: and the spirit shall return unto God who gave it. (Ecclesiastes 12:7)

[67] And Moses returned unto the LORD, and said, Oh, this people have sinned a great sin, and have made them gods of gold. Yet now, if thou wilt forgive their sin—; and if not, blot me, I pray thee, out of thy book which thou hast written. And the LORD said unto Moses, Whosoever hath sinned against me, him will I blot out of my book. (Exodus 32:31-33)

The face of the LORD is against them that do evil, to cut off the remembrance of them from the earth. (Psalm 34:16)

[68] That the trial of your faith, being much more precious than of gold that perisheth, though it be tried with fire, might be found unto praise and honour and glory at the appearing of Jesus Christ: (1Peter 1:7)

I counsel thee to buy of me gold tried in the fire, that thou mayest be rich; and white raiment, that thou mayest be clothed, and that the shame of thy nakedness do not appear; and anoint thine eyes with eyesalve, that thou mayest see. (Revelation 3:18)

[69] And I went out by night by the gate of the valley, even before the dragon well, and to the dung port, and viewed the walls of Jerusalem, which were broken down, and the gates thereof were consumed with fire. (Nehemiah 2:13)

But the day of the Lord will come as a thief in the night; in the which the heavens shall pass away with a great noise, and the elements shall melt with fervent heat, the earth also and the works that are therein shall be burned up. Seeing then that all these things shall be dissolved, what manner of persons ought ye to be in all holy conversation and godliness, Looking for and hasting unto the coming of the day of God, wherein the heavens being on fire shall be dissolved, and the elements shall melt with fervent heat? (2Peter 3:10-12)

For, behold, the day cometh, that shall burn as an oven; and all the proud, yea, and all that do wickedly, shall be stubble: and the day that cometh shall burn them up, saith the LORD of hosts, that it shall leave them neither root nor branch. But unto you that fear my name shall the Sun of righteousness arise with healing in his wings; and ye shall go forth, and grow up as calves of the stall. And ye shall tread down the wicked; for they shall be ashes under the soles of your feet in the day that I shall do this, saith the LORD of hosts. (Malachi 4:1-3)

[70] And if thy hand offend thee, cut it off: it is better for thee to enter into life maimed, than having two hands to go into hell, into the fire that never shall be quenched: Where their worm dieth not, and the fire is not quenched. And if thy foot offend thee, cut it off: it is better for thee to enter halt into life, than having two feet to be cast into hell, into the fire that never shall be quenched: Where their worm dieth not, and the fire is not quenched. And if thine eye offend thee, pluck it out: it is better for thee to enter into the kingdom of God with one eye, than having two eyes to be cast into hell fire: Where their worm dieth not, and the fire is not quenched. (Mark 9:43-48)

[71] For the living know that they shall die: but the dead know not any thing, neither have they any more a reward; for the memory of them is forgotten. Also their love, and their hatred, and their envy, is now perished; neither have they any more a portion for ever in any thing that is done under the sun. (Ecclesiastes 9:5; 6)

[72] The Son of man shall send forth his angels, and they shall gather out of his kingdom all things that offend, and them which do iniquity; And shall cast them into a furnace of fire: there shall be wailing and gnashing of teeth. (Matthew 13:41; 42)

[73] But, beloved, be not ignorant of this one thing, that one day is with the Lord as a thousand years, and a thousand years as one day. (2Peter 3:8)

[74] But these, as natural brute beasts, made to be taken and destroyed, speak evil of the things that they understand not; and shall utterly perish in their own corruption; (2Peter 2:12)

[75] It is a fearful thing to fall into the hands of the living God. (Hebrews 10:31)

[76] And the Spirit and the bride say, Come. And let him that heareth say, Come. And let him that is athirst come. And whosoever will, let him take the water of life freely. (Revelation 22:17)

[77] For whom he did foreknow, he also did predestinate to be conformed to the image of his Son, that he might be the firstborn among many brethren. Moreover whom he did predestinate, them he also called: and whom he called, them he also justified: and whom he justified, them he also glorified. (Romans 8:29-30)

[78] All that the Father giveth me shall come to me; and him that cometh to me I will in no wise cast out. (John 6:37)

No man can come to me, except the Father which hath sent me draw him: and I will raise him up at the last day. (John 6:44)

[79] For God so loved the world (men and women of every tribe, nation and tongue), that he gave his only begotten Son, that whosoever believeth in him should not perish, but have everlasting life. (John 3:16)

CHAPTER TWO

[1] God, who at sundry times and in divers manners spake in time past unto the fathers by the prophets, Hath in these last days spoken unto us by his Son, whom he hath appointed heir of all things, by whom also he made the worlds; (Hebrews 1:1)

[2] In the beginning was the Word, and the Word was with God, and the Word was God. And the Word was made flesh, and dwelt among us, (and we beheld his glory, the glory as of the only begotten of the Father,) full of grace and truth. (John 1:1; 14)

[3] And without controversy great is the mystery of godliness: God was manifest in the flesh, justified in the Spirit, seen of angels, preached unto the Gentiles, believed on in the world, received up into glory. (1Timothy 3:16)

[4] Who being the brightness of his glory, and the express image of his person, and upholding all things by the word of his power, when he had by himself purged our sins, sat down on the right hand of the Majesty on high; (Hebrews 1:3)

[5] Beware lest any man spoil you through philosophy and vain deceit, after the tradition of men, after the rudiments of the world, and not after Christ. For in him dwelleth all the fulness of the Godhead bodily. (Colossians 2:8)

[6] Whereby are given unto us exceeding great and precious promises: that by these ye might be partakers of the divine nature, having escaped the corruption that is in the world through lust. (2Peter 1:4)

[7] But the hour cometh, and now is, when the true worshippers shall worship the Father in spirit and in truth: for the Father seeketh such to worship him. (John 4:23)

[8] Sanctify them through thy truth: thy word is truth. (John 17:17)

[9] Who being the brightness of his glory, and the express image of his person, and upholding all things by the word of his power, when he

had by himself purged our sins, sat down on the right hand of the Majesty on high; (Hebrews 1:3)

[10] For God, who commanded the light to shine out of darkness, hath shined in our hearts, to give the light of the knowledge of the glory of God in the face of Jesus Christ. (2Corinthians 4:6)

All things are delivered unto me of my Father: and no man knoweth the Son, but the Father; neither knoweth any man the Father, save the Son, and he to whomsoever the Son will reveal him. (Matthew 11:27)

[11] Verily I say unto you, All sins shall be forgiven unto the sons of men, and blasphemies wherewith soever they shall blaspheme: But he that shall blaspheme against the Holy Ghost hath never forgiveness, but is in danger of eternal damnation: Because they said, He hath an unclean spirit. (Mark 3:28-30)

[12] But Peter said, Ananias, why hath Satan filled thine heart to lie to the Holy Ghost, andto keep back part of the price of the land? Whiles it remained, was it not thine own? and after it was sold, was it not in thine own power? why hast thou conceived this thing in thine heart? thou hast not lied unto men, but unto God. (Acts 5:3; 4)

[13] According as his divine power hath given unto us all things that pertain unto life and godliness, through the knowledge of him that hath called us to glory and virtue: (2Peter 1:3)

[14] Then he answered and spake unto me, saying, This is the word of the LORD unto Zerubbabel, saying, Not by might, nor by power, but by my spirit, saith the LORD of hosts. (Zechariah 4:6)

[15] After these things the word of the LORD came unto Abram in a vision, saying, Fear not, Abram: I am thy shield, and thy exceeding great reward. (Genesis 15:1)

But the Spirit of the LORD came upon Gideon, and he blew a trumpet; and Abiezer was gathered after him. (Judges 6:34)

[16] All things are delivered unto me of my Father: and no man knoweth the Son, but the Father; neither knoweth any man the Father, save

the Son, and he to whomsoever the Son will reveal him. (Matthew 11:27)

[17] No man hath seen God at any time; the only begotten Son, which is in the bosom of the Father, he hath declared him. (John 1:18)

[18] Jesus saith unto him, Have I been so long time with you, and yet hast thou not known me, Philip? he that hath seen me hath seen the Father; and how sayest thou then, Shew us the Father? (John 14:9)

[19] Jesus saith unto him, I am the way, the truth, and the life: no man cometh unto the Father, but by me. (John 14:6)

[20] Who is the image of the invisible God, the firstborn of every creature: For by him were all things created, that are in heaven, and that are in earth, visible and invisible, whether they be thrones, or dominions, or principalities, or powers: all things were created by him, and for him. (Colossians 1:15-16)

[21] And without controversy great is the mystery of godliness: God was manifest in the flesh, justified in the Spirit, seen of angels, preached unto the Gentiles, believed on in the world, received up into glory. (1Timothy 3:16)

[22] Him, being delivered by the determinate counsel and foreknowledge of God, ye have taken, and by wicked hands have crucified and slain: (Acts 2:23)

[23] In the beginning was the Word, and the Word was with God, and the Word was God. And the Word was made flesh, and dwelt among us, (and we beheld his glory, the glory as of the only begotten of the Father,) full of grace and truth. (John 1:1; 14)

[24] And the angel answered and said unto her, The Holy Ghost shall come upon thee, and the power of the Highest shall overshadow thee: therefore also that holy thing which shall be born of thee shall be called the Son of God. (Luke 1:35)

[25] Now the Lord is that Spirit: and where the Spirit of the Lord is, there is liberty. (2Corinthians 3:17)

And so it is written, The first man Adam was made a living soul; the last Adam was made a quickening spirit. (1Corinthians 15:45)

[26] And without controversy great is the mystery of godliness: God was manifest in the flesh, justified in the Spirit, seen of angels, preached unto the Gentiles, believed on in the world, received up into glory. (1Timothy 3:16)

[27] And so it is written, The first man Adam was made a living soul; the last Adam was made a quickening (life giving) spirit. (1Corinthians 15:45)

[28] For there are three that bear record in heaven, the Father, the Word, and the Holy Ghost: and these three are one. (1John 5:7)

And he was clothed with a vesture dipped in blood: and his name is called The Word of God. (Revelation 19:13)

[29] Him, being delivered by the determinate counsel and foreknowledge of God, ye have taken, and by wicked hands have crucified and slain: (Acts 2:23)

[30] And no man hath ascended up to heaven, but he that came down from heaven, even the Son of man which is in heaven. (John 3:13)

[31] That which hath been is now; and that which is to be hath already been; and God requireth that which is past. (Ecclesiastes 3:15)

[32] Even when we were dead in sins, hath quickened us together with Christ, (by grace ye are saved;) And hath raised us up together, and made us sit together in heavenly places in Christ Jesus: (Ephesians 2:5; 6)

[33] Who opposeth and exalteth himself above all that is called God, or that is worshipped; so that he as God sitteth in the temple of God, shewing himself that he is God. (2Thessalonians 2:4)

[34] It is sown a natural body; it is raised a spiritual body. There is a natural body, and there is a spiritual body. And so it is written, The first man Adam was made a living soul; the last Adam was made a quickening spirit. Howbeit that was not first which is spiritual, but that which is natural; and afterward that which is spiritual. (1Corinthians 15:44-46)

[35] Him, being delivered by the determinate counsel and foreknowledge of God, ye have taken, and by wicked hands have crucified and slain: (Acts 2:23)

For whom he did foreknow, he also did predestinate to be conformed to the image of his Son, that he might be the firstborn among many brethren. (Romans 8:29)

Peter, an apostle of Jesus Christ, to the strangers scattered throughout Pontus, Galatia, Cappadocia, Asia, and Bithynia, Elect according to the foreknowledge of God the Father, through sanctification of the Spirit, unto obedience and sprinkling of the blood of Jesus Christ: Grace unto you, and peace, be multiplied. (1Peter 1:1; 2)

[36] For my thoughts are not your thoughts, neither are your ways my ways, saith the LORD. For as the heavens are higher than the earth, so are my ways higher than your ways, and my thoughts than your thoughts. (Isaiah 55:8; 9)

[37] But the natural man receiveth not the things of the Spirit of God: for they are foolishness unto him: neither can he know them, because they are spiritually discerned. (1Corinthians 2:14)

[38] (As it is written, I have made thee a father of many nations,) before him whom he believed, even God, who quickeneth the dead, and calleth those things which be not as though they were. (Romans 4:17)

[39] Remember the former things of old: for I am God, and there is none else; I am God, and there is none like me, Declaring the end from the beginning, and from ancient times the things that are not yet done, saying, My counsel shall stand, and I will do all my pleasure: (Isaiah 46:9; 10)

[40] He that sitteth in the heavens shall laugh: the Lord shall have them in derision. (Psalm 2:4)

The wicked plotteth against the just, and gnasheth upon him with his teeth. The Lord shall laugh at him: for he seeth that his day is coming. (Psalm 37:12; 13)

[41] For verily I say unto you, Till heaven and earth pass, one jot or one tittle shall in no wise pass from the law, till all be fulfilled. (Matthew 5:18)

But the day of the Lord will come as a thief in the night; in the which the heavens shall pass away with a great noise, and the elements shall melt with fervent heat, the earth also and the works that are therein shall be burned up. (2Peter 3:10)

[42] And I saw a new heaven and a new earth: for the first heaven and the first earth were passed away; and there was no more sea. (Revelation 21:1)

[43] The thing that hath been, it is that which shall be; and that which is done is that which shall be done: and there is no new thing under the sun. (Ecclesiastes 1:9)

[44] Again, he limiteth a certain day, saying in David, To day, after so long a time; as it is said, To day if ye will hear his voice, harden not your hearts. (Hebrews 4:7)

[45] And God said unto Moses, I AM THAT I AM: and he said, Thus shalt thou say unto the children of Israel, I AM hath sent me unto you. (Exodus 3:14)

[46] So also is the resurrection of the dead. It is sown in corruption; it is raised in incorruption: It is sown in dishonour; it is raised in glory: it is sown in weakness; it is raised in power: (1Corintians 15:42; 43)

[47] And the earth was without form, and void; and darkness was upon the face of the deep. And the Spirit of God moved upon the face of the waters. And God said, Let there be light: and there was light. (Genesis 1:2; 3)

For God, who commanded the light to shine out of darkness, hath shined in our hearts, to give the light of the knowledge of the glory of God in the face of Jesus Christ. (2Corintians 4:6)

[48] And so it is written, The first man Adam was made a living soul; the last Adam was made a quickening spirit. Howbeit that was not first which is spiritual, but that which is natural; and afterward that which is spiritual. The first man is of the earth, earthy: the second

man is the Lord from heaven. As is the earthy, such are they also that are earthy: and as is the heavenly, such are they also that are heavenly. And as we have borne the image of the earthy, we shall also bear the image of the heavenly. (1Corinthians 15:45-49)

[49] Verily, verily, I say unto you, Except a corn of wheat fall into the ground and die, it abideth alone: but if it die, it bringeth forth much fruit. (John 12:24)

[50] In that he saith, A new covenant, he hath made the first old. Now that which decayeth and waxeth old is ready to vanish away. (Hebrews 8:13)

[51] When the ruler of the feast had tasted the water that was made wine, and knew not whence it was: (but the servants which drew the water knew;) the governor of the feast called the bridegroom, And saith unto him, Every man at the beginning doth set forth good wine; and when men have well drunk, then that which is worse: but thou hast kept the good wine until now. (John 2:9; 10)

[52] The thing that hath been, it is that which shall be; and that which is done is that which shall be done: and there is no new thing under the sun. Is there any thing whereof it may be said, See, this is new? it hath been already of old time, which was before us. (Ecclesiastes 1:9; 10)

That which hath been is now; and that which is to be hath already been; and God requireth that which is past. (Ecclesiastes 3:15)

[53] But as it is written, Eye hath not seen, nor ear heard, neither have entered into the heart of man, the things which God hath prepared for them that love him. But God hath revealed them unto us by his Spirit: for the Spirit searcheth all things, yea, the deep things of God. (1Corinthians 2:9; 10)

Which in other ages was not made known unto the sons of men, as it is now revealed unto his holy apostles and prophets by the Spirit; (Ephesians 3:5)

[54] And now, O Father, glorify thou me with thine own self with the glory which I had with thee before the world was. (John 17:5)

And he was clothed with a vesture dipped in blood: and his name is called The Word of God. (Revelation 19:13)

[55] I and my Father are one. (John 10:30)

And now I am no more in the world, but these are in the world, and I come to thee. Holy Father, keep through thine own name those whom thou hast given me, that they may be one, as we are. (John 17:11)

[56] For unto us a child is born, unto us a son is given: and the government shall be upon his shoulder: and his name shall be called Wonderful, Counsellor, The mighty God, The everlasting Father, The Prince of Peace. (Isaiah 9:6)

Now the Lord is that Spirit: and where the Spirit of the Lord is, there is liberty. (2Corinthians 3:17)

[57] Therefore let all the house of Israel know assuredly, that God hath made that same Jesus, whom ye have crucified, both Lord and Christ. (Acts 2:36)

[58] And the Word was made flesh, and dwelt among us, (and we beheld his glory, the glory as of the only begotten of the Father,) full of grace and truth. (John 1:14)

He that hath an ear, let him hear what the Spirit saith unto the churches; To him that overcometh will I give to eat of the tree of life, which is in the midst of the paradise of God. (Revelation 2:7)

[59] I am Alpha and Omega, the beginning and the ending, saith the Lord, which is, and which was, and which is to come, the Almighty. (Revelation 1:8)

[60] And Jesus came and spake unto them, saying, All power is given unto me in heaven and in earth. (Matthew 28:18)

[61] To whom God would make known what is the riches of the glory of this mystery among the Gentiles; which is Christ in you, the hope of glory: (Colossians 1:27)

[62] (But this spake he of the Spirit, which they that believe on him should receive: for the Holy Ghost was not yet given; because that Jesus was not yet glorified.) (John 7:39)

[63] For there is one God, and one mediator between God and men, the man Christ Jesus; (1Timothy 2:5)

To him that overcometh will I grant to sit with me in my throne, even as I also overcame, and am set down with my Father in his throne. (Revelation 3:21)

[64] And hath raised us up together, and made us sit together in heavenly places in Christ Jesus: (Ephesians 2:6)

[65] The thing that hath been, it is that which shall be; and that which is done is that which shall be done: and there is no new thing under the sun. (Ecclesiastes 1:9)

[66] While we look not at the things which are seen, but at the things which are not seen: for the things which are seen are temporal; but the things which are not seen are eternal. (2Corinthians 4:18)

[67] Herein is our love made perfect, that we may have boldness in the day of judgment: because as he is, so are we in this world. (1John 4:17)

[68] For it pleased the Father that in him (Christ and his church) should all fulness dwell; (Colossians 1:19)

[69] I and my Father are one. (John 10:30)

[70] If I do not the works of my Father, believe me not. But if I do, though ye believe not me, believe the works: that ye may know, and believe, that the Father is in me, and I in him. (John 10:37; 38)

[71] I am Alpha and Omega, the beginning and the ending, saith the Lord, which is, and which was, and which is to come, the Almighty. (Revelation 1:8)

[72] But unto the Son he saith, Thy throne, O God, is for ever and ever: a sceptre of righteousness is the sceptre of thy kingdom. Thou hast loved righteousness, and hated iniquity; therefore God, even thy God, hath anointed thee with the oil of gladness above thy fellows. (Hebrews 1:8; 9)

[73] Jesus Christ the same yesterday, and to day, and forever. (Hebrews 13:8)

[74] Wherefore when he cometh into the world, he saith, Sacrifice and offering thou wouldest not, but a body hast thou prepared me: (Hebrews 10:5)

[75] In the beginning was the Word, and the Word was with God, and the Word was God. (*Not just a god as some would have us believe*) And the Word was made flesh, and dwelt among us, (and we beheld his glory, the glory as of the only begotten of the Father,) full of grace and truth. (John 1:1; 14)

[76] It is the spirit that quickeneth; the flesh profiteth nothing: the words that I speak unto you, they are spirit, and they are life. (John 6:63)

[77] Believest thou not that I am in the Father, and the Father in me? the words that I speak unto you I speak not of myself: but the Father that dwelleth in me, he doeth the works. (John 14:10)

[78] And the angel answered and said unto her, The Holy Ghost shall come upon thee, and the power of the Highest shall overshadow thee: therefore also that holy thing which shall be born of thee shall be called the Son of God. (Luke 1:35)

[79] Then said Jesus unto them, When ye have lifted up the Son of man, then shall ye know that I am he, and that I do nothing of myself; but as my Father hath taught me, I speak these things. (John 8:28)

[80] So shall my word be that goeth forth out of my mouth: it shall not return unto me void, but it shall accomplish that which I please, and it shall prosper in the thing whereto I sent it. (Isaiah 55:11)

[81] But he answered and said, It is written, Man shall not live by bread alone, but by every word that proceedeth out of the mouth of God. (Matthew 4:4)

Then he answered and spake unto me, saying, This is the word of the LORD unto Zerubbabel, saying, Not by might, nor by power, but by my spirit, saith the LORD of hosts. (Zechariah 4:6)

[82] Believest thou not that I am in the Father, and the Father in me? the words that I speak unto you I speak not of myself: but the Father that dwelleth in me, he doeth the works. (John 14:10)

[83] And all things are of God, who hath reconciled us to himself by Jesus Christ, and hath given to us the ministry of reconciliation; To wit, that God was in Christ, reconciling the world unto himself, not imputing their trespasses unto them; and hath committed unto us the word of reconciliation. (2Corinthians 5:18-19)

[84] For in him dwelleth all the fulness of the Godhead bodily. And ye are complete in him, which is the head of all principality and power: (Colossians 2:9; 10)

[85] He that heareth you heareth me; and he that despiseth you despiseth me; and he that despiseth me despiseth him that sent me. (Luke 10:16)

[86] And again, when he bringeth in the firstbegotten into the world, he saith, And let all the angels of God worship him. (Hebrews 1:6)

[87] Wherefore God also hath highly exalted him, and given him a name which is above every name: That at the name of Jesus every knee should bow, of things in heaven, and things in earth, and things under the earth; And that every tongue should confess that Jesus Christ is Lord, to the glory of God the Father. (Philippians 2:9-11)

[88] For he whom God hath sent speaketh the words of God: for God giveth not the Spirit by measure unto him. (John 3:34)

[89] And in that day ye shall ask me nothing. Verily, verily, I say unto you, Whatsoever ye shall ask the Father in my name, he will give it you. (John 16:23)

[90] And whatsoever ye shall ask in my name, that will I do, that the Father may be glorified in the Son. If ye shall ask any thing in my name, I will do it. (John 14:13; 14)

[91] After this manner therefore pray ye: Our Father which art in heaven, Hallowed be thy name. (Matthew 6:9)

[92] Jesus saith unto him, I am the way, the truth, and the life: no man cometh unto the Father, but by me. (John 14:6)

[93] And Jesus came and spake unto them, saying, All power is given unto me in heaven and in earth. (Matthew 28:18)

[94] And without controversy great is the mystery of godliness: God was manifest in the flesh, justified in the Spirit, seen of angels, preached unto the Gentiles, believed on in the world, received up into glory. (1Timothy 3:16)

[95] At that time Jesus answered and said, I thank thee, O Father, Lord of heaven and earth, because thou hast hid these things from the wise and prudent, and hast revealed them unto babes. (Matthew 11:25)

But we speak the wisdom of God in a mystery, even the hidden wisdom, which God ordained before the world unto our glory: (1Corinthians 2:7)

[96] Now Israel loved Joseph more than all his children, because he was the son of his old age: and he made him a coat of many colours. And when his brethren saw that their father loved him more than all his brethren, they hated him, and could not speak peaceably unto him. And Joseph dreamed a dream, and he told it his brethren: and they hated him yet the more. And he said unto them, Hear, I pray you, this dream which I have dreamed: For, behold, we were binding sheaves in the field, and, lo, my sheaf arose, and also stood upright; and, behold, your sheaves stood round about, and made obeisance to my sheaf. And his brethren said to him, Shalt thou indeed reign over us? or shalt thou indeed have dominion over us? And they hated him yet the more for his dreams, and for his words. (Genesis 37:3-8)

[97] Hear another parable: There was a certain householder, which planted a vineyard, and hedged it round about, and digged a winepress in it, and built a tower, and let it out to husbandmen, and went into a far country: And when the time of the fruit drew near, he sent his servants to the husbandmen, that they might receive the fruits of it. And the husbandmen took his servants, and beat one, and killed another, and stoned another. Again, he sent other servants more than the first: and they did unto them likewise. But last of all he sent unto them his son, saying, They will reverence my son. But when the husbandmen saw the son, they said among themselves, This is the heir; come, let us kill him, and let us seize on his inheritance. And they caught him, and cast him out of the vineyard, and slew him. (Matthew 21:33-39)

[98] How art thou fallen from heaven, O Lucifer, son of the morning! how art thou cut down to the ground, which didst weaken the nations! For thou hast said in thine heart, I will ascend into heaven, I will exalt my throne above the stars of God: I will sit also upon the mount of the congregation, in the sides of the north: I will ascend above the heights of the clouds; I will be like the most High. (Isaiah 14:12-14)

[99] And when he was come into the temple, the chief priests and the elders of the people came unto him as he was teaching, and said, By what authority doest thou these things? and who gave thee this authority? (Matthew 21:23)

[100] As it is written, Jacob have I loved, but Esau have I hated. What shall we say then? Is there unrighteousness with God? God forbid. For he saith to Moses, I will have mercy on whom I will have mercy, and I will have compassion on whom I will have compassion. So then it is not of him that willeth, nor of him that runneth, but of God that sheweth mercy. For the scripture saith unto Pharaoh, Even for this same purpose have I raised thee up, that I might shew my power in thee, and that my name might be declared throughout all the earth. Therefore hath he mercy on whom he will have mercy, and whom he will he hardeneth. (Romans 9:13-18)

[101] But God hath chosen the foolish things of the world to confound the wise; and God hath chosen the weak things of the world to confound the things which are mighty; And base things of the world, and things which are despised, hath God chosen, yea, and things which are not, to bring to nought things that are: That no flesh should glory in his presence. (1Corinthians 1:29)

[102] Jesus saith unto them, Did ye never read in the scriptures, The stone which the builders rejected, the same is become the head of the corner: this is the Lord's doing, and it is marvellous in our eyes? (Matthew 21:42)

[103] (For the children being not yet born, neither having done any good or evil, that the purpose of God according to election might stand, not of works, but of him that calleth;) It was said unto her, The elder shall serve the younger. (Romans 9:11-12)

[104] And every one that hath forsaken houses, or brethren, or sisters, or father, or mother, or wife, or children, or lands, for my name's sake, shall receive an hundredfold, and shall inherit everlasting life. But many that are first shall be last; and the last shall be first. (Matthew 19:29; 30)

[105] And the LORD said unto Cain, Where is Abel thy brother? And he said, I know not: Am I my brother's keeper? And he said, What hast thou done? the voice of thy brother's blood crieth unto me from the ground. (Genesis 4:10)

[106] But ye are come unto mount Sion, and unto the city of the living God, the heavenly Jerusalem, and to an innumerable company of angels, To the general assembly and church of the firstborn, which are written in heaven, and to God the Judge of all, and to the spirits of just men made perfect, And to Jesus the mediator of the new covenant, and to the blood of sprinkling, that speaketh better things than that of Abel. (Hebrews 12:22-24)

[107] And fear not them which kill the body, but are not able to kill the soul: but rather fear him which is able to destroy both soul and body in hell. (Matthew 10:28)

[108] For I will pass through the land of Egypt this night, and will smite all the firstborn in the land of Egypt, both man and beast; and against all the gods of Egypt I will execute judgment: I am the LORD. And the blood shall be to you for a token upon the houses where ye are: and when I see the blood, I will pass over you, and the plague shall not be upon you to destroy you, when I smite the land of Egypt. (Exodus 12:12; 13)

[109] For when Moses had spoken every precept to all the people according to the law, he took the blood of calves and of goats, with water, and scarlet wool, and hyssop, and sprinkled both the book, and all the people, Saying, This is the blood of the testament which God hath enjoined unto you. Moreover he sprinkled with blood both the tabernacle, and all the vessels of the ministry. And almost all things are by the law purged with blood; and without shedding of blood is no remission. (Hebrews 9:19-22)

[110] Who hath believed our report? and to whom is the arm of the LORD revealed? For he shall grow up before him as a tender plant, and as a root out of a dry ground: he hath no form nor comeliness; and when we shall see him, there is no beauty that we should desire him. He is despised and rejected of men; a man of sorrows, and acquainted with grief: and we hid as it were our faces from him; he was despised, and we esteemed him not. Surely he hath borne our griefs, and carried our sorrows: yet we did esteem him stricken, smitten of God, and afflicted. But he was wounded for our transgressions, he was bruised for our iniquities: the chastisement of our peace was upon him; and with his stripes we are healed. All we like sheep have gone astray; we have turned every one to his own way; and the LORD hath laid on him the iniquity of us all. (Isaiah 53:1-6)

CHAPTER THREE

[1] Blessed is the man that walketh not in the counsel of the ungodly, nor standeth in the way of sinners, nor sitteth in the seat of the scornful. But his delight is in the law of the LORD; and in his law doth he meditate day and night. And he shall be like a tree planted by the rivers of water, that bringeth forth his fruit in his season; his leaf also shall not wither; and whatsoever he doeth shall prosper. (Psalm 1:1-3)

[2] And God saw every thing that he had made, and, behold, it was very good. And the evening and the morning were the sixth day. (Genesis 1:31)

[3] He hath made every thing beautiful in his time: also he hath set the world in their heart, so that no man can find out the work that God maketh from the beginning to the end. (Ecclesiastes 3:11)

[4] And out of the ground made the LORD God to grow every tree that is pleasant to the sight, and good for food; the tree of life also in the midst of the garden, and the tree of knowledge of good and evil. (Genesis 2:9)

[5] And when the woman saw that the tree was good for food, and that it was pleasant to the eyes, and a tree to be desired to make one

wise, she took of the fruit thereof, and did eat, and gave also unto her husband with her; and he did eat. (Genesis 3:6)

[6] And the LORD God commanded the man, saying, Of every tree of the garden thou mayest freely eat: But of the tree of the knowledge of good and evil, thou shalt not eat of it: for in the day that thou eatest thereof thou shalt surely die. (Genesis 2:16)

[7] To every thing there is a season, and a time to every purpose under the heaven: (Ecclesiastes 3:1)

[8] And they were both naked, the man and his wife, and were not ashamed. (Genesis 2:25)

And he said, Who told thee that thou wast naked? Hast thou eaten of the tree, whereof I commanded thee that thou shouldest not eat? (Genesis 3:11)

[9] And the LORD God said, Behold, the man is become as one of us, to know good and evil: and now, lest he put forth his hand, and take also of the tree of life, and eat, and live for ever: (Genesis 3:22)

[10] Search the scriptures; for in them ye think ye have eternal life: and they are they which testify of me. (John 5:39)

[11] And Adam called his wife's name Eve; because she was the mother of all living. (Genesis 3:20)

[12] Wherefore they are no more twain, but one flesh. What therefore God hath joined together, let not man put asunder. (Matthew 19:6)

[13] According as he hath chosen us in him before the foundation of the world, that we should be holy and without blame before him in love: (Ephesians 1:4)

[14] Who also hath made us able ministers of the new testament; not of the letter, but of the spirit: for the letter killeth, but the spirit giveth life. (2Corinthians 3:6)

[15] And they were both naked, the man and his wife, and were not ashamed. (Genesis 2:25)

[16] But the hour cometh, and now is, when the true worshippers shall worship the Father in spirit and in truth: for the Father seeketh such to

worship him. God is a Spirit: and they that worship him must worship him in spirit and in truth. (John 4:23)

[17] For we know that if our earthly house of this tabernacle were dissolved, we have a building of God, an house not made with hands, eternal in the heavens. For in this we groan, earnestly desiring to be clothed upon with our house which is from heaven: If so be that being clothed we shall not be found naked. For we that are in this tabernacle do groan, being burdened: not for that we would be unclothed, but clothed upon, that mortality might be swallowed up of life. Now he that hath wrought us for the selfsame thing is God, who also hath given unto us the earnest of the Spirit. Therefore we are always confident, knowing that, whilst we are at home in the body, we are absent from the Lord: (2Corinthians 5:1-6)

[18] And Jesus said, Are ye also yet without understanding? Do not ye yet understand, that whatsoever entereth in at the mouth goeth into the belly, and is cast out into the draught? But those things which proceed out of the mouth come forth from the heart; and they defile the man. For out of the heart proceed evil thoughts, murders, adulteries, fornications, thefts, false witness, blasphemies: These are the things which defile a man: but to eat with unwashen hands defileth not a man. (Matthew 15:16)

[19] Unto Adam also and to his wife did the LORD God make coats of skins, and clothed them. (Genesis 3:21)

[20] And almost all things are by the law purged with blood; and without shedding of blood is no remission. (Hebrews 9:22)

[21] And the LORD God commanded the man, saying, Of every tree of the garden thou mayest freely eat: But of the tree of the knowledge of good and evil, thou shalt not eat of it: for in the day that thou eatest thereof thou shalt surely die. (Genesis 2:16)

And you, being dead in your sins and the uncircumcision of your flesh, hath he quickened together with him, having forgiven you all trespasses. (Colossians 2:13)

[22] Because thou sayest, I am rich, and increased with goods, and have need of nothing; and knowest not that thou art wretched, and

miserable, and poor, and blind, and naked: I counsel thee to buy of me gold tried in the fire, that thou mayest be rich; and white raiment, that thou mayest be clothed, and that the shame of thy nakedness do not appear; and anoint thine eyes with eyesalve, that thou mayest see. (Revelation 3:17; 18)

²³ While we look not at the things which are seen, but at the things which are not seen: for the things which are seen are temporal; but the things which are not seen are eternal. (2Corinthians 4:18)

²⁴ But God giveth it a body as it hath pleased him, and to every seed his own body. All flesh is not the same flesh: but there is one kind of flesh of men, another flesh of beasts, another of fishes, and another of birds. (1Corinthians 15:38)

²⁵ The life is more than meat, and the body is more than raiment. (Luke 12:23)

Consider the lilies how they grow: they toil not, they spin not; and yet I say unto you, that Solomon in all his glory was not arrayed like one of these. If then God so clothe the grass, which is to day in the field, and to morrow is cast into the oven; how much more will he clothe you, O ye of little faith? (Luke 12:27; 28)

²⁶ Furthermore we have had fathers of our flesh which corrected us, and we gave them reverence: shall we not much rather be in subjection unto the Father of spirits, and live? (Hebrews 12:9)

²⁷ Wherefore when he cometh into the world, he saith, Sacrifice and offering thou wouldest not, but a body hast thou prepared me: (Hebrews 10:5)

²⁸ For thou hast said in thine heart, I will ascend into heaven, I will exalt my throne above the stars of God: I will sit also upon the mount of the congregation, in the sides of the north: I will ascend above the heights of the clouds; I will be like the most High. (Isaiah 14:13)

²⁹ And the serpent said unto the woman, Ye shall not surely die: For God doth know that in the day ye eat thereof, then your eyes shall be opened, and ye shal l be as gods, knowing good and evil. (Genesis 3:4; 5)

[30] Then he answered and spake unto me, saying, This is the word of the LORD unto Zerubbabel, saying, Not by might, nor by power, but by my spirit, saith the LORD of hosts. (Zechariah 4:6)

[31] Thou hast been in Eden the garden of God; every precious stone was thy covering, the sardius, topaz, and the diamond, the beryl, the onyx, and the jasper, the sapphire, the emerald, and the carbuncle, and gold: the workmanship of thy tabrets and of thy pipes was prepared in thee in the day that thou wast created. Thou art the anointed cherub that covereth; and I have set thee so: thou wast upon the holy mountain of God; thou hast walked up and down in the midst of the stones of fire. Thou wast perfect in thy ways from the day that thou wast created, till iniquity was found in thee. (Ezekiel 28:13-15)

[32] How art thou fallen from heaven, O Lucifer, son of the morning! how art thou cut down to the ground, which didst weaken the nations! (Isaiah 14:12)

[33] And the LORD God said unto the serpent, Because thou hast done this, thou art cursed above all cattle, and above every beast of the field; upon thy belly shalt thou go, and dust shalt thou eat all the days of thy life: And I will put enmity between thee and the woman, and between thy seed and her seed; it shall bruise thy head, and thou shalt bruise his heel. (Genesis 3:15)

[34] But he answered and said, I am not sent but unto the lost sheep of the house of Israel. (Matthew 15:24)

[35] These twelve Jesus sent forth, and commanded them, saying, Go not into the way of the Gentiles, and into any city of the Samaritans enter ye not: But go rather to the lost sheep of the house of Israel. And as ye go, preach, saying, The kingdom of heaven is at hand. Heal the sick, cleanse the lepers, raise the dead, cast out devils: freely ye have received, freely give. (Matthew 10:5-8)

[36] For this cause I Paul, the prisoner of Jesus Christ for you Gentiles, If ye have heard of the dispensation of the grace of God which is given me to you-ward: How that by revelation he made known unto me the mystery; (as I wrote afore in few words, Whereby, when ye read, ye may understand my knowledge in the mystery of Christ) Which in other ages was not made known unto the sons of men, as it is now

revealed unto his holy apostles and prophets by the Spirit; That the Gentiles should be fellowheirs, and of the same body, and partakers of his promise in Christ by the gospel: (Ephesians 3:1-6)

[37] Let no man therefore judge you in meat, or in drink, or in respect of an holyday, or of the new moon, or of the sabbath days: Which are a shadow of things to come; but the body is of Christ. (Colossians 2:16)

For the law having a shadow of good things to come, and not the very image of the things, can never with those sacrifices which they offered year by year continually make the comers thereunto perfect. (Hebrews 10:1)

[38] For finding fault with them, he saith, Behold, the days come, saith the Lord, when I will make a new covenant with the house of Israel and with the house of Judah: Not according to the covenant that I made with their fathers in the day when I took them by the hand to lead them out of the land of Egypt; because they continued not in my covenant, and I regarded them not, saith the Lord. For this is the covenant that I will make with the house of Israel after those days, saith the Lord; I will put my laws into their mind, and write them in their hearts: and I will be to them a God, and they shall be to me a people: (Hebrews 8:8-10)

Hath not the potter power over the clay, of the same lump to make one vessel unto honour, and another unto dishonour? What if God, willing to shew his wrath, and to make his power known, endured with much longsuffering the vessels of wrath fitted to destruction: And that he might make known the riches of his glory on the vessels of mercy, which he had afore prepared unto glory, Even us, whom he hath called, not of the Jews only, but also of the Gentiles? As he saith also in Osee, I will call them my people, which were not my people; and her beloved, which was not beloved. And it shall come to pass, that in the place where it was said unto them, Ye are not my people; there shall they be called the children of the living God. (Romans 9:21-26)

[39] Wherefore remember, that ye being in time past Gentiles in the flesh, who are called Uncircumcision by that which is called the Circumcision in the flesh made by hands; That at that time ye were

without Christ, being aliens from the commonwealth of Israel, and strangers from the covenants of promise, having no hope, and without God in the world: But now in Christ Jesus ye who sometimes were far off are made nigh by the blood of Christ. For he is our peace, who hath made both one, and hath broken down the middle wall of partition between us; Having abolished in his flesh the enmity, even the law of commandments contained in ordinances; for to make in himself of twain one new man, so making peace; And that he might reconcile both unto God in one body by the cross, having slain the enmity thereby: And came and preached peace to you which were afar off, and to them that were nigh. For through him we both have access by one Spirit unto the Father. (Ephesians 2:11-18)

[40] Therefore if the uncircumcision keep the righteousness of the law, shall not his uncircumcision be counted for circumcision? And shall not uncircumcision which is by nature, if it fulfil the law, judge thee, who by the letter and circumcision dost transgress the law? For he is not a Jew, which is one outwardly; neither is that circumcision, which is outward in the flesh: But he is a Jew, which is one inwardly; and circumcision is that of the heart, in the spirit, and not in the letter; whose praise is not of men, but of God. (Romans 2:26-29)

Tell me, ye that desire to be under the law, do ye not hear the law? For it is written, that Abraham had two sons, the one by a bondmaid, the other by a freewoman. But he who was of the bondwoman was born after the flesh; but he of the freewoman was by promise. Which things are an allegory: for these are the two covenants; the one from the mount Sinai, which gendereth to bondage, which is Agar. For this Agar is mount Sinai in Arabia, and answereth to Jerusalem which now is, and is in bondage with her children. But Jerusalem which is above is free, which is the mother of us all. For it is written, Rejoice, thou barren that bearest not; break forth and cry, thou that travailest not: for the desolate hath many more children than she which hath an husband. Now we, brethren, as Isaac was, are the children of promise. But as then he that was born after the flesh persecuted him that was born after the Spirit, even so it is now. Nevertheless what saith the scripture? Cast out the bondwoman and her son: for the son of the bondwoman shall not be heir with the son of the freewoman.

So then, brethren, we are not children of the bondwoman, but of the free. (Galatians 4:21-31)

[41] Therefore the Jews sought the more to kill him, because he not only had broken the sabbath, but said also that God was his Father, making himself equal with God. (John 5:18)

The disciple is not above his master: but every one that is perfect shall be as his master. (Luke 6:40)

Let this mind be in you, which was also in Christ Jesus: Who, being in the form of God, thought it not robbery to be equal with God: But made himself of no reputation, and took upon him the form of a servant, and was made in the likeness of men: (Philippians 2:5-7)

[42] But he answered and said, It is written, Man shall not live by bread alone, but by every word that proceedeth out of the mouth of God. (Matthew 4:4)

Search the scriptures; for in them ye think ye have eternal life: and they are they which testify of me. And ye will not come to me, that ye might have life. (John 5:39; 40)

Being born again, not of corruptible seed, but of incorruptible, by the word of God, which liveth and abideth for ever. (1Peter 1:23)

[43] But ye shall receive power, after that the Holy Ghost is come upon you: and ye shall be witnesses unto me both in Jerusalem, and in all Judaea, and in Samaria, and unto the uttermost part of the earth. (Acts 1:8)

[44] Now as touching things offered unto idols, we know that we all have knowledge. Knowledge puffeth up, but charity edifieth. And if any man think that he knoweth any thing, he knoweth nothing yet as he ought to know. 1Corinthians 8:1; 2)

[45] For thou hast said in thine heart, I will ascend into heaven, I will exalt my throne above the stars of God: I will sit also upon the mount of the congregation, in the sides of the north: I will ascend above the heights of the clouds; I will be like the most High. (Isaiah 14:13)

[46] But ye shall receive power, after that the Holy Ghost is come upon you: and ye shall be witnesses unto me both in Jerusalem, and in

all Judaea, and in Samaria, and unto the uttermost part of the earth. (Acts 1:8)

[47] According as his divine power hath given unto us all things that pertain unto life and godliness, through the knowledge of him that hath called us to glory and virtue: Whereby are given unto us exceeding great and precious promises: that by these ye might be partakers of the divine nature, having escaped the corruption that is in the world through lust. (2Peter 1:3; 14)

[48] After these things the word of the LORD came unto Abram in a vision, saying, Fear not, Abram: I am thy shield, and thy exceeding great reward. (Genesis 15:1)

[49] That the God of our Lord Jesus Christ, the Father of glory, may give unto you the spirit of wisdom and revelation in the knowledge of him: The eyes of your understanding being enlightened; that ye may know what is the hope of his calling, and what the riches of the glory of his inheritance in the saints, And what is the exceeding greatness of his power to us-ward who believe, according to the working of his mighty power, Which he wrought in Christ, when he raised him from the dead, and set him at his own right hand in the heavenly places, Far above all principality, and power, and might, and dominion, and every name that is named, not only in this world, but also in that which is to come: And hath put all things under his feet, and gave him to be the head over all things to the church, Which is his body, the fulness of him that filleth all in all. Ephesians 1:17-23)

But God, who is rich in mercy, for his great love wherewith he loved us, Even when we were dead in sins, hath quickened us together with Christ, (by grace ye are saved;) And hath raised us up together, and made us sit together in heavenly places in Christ Jesus: (Ephesians 2:4-6)

To him that overcometh will I grant to sit with me in my throne, even as I also overcame, and am set down with my Father in his throne. He that hath an ear, let him hear what the Spirit saith unto the churches. (Revelation 3:21-22)

[50] No man putteth a piece of new cloth unto an old garment, for that which is put in to fill it up taketh from the garment, and the rent is

made worse. Neither do men put new wine into old bottles: else the bottles break, and the wine runneth out, and the bottles perish: but they put new wine into new bottles, and both are preserved. (Matthew 9:16-17)

[51] And he said, I beseech thee, shew me thy glory. And he said, I will make all my goodness pass before thee, and I will proclaim the name of the LORD before thee; and will be gracious to whom I will be gracious, and will shew mercy on whom I will shew mercy. And he said, Thou canst not see my face: for there shall no man see me, and live. (Exodus 33:18-20)

[52] And God said, Let us make man in our image, after our likeness: and let them have dominion over the fish of the sea, and over the fowl of the air, and over the cattle, and over all the earth, and over every creeping thing that creepeth upon the earth. (Genesis 1:26)

[53] And the LORD God said, Behold, the man is become as one of us, to know good and evil: and now, lest he put forth his hand, and take also of the tree of life, and eat, and live for ever: Therefore the LORD God sent him forth from the garden of Eden, to till the ground from whence he was taken. So he drove out the man; and he placed at the east of the garden of Eden Cherubims, and a flaming sword which turned every way, to keep the way of the tree of life. (Genesis 3:22-24)

[54] I call heaven and earth to record this day against you, that I have set before you life and death, blessing and cursing: therefore choose life, that both thou and thy seed may live: (Deuteronomy 30:19)

[55] But the Spirit of the LORD came upon Gideon, and he blew a trumpet; and Abiezer was gathered after him. (Judges 6:34)

[56] Even the Spirit of truth; whom the world cannot receive, because it seeth him not, neither knoweth him: but ye know him; for he dwelleth with you, and shall be in you. (John 14:17)

[57] For as the Father hath life in himself; so hath he given to the Son to have life in himself; (John 5:26)

[58] In the beginning was the Word, and the Word was with God, and the Word was God. The same was in the beginning with God. All

things were made by him; and without him was not any thing made that was made. And the Word was made flesh, and dwelt among us, (and we beheld his glory, the glory as of the only begotten of the Father) full of grace and truth. (John 1:1-3; 14)

For by him were all things created, that are in heaven, and that are in earth, visible and invisible, whether they be thrones, or dominions, or principalities, or powers: all things were created by him, and for him: (Colossians 1:16)

[59] Behold, a virgin shall be with child, and shall bring forth a son, and they shall call his name Emmanuel, which being interpreted is, God with us. (Matthew 1:23)

[60] Then answered Jesus and said unto them, Verily, verily, I say unto you, The Son can do nothing of himself, but what he seeth the Father do: for what things soever he doeth, these also doeth the Son likewise. (John 5:19)

[61] And without controversy great is the mystery of godliness: God was manifest in the flesh, justified in the Spirit, seen of angels, preached unto the Gentiles, believed on in the world, received up into glory. (1Timothy 3:16)

To wit, that God was in Christ, reconciling the world unto himself, not imputing their trespasses unto them; and hath committed unto us the word of reconciliation. (2Corinthians 5:19)

[62] Then cometh the end, when he shall have delivered up the kingdom to God, even the Father; when he shall have put down all rule and all authority and power. (1Corinthians 15:24)

[63] And without controversy great is the mystery of godliness: God was manifest in the flesh, justified in the Spirit, seen of angels, preached unto the Gentiles, believed on in the world, received up into glory. (1Timothy 3:16)

[64] Wherefore they are no more twain, but one flesh. What therefore God hath joined together, let not man put asunder. (Matthew 19:6)

.

⁶⁵ What? know ye not that he which is joined to an harlot is one body? for two, saith he, shall be one flesh. But he that is joined unto the Lord is one spirit. (1Corinthians 6:16)

⁶⁶ And the angel that talked with me came again, and waked me, as a man that is wakened out of his sleep, And said unto me, What seest thou? And I said, I have looked, and behold a candlestick all of gold, with a bowl upon the top of it, and his seven lamps thereon, and seven pipes to the seven lamps, which are upon the top thereof: And two olive trees by it, one upon the right side of the bowl, and the other upon the left side thereof. So I answered and spake to the angel that talked with me, saying, What are these, my lord? Then the angel that talked with me answered and said unto me, Knowest thou not what these be? And I said, No, my lord. Then he answered and spake unto me, saying, This is the word of the LORD unto Zerubbabel, saying, Not by might, nor by power, but by my spirit, saith the LORD of hosts. (Zechariah 4: 1-6)

And I will give power unto my two witnesses, and they shall prophesy a thousand two hundred and threescore days, clothed in sackcloth. These are the two olive trees, and the two candlesticks standing before the God of the earth. (Revelation 11:3)

⁶⁷ There is one body, and one Spirit, even as ye are called in one hope of your calling; (Ephesians 4:4)

⁶⁸ That which was from the beginning, which we have heard, which we have seen with our eyes, which we have looked upon, and our hands have handled, of the Word of life; (For the life was manifested, and we have seen it, and bear witness, and shew unto you that eternal life, which was with the Father, and was manifested unto us;) (1John 1:1-2)

And this is the record, that God hath given to us eternal life, and this life is in his Son. He that hath the Son hath life; and he that hath not the Son of God hath not life. (1John 5:11; 12)

⁶⁹ The thief cometh not, but for to steal, and to kill, and to destroy: I am come that they might have life, and that they might have it more abundantly. (John 10:10)

[70] Howbeit when he, the Spirit of truth, is come, he will guide you into all truth: for he shall not speak of himself; but whatsoever he shall hear, that shall he speak: and he will shew you things to come. (John 16:13)

[71] But of the tree of the knowledge of good and evil, thou shalt not eat of it: for in the day that thou eatest thereof thou shalt surely die. (Genesis 2:17)

CHAPTER FOUR

[1] That Christ may dwell in your hearts by faith; that ye, being rooted and grounded in love, May be able to comprehend with all saints what is the breadth, and length, and depth, and height; (Ephesians 3:18)

[2] Because the carnal mind is enmity against God: for it is not subject to the law of God, neither indeed can be. (Romans 8:7)

[3] But the natural man receiveth not the things of the Spirit of God: for they are foolishness unto him: neither can he know them, because they are spiritually discerned. (1Corinthians 2:14)

[4] For the Jews require a sign, and the Greeks seek after wisdom: But we preach Christ crucified, unto the Jews a stumblingblock, and unto the Greeks foolishness; (1Corinthians 1:22; 23)

[5] While we look not at the things which are seen, but at the things which are not seen: for the things which are seen are temporal; but the things which are not seen are eternal. (2Corinthians 4:18)

[6] But God, who is rich in mercy, for his great love wherewith he loved us, Even when we were dead in sins, hath quickened us together with Christ, (by grace ye are saved;) And hath raised us up together, and made us sit together in heavenly places in Christ Jesus: (Ephesians 2: 4; 5)

[7] Jesus answered and said unto him, Verily, verily, I say unto thee, Except a man be born again, he cannot see the kingdom of God. (John 3:3)

[8] But the natural man receiveth not the things of the Spirit of God: for they are foolishness unto him: neither can he know them, because they are spiritually discerned. But he that is spiritual judgeth all things, yet he himself is judged of no man. For who hath known the mind of the Lord, that he may instruct him? But we have the mind of Christ. (1Corinthians 2:14-16)

[9] But God hath revealed them unto us by his Spirit: for the Spirit searcheth all things, yea, the deep things of God. For what man knoweth the things of a man, save the spirit of man which is in him? even so the things of God knoweth no man, but the Spirit of God. Now we have received, not the spirit of the world, but the spirit which is of God; that we might know the things that are freely given to us of God. (1Corinthians 2:10-12)

[10] The Lord knoweth how to deliver the godly out of temptations, and to reserve the unjust unto the day of judgment to be punished: But chiefly them that walk after the flesh in the lust of uncleanness, and despise government. Presumptuous are they, selfwilled, they are not afraid to speak evil of dignities. Whereas angels, which are greater in power and might, bring not railing accusation against them before the Lord. But these, as natural brute beasts, made to be taken and destroyed, speak evil of the things that they understand not; and shall utterly perish in their own corruption; (2Peter 2:9—12)

Yet Michael the archangel, when contending with the devil he disputed about the body of Moses, durst not bring against him a railing accusation, but said, The Lord rebuke thee. But these speak evil of those things which they know not: but what they know naturally, as brute beasts, in those things they corrupt themselves. (Jude 1:9; 10)

[11] Howbeit we speak wisdom among them that are perfect: yet not the wisdom of this world, nor of the princes of this world, that come to nought: But we speak the wisdom of God in a mystery, even the hidden wisdom, which God ordained before the world unto our glory: Which none of the princes of this world knew: for had they known it, they would not have crucified the Lord of glory. But as it is written, Eye hath not seen, nor ear heard, neither have entered into the heart of man, the things which God hath prepared for them that love him. But

God hath revealed them unto us by his Spirit: for the Spirit searcheth all things, yea, the deep things of God. (1Corinthians 2:6-10)

[12] I knew a man in Christ above fourteen years ago, (whether in the body, I cannot tell; or whether out of the body, I cannot tell: God knoweth;) such an one caught up to the third heaven. And I knew such a man, (whether in the body, or out of the body, I cannot tell: God knoweth;) How that he was caught up into paradise, and heard unspeakable words, which it is not lawful for a man to utter. (2Corinthians 12:2-4)

[13] I was in the Spirit on the Lord's day, and heard behind me a great voice, as of a trumpet, (Revelation 1:10)

After this I looked, and, behold, a door was opened in heaven: and the first voice which I heard was as it were of a trumpet talking with me; which said, Come up hither, and I will shew thee things which must be hereafter. And immediately I was in the spirit: and, behold, a throne was set in heaven, and one sat on the throne. Revelation 4:1; 2)

[14] I beseech you therefore, brethren, by the mercies of God, that ye present your bodies a living sacrifice, holy, acceptable unto God, which is your reasonable service. And be not conformed to this world: but be ye transformed by the renewing of you mind, that ye may prove what is that good, and acceptable, and perfect, will of God. (Romans 12:1; 2)

[15] And the LORD God planted a garden eastward in Eden; and there he put the man whom he had formed. (Genesis 2:8)

[16] And a river went out of Eden to water the garden; and from thence it was parted, and became into four heads. (Genesis 2:10)

[17] In the last day, that great day of the feast, Jesus stood and cried, saying, If any man thirst, let him come unto me, and drink. He that believeth on me, as the scripture hath said, out of his belly shall flow rivers of living water. (But this spake he of the Spirit, which they that believe on him should receive: for the Holy Ghost was not yet given; because that Jesus was not yet glorified.) (John 7:37-39)

[18] And he shewed me a pure river of water of life, clear as crystal, proceeding out of the throne of God and of the Lamb. In the midst of the street of it, and on either side of the river, was there the tree of life, which bare twelve manner of fruits, and yielded her fruit every month: and the leaves of the tree were for the healing of the nations. (Rev 22:1-2)

[19] And then shall he send his angels, and shall gather together his elect from the four winds, from the uttermost part of the earth to the uttermost part of heaven. (Mark 13:27)

That Christ may dwell in your hearts by faith; that ye, being rooted and grounded in love, May be able to comprehend with all saints what is the breadth, and length, and depth, and height; (Eph 3:17; 18)

[20] But I say unto you, Swear not at all; neither by heaven; for it is God's throne: (Matthew 5:34)

Heaven is my throne, and earth is my footstool: what house will ye build me? saith the Lord: or what is the place of my rest? (Acts 7:49)

And he shewed me a pure river of water of life, clear as crystal, proceeding out of the throne of God and of the Lamb. In the midst of the street of it, and on either side of the river, was there the tree of life, which bare twelve manner of fruits, and yielded her fruit every month: and the leaves of the tree were for the healing of the nations. And there shall be no more curse: but the throne of God and of the Lamb shall be in it; and his servants shall serve him: (Revelation 22:1-4)

And a river went out of Eden to water the garden; and from thence it was parted, and became into four heads. (Genesis 2:10)

[21] Behold, the heaven and the heaven of heavens is the LORD'S thy God, the earth also, with all that therein is. (Deuteronomy 10:14)

But will God indeed dwell on the earth? behold, the heaven and heaven of heavens cannot contain thee; how much less this house that I have builded? (1Kings 8:27)

[22] To him that overcometh will I grant to sit with me in my throne, even as I also overcame, and am set down with my Father in his throne. (Revelation 3:21)

[23] And he shewed me a pure river of water of life, clear as crystal, proceeding out of the throne of God and of the Lamb. (Revelation 22:1)

[24] But God, who is rich in mercy, for his great love wherewith he loved us, Even when we were dead in sins, hath quickened us together with Christ, (by grace ye are saved;) And hath raised us up together, and made us sit together in heavenly places in Christ Jesus: That in the ages to come he might shew the exceeding riches of his grace in his kindness toward us through Christ Jesus. (Ephesians 2:4-7)

[25] But I would have you know, that the head of every man is Christ; and the head of the woman is the man; and the head of Christ is God. (1Corinthians 11:3)

[26] For he hath put all things under his feet. But when he saith all things are put under him, it is manifest that he is excepted, which did put all things under him. And when all things shall be subdued unto him, then shall the Son also himself be subject unto him that put all things under him, that God may be all in all. (1Corinthians 15:27; 28)

For the husband is the head of the wife, even as Christ is the head of the church: and he is the saviour of the body. Therefore as the church is subject unto Christ, so let the wives be to their own husbands in every thing. (Ephesians 5:23-24)

[27] And the LORD God planted a garden eastward in Eden; and there he put the man whom he had formed. And the LORD God took the man, and put him into the garden of Eden to dress it and to keep it. And they heard the voice of the LORD God walking in the garden in the cool of the day: and Adam and his wife hid themselves from the presence of the LORD God amongst the trees of the garden. Genesis 2:8; 2:15; 3:8

[28] And the LORD God planted a garden eastward in Eden; and there he put the man whom he had formed. (Genesis 2:8)

Thou hast been in Eden the garden of God; every precious stone was thy covering, the sardius, topaz, and the diamond, the beryl, the onyx, and the jasper, the sapphire, the emerald, and the carbuncle, and gold: the workmanship of thy tabrets and of thy pipes was prepared in thee in the day that thou wast created. Thou art the anointed cherub that covereth; and I have set thee so: thou wast upon the holy mountain of God; thou hast walked up and down in the midst of the stones of fire. Thou wast perfect in thy ways from the day that thou wast created, till iniquity was found in thee. (Ezekiel 28:13-15)

[29] I knew a man in Christ above fourteen years ago, (whether in the body, I cannot tell; or whether out of the body, I cannot tell: God knoweth;) such an one caught up to the third heaven. And I knew such a man, (whether in the body, or out of the body, I cannot tell: God knoweth;) How that he was caught up into paradise, and heard unspeakable words, which it is not lawful for a man to utter. (2Corinthians 12:2-4)

[30] He that hath an ear, let him hear what the Spirit saith unto the churches; To him that overcometh will I give to eat of the tree of life, which is in the midst of the paradise of God. (Revelation 2:7)

[31] And Jesus said unto him, Verily I say unto thee, To day shalt thou be with me in paradise. (Luke 23:43)

[32] All things are delivered unto me of my Father: and no man knoweth the Son, but the Father; neither knoweth any man the Father, save the Son, and he to whomsoever the Son will reveal him. (Matthew 11:27)

Jesus saith unto him, I am the way, the truth, and the life: no man cometh unto the Father, but by me. (John 14:6)

[33] How art thou fallen from heaven, O Lucifer, son of the morning! how art thou cut down to the ground, which didst weaken the nations! For thou hast said in thine heart, I will ascend into heaven, I will exalt my throne above the stars of God: I will sit also upon the mount of the congregation, in the sides of the north: I will ascend above the heights of the clouds; I will be like the most High. (Isaiah 14:12-14)

And he said unto them, I beheld Satan as lightning fall from heaven. (Luke 10:18)

[34] Therefore rejoice, ye heavens, and ye that dwell in them. Woe to the inhabiters of the earth and of the sea! for the devil is come down unto you, having great wrath, because he knoweth that he hath but a short time. (Revelation 12:12)

And the LORD said unto Satan, Whence comest thou? Then Satan answered the LORD, and said, From going to and fro in the earth, and from walking up and down in it. (Job 1:7)

[35] How art thou fallen from heaven, O Lucifer, son of the morning! how art thou cut down to the ground, which didst weaken the nations! For thou hast said in thine heart, I will ascend into heaven, I will exalt my throne above the stars of God: I will sit also upon the mount of the congregation, in the sides of the north: I will ascend above the heights of the clouds; I will be like the most High. Yet thou shalt be brought down to hell, to the sides of the pit. (Isaiah 14:12-15)

And I saw an angel come down from heaven, having the key of the bottomless pit and a great chain in his hand. And he laid hold on the dragon, that old serpent, which is the Devil, and Satan, and bound him a thousand years, And cast him into the bottomless pit, and shut him up, and set a seal upon him, that he should deceive the nations no more, till the thousand years should be fulfilled: and after that he must be loosed a little season. (Revelation 20:1-3)

[36] And a river went out of Eden to water the garden; and from thence it was parted, and became into four heads. (Genesis 2:10)

And he shewed me a pure river of water of life, clear as crystal, proceeding out of the throne of God and of the Lamb. (Revelation 22:1)

[37] To him that overcometh will I grant to sit with me in my throne, even as I also overcame, and am set down with my Father in his throne. (Revelation 3:21)

[38] For our God is a consuming fire. (Hebrews 12:29)

[39] I am Alpha and Omega, the beginning and the ending, saith the Lord, which is, and which was, and which is to come, the Almighty. (Revelation 1:8)

[40] Therefore are they before the throne of God, and serve him day and night in his temple: and he that sitteth on the throne shall dwell among them. (Revelation 7:15)

And they sung as it were a new song before the throne, and before the four beasts, and the elders: and no man could learn that song but the hundred and forty and four thousand, which were redeemed from the earth. (Revelation 14:3)

[41] For unto us a child is born, unto us a son is given: and the government shall be upon his shoulder: and his name shall be called Wonderful, Counsellor, The mighty God, The everlasting Father, The Prince of Peace. (Isaiah 9:6)

[42] That in the dispensation of the fulness of times he might gather together in one all things in Christ, both which are in heaven, and which are on earth; even in him: (Ephesians 1:10)

[43] Take heed that ye despise not one of these little ones; for I say unto you, That in heaven their angels do always behold the face of my Father which is in heaven. (Matthew 18:10)

[44] If ye had known me, ye should have known my Father also: and from henceforth ye know him, and have seen him. Philip saith unto him, Lord, shew us the Father, and it sufficeth us. Jesus saith unto him, Have I been so long time with you, and yet hast thou not known me, Philip? he that hath seen me hath seen the Father; and how sayest thou then, Shew us the Father? (John 14:7-9)

[45] For God, who commanded the light to shine out of darkness, hath shined in our hearts, to give the light of the knowledge of the glory of God in the face of Jesus Christ. (2Corinthians 4:6)

[46] God, who at sundry times and in divers manners spake in time past unto the fathers by the prophets, Hath in these last days spoken unto us by his Son, whom he hath appointed heir of all things, by whom also he made the worlds; Who being the brightness of his glory, and the express image of his person, and upholding all things by the word

of his power, when he had by himself purged our sins, sat down on the right hand of the Majesty on high; (Hebrews 1:1-3)

[47] And the LORD God planted a garden eastward in Eden; and there he put the man whom he had formed. (Genesis 2:8)

[48] And they heard the voice of the LORD God walking in the garden in the cool of the day: and Adam and his wife hid themselves from the presence of the LORD God amongst the trees of the garden. (Genesis 3:8)

[49] Now the serpent was more subtil than any beast of the field which the LORD God had made. And he said unto the woman, Yea, hath God said, Ye shall not eat of every tree of the garden? (Genesis 3:1)

Thou hast been in Eden the garden of God; every precious stone was thy covering, the sardius, topaz, and the diamond, the beryl, the onyx, and the jasper, the sapphire, the emerald, and the carbuncle, and gold: the workmanship of thy tabrets and of thy pipes was prepared in thee in the day that thou wast created. (Ezekiel 28:13)

[50] For when they shall rise from the dead, they neither marry, nor are given in marriage; but are as the angels which are in heaven. (Mark 12:25)

[51] Dare any of you, having a matter against another, go to law before the unjust, and not before the saints? Do ye not know that the saints shall judge the world? and if the world shall be judged by you, are ye unworthy to judge the smallest matters? Know ye not that we shall judge angels? how much more things that pertain to this life? (1Corinthians 6:1—3)

[52] But he that is joined unto the Lord is one spirit. (1Corinthians 6:17)

[53] And there came unto me one of the seven angels which had the seven vials full of the seven last plagues, and talked with me, saying, Come hither, I will shew thee the bride, the Lamb's wife. And he carried me away in the spirit to a great and high mountain, and shewed me that great city, the holy Jerusalem, descending out of heaven from God, (Revelation 21:9; 10)

[54] Verily, verily, I say unto you, Except a corn of wheat fall into the ground and die, it abideth alone: but if it die, it bringeth forth much fruit. (John 12:24)

[55] So also is the resurrection of the dead. It is sown in corruption; it is raised in incorruption: It is sown in dishonour; it is raised in glory: it is sown in weakness; it is raised in power: It is sown a natural body; it is raised a spiritual body. There is a natural body, and there is a spiritual body. And so it is written, The first man Adam was made a living soul; the last Adam was made a quickening spirit. Howbeit that was not first which is spiritual, but that which is natural; and afterward that which is spiritual. (1Co 15:42-46)

[56] Let no man therefore judge you in meat, or in drink, or in respect of an holyday, or of the new moon, or of the sabbath days: Which are a shadow of things to come; but the body is of Christ. (Colossians 2:16; 17)

For the law having a shadow of good things to come, and not the very image of the things, can never with those sacrifices which they offered year by year continually make the comers thereunto perfect. (Hebrews 10:1)

[57] And saith unto him, Every man at the beginning doth set forth good wine; and when men have well drunk, then that which is worse: but thou hast kept the good wine until now. (John 2:10)

[58] And he saith unto him, Verily, verily, I say unto you, Hereafter ye shall see heaven open, and the angels of God ascending and descending upon the Son of man. (John 1:51)

[59] But Abraham said, Son, remember that thou in thy lifetime receivedst thy good things, and likewise Lazarus evil things: but now he is comforted, and thou art tormented. And beside all this, between us and you there is a great gulf fixed: so that they which would pass from hence to you cannot; neither can they pass to us, that would come from thence. (Luke 16:25; 26)

[60] Then said Jesus unto them again, Verily, verily, I say unto you, I am the door of the sheep. All that ever came before me are thieves and robbers: but the sheep did not hear them. I am the door: by me if

any man enter in, he shall be saved, and shall go in and out, and find pasture. (John 10:7-9)

[61] And Jesus came and spake unto them, saying, All power is given unto me in heaven and in earth. (Matthew 28:18)

[62] That they all may be one; as thou, Father, art in me, and I in thee, that they also may be one in us: that the world may believe that thou hast sent me. (John 17:21)

[63] He that dwelleth in the secret place of the most High shall abide under the shadow of the Almighty. (Psalm 91:1)

[64] Jesus saith unto him, I am the way, the truth, and the life: no man cometh unto the Father, but by me. (John 14:6)

[65] And the LORD God planted a garden eastward in Eden; and there he put the man whom he had formed. (Genesis 2:8)

[66] Without father, without mother, without descent, having neither beginning of days, nor end of life; but made like unto the Son of God; abideth a priest continually. (Hebrews 7:3)

Jesus Christ the same yesterday, and to day, and for ever. (Hebrews 13:8)

[67] And the LORD God said, Behold, the man is become as one of us, to know good and evil: and now, lest he put forth his hand, and take also of the tree of life, and eat, and live for ever: Therefore the LORD God sent him forth from the garden of Eden, to till the ground from whence he was taken. So he drove out the man; and he placed at the east of the garden of Eden Cherubims, and a flaming sword which turned every way, to keep the way of the tree of life. (Genesis 3:22-24)

[68] Giving thanks unto the Father, which hath made us meet to be partakers of the inheritance of the saints in light: Who hath delivered us from the power of darkness, and hath translated us into the kingdom of his dear Son: In whom we have redemption through his blood, even the forgiveness of sins: (Colossians 1:12-14)

[69] And the LORD God formed man of the dust of the ground, and breathed into his nostrils the breath of life; and man became a living

soul. And the LORD God planted a garden eastward in Eden; and there he put the man whom he had formed. (Genesis 2:7; 8)

[70] And a river went out of Eden to water the garden; and from thence it was parted, and became into four heads. (Genesis 2:10)

[71] And every plant of the field before it was in the earth, and every herb of the field before it grew: for the LORD God had not caused it to rain upon the earth, and there was not a man to till the ground. But there went up a mist from the earth, and watered the whole face of the ground. (Genesis 2:5; 6)

[72] And there appeared a great wonder in heaven; a woman clothed with the sun, and the moon under her feet, and upon her head a crown of twelve stars: (Revelation 12:1)

[73] And the Spirit and the bride say, Come. And let him that heareth say, Come. And let him that is athirst come. And whosoever will, let him take the water of life freely. (Revelation 22:17)

[74] For as the body without the spirit is dead, so faith without works is dead also. (James 2:26)

[75] And the LORD God planted a garden eastward in Eden; and there he put the man whom he had formed. (Genesis 2:8)

[76] And he carried me away in the spirit to a great and high mountain, and shewed me that great city, the holy Jerusalem, descending out of heaven from God, (Revelation 21:10)

[77] And the LORD God caused a deep sleep to fall upon Adam, and he slept: and he took one of his ribs, and closed up the flesh instead thereof; And the rib, which the LORD God had taken from man, made he a woman, and brought her unto the man. (Genesis 2:21; 22)

[78] And Adam said, This is now bone of my bones, and flesh of my flesh: she shall be called Woman, because she was taken out of Man. Therefore shall a man leave his father and his mother, and shall cleave unto his wife: and they shall be one flesh. (Genesis 2:23; 24)

[79] Wherefore they are no more twain, but one flesh. What therefore God hath joined together, let not man put asunder. (Matthew 19:6)

[80] Blessed be the God and Father of our Lord Jesus Christ, who hath blessed us with all spiritual blessings in heavenly places in Christ: According as he hath chosen us in him before the foundation of the world, that we should be holy and without blame before him in love: (Ephesians 1:3; 4)

[81] That he might present it to himself a glorious church, not having spot, or wrinkle, or any such thing; but that it should be holy and without blemish. (Ephesians 5:27)

[82] But he that is joined unto the Lord is one spirit. (1Corinthians 6:17)

For no man ever yet hated his own flesh; but nourisheth and cherisheth it, even as the Lord the church: For we are members of his body, of his flesh, and of his bones. (Ephesians 5:29)

[83] That the God of our Lord Jesus Christ, the Father of glory, may give unto you the spirit of wisdom and revelation in the knowledge of him: The eyes of your understanding being enlightened; that ye may know what is the hope of his calling, and what the riches of the glory of his inheritance in the saints, And what is the exceeding greatness of his power to us-ward who believe, according to the working of his mighty power, Which he wrought in Christ, when he raised him from the dead, and set him at his own right hand in the heavenly places, Far above all principality, and power, and might, and dominion, and every name that is named, not only in this world, but also in that which is to come: And hath put all things under his feet, and gave him to be the head over all things to the church, Which is his body, the fulness of him that filleth all in all. (Ephesians 1:17-23)

But God, who is rich in mercy, for his great love wherewith he loved us, Even when we were dead in sins, hath quickened us together with Christ, (by grace ye are saved;) And hath raised us up together, and made us sit together in heavenly places in Christ Jesus: That in the ages to come he might shew the exceeding riches of his grace in his kindness toward us through Christ Jesus. (Ephesians 2:4-7)

[84] And God said, Let us make man in our image, after our likeness: and let them have dominion over the fish of the sea, and over the fowl

of the air, and over the cattle, and over all the earth, and over every creeping thing that creepeth upon the earth. (Genesis 1:26)

[85] And Jesus came and spake unto them, saying, All power is given unto me in heaven and in earth. Go ye therefore, and teach all nations, baptizing them in the name of the Father, and of the Son, and of the Holy Ghost: Teaching them to observe all things whatsoever I have commanded you: and, lo, I am with you alway, even unto the end of the world. Amen. (Matthew 28:18-20)

Dare any of you, having a matter against another, go to law before the unjust, and not before the saints? Do ye not know that the saints shall judge the world? and if the world shall be judged by you, are ye unworthy to judge the smallest matters? Know ye not that we shall judge angels? how much more things that pertain to this life? If then ye have judgments of things pertaining to this life, set them to judge who are least esteemed in the church. (1Corinthians 6:1-4)

[86] Having made known unto us the mystery of his will, according to his good pleasure which he hath purposed in himself: That in the dispensation of the fulness of times he might gather together in one all things in Christ, both which are in heaven, and which are on earth; even in him: (Ephesians 1:9; 10)

[87] And to make all men see what is the fellowship of the mystery, which from the beginning of the world hath been hid in God, who created all things by Jesus Christ: To the intent that now unto the principalities and powers in heavenly places might be known by the church the manifold wisdom of God, According to the eternal purpose which he purposed in Christ Jesus our Lord: (Ephesians 3:9-11)

[88] What therefore God hath joined together, let not man put asunder. (Mark 10:9)

[89] These are spots in your feasts of charity, when they feast with you, feeding themselves without fear: clouds they are without water, carried about of winds; trees whose fruit withereth, without fruit, twice dead, plucked up by the roots; (Jude 1:12)

[90] Study to shew thyself approved unto God, a workman that needeth not to be ashamed, rightly dividing the word of truth. (2Timothy 2:15)

[91] For whom he did foreknow, he also did predestinate to be conformed to the image of his Son, that he might be the firstborn among many brethren. Moreover whom he did predestinate, them he also called: and whom he called, them he also justified: and whom he justified, them he also glorified. (Romans 8:29; 29)

[92] Seeing ye have purified your souls in obeying the truth through the Spirit unto unfeigned love of the brethren, see that ye love one another with a pure heart fervently: Being born again, not of corruptible seed, but of incorruptible, by the word of God, which liveth and abideth for ever. (1Peter 1:22; 23)

[93] For unto which of the angels said he at any time, Thou art my Son, this day have I begotten thee? And again, I will be to him a Father, and he shall be to me a Son? (Hebrews 1:5)

[94] For verily he took not on him the nature of angels; but he took on him the seed of Abraham. (Hebrews 2:16)

[95] For the Lord himself shall descend from heaven with a shout, with the voice of the archangel, and with the trump of God: and the dead in Christ shall rise first: (1Thessalonians 4:16)

And there was war in heaven: Michael and his angels fought against the dragon; and the dragon fought and his angels, (Revelation12:7)

And I saw heaven opened, and behold a white horse; and he that sat upon him was called Faithful and True, and in righteousness he doth judge and make war. His eyes were as a flame of fire, and on his head were many crowns; and he had a name written, that no man knew, but he himself. And he was clothed with a vesture dipped in blood: and his name is called The Word of God. And the armies which were in heaven followed him upon white horses, clothed in fine linen, white and clean. And out of his mouth goeth a sharp sword, that with it he should smite the nations: and he shall rule them with a rod of iron: and he treadeth the winepress of the fierceness and wrath of Almighty God. And he hath on his vesture and on his thigh a name written, KING OF KINGS, AND LORD OF LORDS. (Revelation 19:11-16)

[96] In the beginning was the Word, and the Word was with God, and the Word was God. And the Word was made flesh, and dwelt among us, (and we beheld his glory, the glory as of the only begotten of the Father,) full of grace and truth. (John 1:1; 14)

[97] But I would have you know, that the head of every man is Christ; and the head of the woman is the man; and the head of Christ is God. (1Corinthians 11:3)

And hath put all things under his feet, and gave him to be the head over all things to the church, (Ephesians 1:22)

[98] Know ye not that we shall judge angels? how much more things that pertain to this life? (1Corinthians 6:3)

And again, when he bringeth in the firstbegotten into the world, he saith, And let all the angels of God worship him. (Hebrews 1:6)

But to which of the angels said he at any time, Sit on my right hand, until I make thine enemies thy footstool? Are they not all ministering spirits, sent forth to minister for them who shall be heirs of salvation? (Hebrews 1:13)

For Christ also hath once suffered for sins, the just for the unjust, that he might bring us to God, being put to death in the flesh, but quickened by the Spirit: By which also he went and preached unto the spirits in prison; Which sometime were disobedient, when once the longsuffering of God waited in the days of Noah, while the ark was a preparing, wherein few, that is, eight souls were saved by water. The like figure whereunto even baptism doth also now save us (not the putting away of the filth of the flesh, but the answer of a good conscience toward God,) by the resurrection of Jesus Christ: Who is gone into heaven, and is on the right hand of God; angels and authorities and powers being made subject unto him. (1Peter 3:18—22)

[99] But one in a certain place testified, saying, What is man, that thou art mindful of him? or the son of man, that thou visitest him? Thou madest him a little lower than the angels; thou crownedst him with

glory and honour, and didst set him over the works of thy hands: Thou hast put all things in subjection under his feet. For in that he put all in subjection under him, he left nothing that is not put under him. But now we see not yet all things put under him. But we see Jesus, who was made a little lower than the angels for the suffering of death, crowned with glory and honour; that he by the grace of God should taste death for every man. (Hebrews 2:6-9)

[100] And without controversy great is the mystery of godliness: God was manifest in the flesh, justified in the Spirit, seen of angels, preached unto the Gentiles, believed on in the world, received up into glory. (1Timothy 3:16)

[101] Wherefore henceforth know we no man after the flesh: yea, though we have known Christ after the flesh, yet now henceforth know we him no more. (2Corinthians 5:16)

[102] The eyes of your understanding being enlightened; that ye may know what is the hope of his calling, and what the riches of the glory of his inheritance in the saints, And what is the exceeding greatness of his power to us-ward who believe, according to the working of his mighty power, Which he wrought in Christ, when he raised him from the dead, and set him at his own right hand in the heavenly places, Far above all principality, and power, and might, and dominion, and every name that is named, not only in this world, but also in that which is to come: And hath put all things under his feet, and gave him to be the head over all things to the church, Which is his body, the fulness of him that filleth all in all. (Ephesians 1:18-23)

But God, who is rich in mercy, for his great love wherewith he loved us, Even when we were dead in sins, hath quickened us together with Christ, (by grace ye are saved;) And hath raised us up together, and made us sit together in heavenly places in Christ Jesus: That in the ages to come he might shew the exceeding riches of his grace in his kindness toward us through Christ Jesus. (Ephesians 2:4-7)

[103] Know ye not that ye are the temple of God, and that the Spirit of God dwelleth in you? (1Corinthians 3:16)

For we know that if our earthly house of this tabernacle were dissolved, we have a building of God, an house not made with hands, eternal in the heavens. (2Corinthians 5:1)

[104] In my Father's house are many mansions: if it were not so, I would have told you. I go to prepare a place for you. And if I go and prepare a place for you, I will come again, and receive you unto myself; that where I am, there ye may be also. (John 14:2; 3)

[105] And Jesus came and spake unto them, saying, All power is given unto me in heaven and in earth. Go ye therefore, and teach all nations, baptizing them in the name of the Father, and of the Son, and of the Holy Ghost: Teaching them to observe all things whatsoever I have commanded you: and, lo, I am with you alway, even unto the end of the world. Amen. (Matthew 28:18-20)

[106] In the beginning was the Word, and the Word was with God, and the Word was God. And the Word was made flesh, and dwelt among us, (and we beheld his glory, the glory as of the only begotten of the Father,) full of grace and truth. (John 1:1; 14)

And so it is written, The first man Adam was made a living soul; the last Adam was made a quickening spirit. (1Corinthians 15:45)

[107] And the angel answered and said unto her, The Holy Ghost shall come upon thee, and the power of the Highest shall overshadow thee: therefore also that holy thing which shall be born of thee shall be called the Son of God. (Luke 1:35)

[108] And the angel answered and said unto her, The Holy Ghost shall come upon thee, and the power of the Highest shall overshadow thee: therefore also that holy thing which shall be born of thee shall be called the Son of God. (Luke 1:35)

[109] The Spirit of the Lord is upon me, because he hath anointed me to preach the gospel to the poor; he hath sent me to heal the brokenhearted, to preach deliverance to the captives, and recovering of sight to the blind, to set at liberty them that are bruised, To preach the acceptable year of the Lord. (Luke 4:18; 19)

[110] What? know ye not that your body is the temple of the Holy Ghost which is in you, which ye have of God, and ye are not your own? (1Corinthians 6:19)

[111] To whom God would make known what is the riches of the glory of this mystery among the Gentiles; which is Christ in you, the hope of glory: (Colossians 1:27)

[112] And no man hath ascended up to heaven, but he that came down from heaven, even the Son of man which is in heaven. (John 3:13)

[113] For there are three that bear record in heaven, the Father, the Word, and the Holy Ghost: and these three are one. (1John 5:7)

And he was clothed with a vesture dipped in blood: and his name is called The Word of God. (Revelation 19:13)

[114] Herein is our love made perfect, that we may have boldness in the day of judgment: because as he is, so are we in this world. (1John 4:17)

[115] It is sown a natural body; it is raised a spiritual body. There is a natural body, and there is a spiritual body. (1Corinthians 15:44)

Wherefore henceforth know we no man after the flesh: yea, though we have known Christ after the flesh, yet now henceforth know we him no more. (2Corinthians 5:16)

[116] But unto the Son he saith, Thy throne, O God, is for ever and ever: a sceptre of righteousness is the sceptre of thy kingdom. Thou hast loved righteousness, and hated iniquity; therefore God, even thy God, hath anointed thee with the oil of gladness above thy fellows. (Hebrews 1:8; 9)

[117] And it is yet far more evident: for that after the similitude of Melchisedec there ariseth another priest, Who is made, not after the law of a carnal commandment, but after the power of an endless life. For he testifieth, Thou art a priest for ever after the order of Melchisedec. (Hebrews 7:15-17)

[118] For the earnest expectation of the creature waiteth for the manifestation of the sons of God. For the creature was made subject to vanity, not willingly, but by reason of him who hath subjected the

same in hope, Because the creature itself also shall be delivered from the bondage of corruption into the glorious liberty of the children of God. For we know that the whole creation groaneth and travaileth in pain together until now. And not only they, but ourselves also, which have the firstfruits of the Spirit, even we ourselves groan within ourselves, waiting for the adoption, to wit, the redemption of our body. (Romans 8:19-23)

[119] If ye then be risen with Christ, seek those things which are above, where Christ sitteth on the right hand of God. Set your affection on things above, not on things on the earth. For ye are dead, and your life is hid with Christ in God. When Christ, who is our life, shall appear, then shall ye also appear with him in glory. (Colossians 3:1-4)

[120] Think not that I am come to send peace on earth: I came not to send peace, but a sword. (Matthew 10:34)

[121] And God called the dry land Earth; and the gathering together of the waters called he Seas: and God saw that it was good. (Genesis 1:10)

[122] And Jesus came and spake unto them, saying, All power is given unto me in heaven and in earth. (Matthew 28:18)

Howbeit the most High dwelleth not in temples made with hands; as saith the prophet, Heaven is my throne, and earth is my footstool: what house will ye build me? saith the Lord: or what is the place of my rest? Hath not my hand made all these things? (Acts 7:48-50)

[123] For by him were all things created, that are in heaven, and that are in earth, visible and invisible, whether they be thrones, or dominions, or principalities, or powers: all things were created by him, and for him: (Colossians 1:16)

[124] Where wast thou when I laid the foundations of the earth? declare, if thou hast understanding. Who hath laid the measures thereof, if thou knowest? or who hath stretched the line upon it? Whereupon are the foundations thereof fastened? or who laid the corner stone thereof; When the morning stars sang together, and all the sons of God shouted for joy? (Job 38:4-7)

[125] For by him were all things created, that are in heaven, and that are in earth, visible and invisible, whether they be thrones, or dominions, or principalities, or powers: all things were created by him, and for him: (Colossians 1:16)

[126] He that answereth a matter before he heareth it, it is folly and shame unto him. (Proverbs 18:13)

[127] For as the body without the spirit is dead, so faith without works is dead also. (James 2:26)

[128] For by him were all things created, that are in heaven, and that are in earth, visible and invisible, whether they be thrones, or dominions, or principalities, or powers: all things were created by him, and for him: (Colossians 1:16)

[129] For in six days the LORD made heaven and earth, the sea, and all that in them is, and rested the seventh day: wherefore the LORD blessed the sabbath day, and hallowed it. (Exodus 20:11)

It is a sign between me and the children of Israel for ever: for in six days the LORD made heaven and earth, and on the seventh day he rested, and was refreshed. (Exodus 31:17)

[130] And he said unto them, Go ye, and tell that fox, Behold, I cast out devils, and I do cures to day and to morrow, and the third day I shall be perfected. (Luke 13:32)

[131] And the earth was without form, and void; and darkness was upon the face of the deep. And the Spirit of God moved upon the face of the waters. (Genesis 1:2)

[132] But Jesus beheld them, and said unto them, With men this is impossible; but with God all things are possible. (Matthew 19:26)

[133] For God is not the author of confusion, but of peace, as in all churches of the saints. (1Corinthians 14:33)

[134] Wisdom is the principal thing; therefore get wisdom: and with all thy getting get understanding. (Proverbs 4:7)

It is the glory of God to conceal a thing: but the honour of kings is to search out a matter. (Proverbs 25:2)

¹³⁵ Charity never faileth: but whether there be prophecies, they shall fail; whether there be tongues, they shall cease; whether there be knowledge, it shall vanish away. For we know in part, and we prophesy in part. But when that which is perfect is come, then that which is in part shall be done away. When I was a child, I spake as a child, I understood as a child, I thought as a child: but when I became a man, I put away childish things. For now we see through a glass, darkly; but then face to face: now I know in part; but then shall I know even as also I am known. And now abideth faith, hope, charity, these three; but the greatest of these is charity. (1Corinthians 13:8-13)

¹³⁶ That Christ may dwell in your hearts by faith; that ye, being rooted and grounded in love, May be able to comprehend with all saints what is the breadth, and length, and depth, and height; (Ephesians 3:17; 18)

¹³⁷ But as it is written, Eye hath not seen, nor ear heard, neither have entered into the heart of man, the things which God hath prepared for them that love him. But God hath revealed them unto us by his Spirit: for the Spirit searcheth all things, yea, the deep things of God. For what man knoweth the things of a man, save the spirit of man which is in him? even so the things of God knoweth no man, but the Spirit of God. Now we have received, not the spirit of the world, but the spirit which is of God; that we might know the things that are freely given to us of God. Which things also we speak, not in the words which man's wisdom teacheth, but which the Holy Ghost teacheth; comparing spiritual things with spiritual. But the natural man receiveth not the things of the Spirit of God: for they are foolishness unto him: neither can he know them, because they are spiritually discerned. But he that is spiritual judgeth all things, yet he himself is judged of no man. For who hath known the mind of the Lord, that he may instruct him? But we have the mind of Christ. (1Corintians 2:9-16)

¹³⁸ In my Father's house are many mansions: if it were not so, I would have told you. I go to prepare a place for you. And if I go and prepare a place for you, I will come again, and receive you unto myself; that where I am, there ye may be also. (John 14:2; 3)

[139] Then the LORD answered Job out of the whirlwind, and said, Who is this that darkeneth counsel by words without knowledge? Gird up now thy loins like a man; for I will demand of thee, and answer thou me. Where wast thou when I laid the foundations of the earth? declare, if thou hast understanding. (Job 38:1-4)

[140] These are the generations of the heavens and of the earth when they were created, in the day that the LORD God made the earth and the heavens, And every plant of the field before it was in the earth, and every herb of the field before it grew: for the LORD God had not caused it to rain upon the earth, and there was not a man to till the ground. But there went up a mist from the earth, and watered the whole face of the ground. (Genesis 2:4-6)

[141] And God said, Let there be a firmament in the midst of the waters, and let it divide the waters from the waters. And God made the firmament, and divided the waters which were under the firmament from the waters which were above the firmament: and it was so. And God called the firmament Heaven. And the evening and the morning were the second day. (Genesis 1:6-8)

[142] And God said, Let there be lights in the firmament of the heaven to divide the day from the night; and let them be for signs, and for seasons, and for days, and years: And let them be for lights in the firmament of the heaven to give light upon the earth: and it was so. And God made two great lights; the greater light to rule the day, and the lesser light to rule the night: he made the stars also. And God set them in the firmament of the heaven to give light upon the earth, And to rule over the day and over the night, and to divide the light from the darkness: and God saw that it was good. And the evening and the morning were the fourth day. (Genesis 1:14-19)

[143] And God said, Let there be light: and there was light. And God saw the light, that it was good: and God divided the light from the darkness. And God called the light Day, and the darkness he called Night. And the evening and the morning were the first day. (Genesis 1:3-5)

[144] For the word of God is quick, and powerful, and sharper than any twoedged sword, piercing even to the dividing asunder of soul and

spirit, and of the joints and marrow, and is a discerner of the thoughts and intents of the heart. (Hebrews 4:12)

[145] For whatsoever things were written aforetime were written for our learning, that we through patience and comfort of the scriptures might have hope. (Romans 15:4)

[146] This then is the message which we have heard of him, and declare unto you, that God is light, and in him is no darkness at all. (1John 1:5)

[147] What I tell you in darkness, that speak ye in light: and what ye hear in the ear, that preach ye upon the housetops. (Matthew 10:27)

[148] Search the scriptures; for in them ye think ye have eternal life: and they are they which testify of me. And ye will not come to me, that ye might have life. (John 5:39-40)

[149] Wherefore God also gave them up to uncleanness through the lusts of their own hearts, to dishonour their own bodies between themselves: Who changed the truth of God into a lie, and worshipped and served the creature more than the Creator, who is blessed for ever. Amen. (Romans 1:24; 25)

[150] He that answereth a matter before he heareth it, it is folly and shame unto him. (Proverbs 18:13)

[151] Let this mind be in you, which was also in Christ Jesus: Who, being in the form of God, thought it not robbery to be equal with God: But made himself of no reputation, and took upon him the form of a servant, and was made in the likeness of men: And being found in fashion as a man, he humbled himself, and became obedient unto death, even the death of the cross. Wherefore God also hath highly exalted him, and given him a name which is above every name: That at the name of Jesus every knee should bow, of things in heaven, and things in earth, and things under the earth. And that every tongue should confess that Jesus Christ is Lord, to the glory of God the Father. (Philippians 2:11)

[152] And when the seven thunders had uttered their voices, I was about to write: and I heard a voice from heaven saying unto me, Seal up those things which the seven thunders uttered, and write them not.

But in the days of the voice of the seventh angel, when he shall begin to sound, the mystery of God should be finished, as he hath declared to his servants the prophets. (Revelation 10:4; 7)

[153] O the depth of the riches both of the wisdom and knowledge of God! how unsearchable are his judgments, and his ways past finding out! For who hath known the mind of the Lord? or who hath been his counsellor? Or who hath first given to him, and it shall be recompensed unto him again? For of him, and through him, and to him, are all things: to whom be glory for ever. Amen. (Romans 11:33-36)

[154] In the beginning God created the heaven and the earth. And the earth was without form, and void; and darkness was upon the face of the deep. And the Spirit of God moved upon the face of the waters. And God said, Let there be light: and there was light. And God saw the light, that it was good: and God divided the light from the darkness. And God called the light Day, and the darkness he called Night. And the evening and the morning were the first day. (Genesis 1:1-5)

[155] Jesus said unto her, I am the resurrection, and the life: he that believeth in me, though he were dead, yet shall he live: (John 11:25)

Verily, verily, I say unto you, Except a corn of wheat fall into the ground and die, it abideth alone: but if it die, it bringeth forth much fruit. (John 12:24)

[156] Jesus answered and said unto them, Destroy this temple, and in three days I will raise it up. (John 2:19)

[157] It was meet that we should make merry, and be glad: for this thy brother was dead, and is alive again; and was lost, and is found. (Luke 15:32)

[158] And we know that all things work together for good to them that love God, to them who are the called according to his purpose. (Romans 8:28)

[159] Howbeit that was not first which is spiritual, but that which is natural; and afterward that which is spiritual. (1Corinthians 15:46)

[160] And saith unto him, Every man at the beginning doth set forth good wine; and when men have well drunk, then that which is worse: but thou hast kept the good wine until now. (John 2:10)

[161] So also is the resurrection of the dead. It is sown in corruption; it is raised in incorruption: (1Corinthians 15:42)

[162] In that he saith, A new covenant, he hath made the first old. Now that which decayeth and waxeth old is ready to vanish away. (Hebrews 8:13)

[163] See now that I, even I, am he, and there is no god with me: I kill, and I make alive; I wound, and I heal: neither is there any that can deliver out of my hand. (Deuteronomy 32:39)

[164] Dearly beloved, avenge not yourselves, but rather give place unto wrath: for it is written, Vengeance is mine; I will repay, saith the Lord. (Romans 12:19)

[165] For the LORD will pass through to smite the Egyptians; and when he seeth the blood upon the lintel, and on the two side posts, the LORD will pass over the door, and will not suffer the destroyer to come in unto your houses to smite you. (Exodus 12:23)

The thief cometh not, but for to steal, and to kill, and to destroy: I am come that they might have life, and that they might have it more abundantly. (John 10:10)

Be sober, be vigilant; because your adversary the devil, as a roaring lion, walketh about, seeking whom he may devour: (1Peter 5:8)

[166] Forasmuch then as the children are partakers of flesh and blood, he also himself likewise took part of the same; that through death he might destroy him that had the power of death, that is, the devil; (Hebrews 2:14)

[167] And the LORD said unto Satan, Behold, he is in thine hand; but save his life. (Job 2:6)

[168] And the sea gave up the dead which were in it; and death and hell delivered up the dead which were in them: and they were judged every man according to their works. And death and hell were cast into the lake of fire. This is the second death. And whosoever was

not found written in the book of life was cast into the lake of fire. (Revelation 20:13-15)

[169] For he must reign, till he hath put all enemies under his feet. The last enemy that shall be destroyed is death. (1Corinthians 15:25; 26)

[170] But I say unto you, Swear not at all; neither by heaven; for it is God's throne: Nor by the earth; for it is his footstool: neither by Jerusalem; for it is the city of the great King. (Matthew 5:34; 35)

And David himself saith in the book of Psalm, The LORD said unto my Lord, Sit thou on my right hand, Till I make thine enemies thy footstool. (Luke 20:42; 43)

[171] And fear not them which kill the body, but are not able to kill the soul: but rather fear him which is able to destroy both soul and body in hell. (Matthew 10:28)

[172] Then shall the dust return to the earth as it was: and the spirit shall return unto God who gave it. (Ecclesiastes 12:7)

[173] They are dead, they shall not live; they are deceased, they shall not rise: therefore hast thou visited and destroyed them, and made all their memory to perish. (Isaiah 26:14)

[174] And the LORD God formed man of the dust of the ground, and breathed into his nostrils the breath of life; and man became a living soul. (Genesis 2:7)

[175] Then shall he say also unto them on the left hand, Depart from me, ye cursed, into everlasting fire, prepared for the devil and his angels: (Matthew 25:41)

[176] Now unto the King eternal, immortal, invisible, the only wise God, be honour and glory for ever and ever. Amen. (1Timothy 1:17)

[177] See now that I, even I, am he, and there is no god with me: I kill, and I make alive; I wound, and I heal: neither is there any that can deliver out of my hand. (Deuteronomy 32:39)

[178] They are dead, they shall not live; they are deceased, they shall not rise: therefore hast thou visited and destroyed them, and made all their memory to perish. (Isaiah 26:14)

[179] Dearly beloved, avenge not yourselves, but rather give place unto wrath: for it is written, Vengeance is mine; I will repay, saith the Lord. (Romans 12:19)

[180] Then shall he say also unto them on the left hand, Depart from me, ye cursed, into everlasting fire, prepared for the devil and his angels: (Matthew 25:41)

Wherefore we receiving a kingdom which cannot be moved, let us have grace, whereby we may serve God acceptably with reverence and godly fear: For our God is a consuming fire. (Hebrews 12:28; 29)

And the devil that deceived them was cast into the lake of fire and brimstone, where the beast and the false prophet are, and shall be tormented day and night for ever and ever. (Revelation 20:10)

[181] But I will forewarn you whom ye shall fear: Fear him, which after he hath killed hath power to cast into hell; yea, I say unto you, Fear him. (Luke 12:5)

[182] Study to shew thyself approved unto God, a workman that needeth not to be ashamed, rightly dividing the word of truth. (2Timothy 2:15)

[183] And the LORD said unto Moses, Whosoever hath sinned against me, him will I blot out of my book. (Exodus 32:33)

There is no remembrance of former things; neither shall there be any remembrance of things that are to come with those that shall come after. (Ecclesiastes 1:11)

The face of the LORD is against them that do evil, to cut off the remembrance of them from the earth. (Psalm 34:16)

[184] That the trial of your faith, being much more precious than of gold that perisheth, though it be tried with fire, might be found unto praise and honour and glory at the appearing of Jesus Christ: (1Peter 1:7)

I counsel thee to buy of me gold tried in the fire, that thou mayest be rich; and white raiment, that thou mayest be clothed, and that the shame of thy nakedness do not appear; and anoint thine eyes with eyesalve, that thou mayest see. (Revelation 3:18)

[185] And I went out by night by the gate of the valley, even before the dragon well, and to the dung port, and viewed the walls of Jerusalem, which were broken down, and the gates thereof were consumed with fire. (Nehemiah 2:13)

For, behold, the day cometh, that shall burn as an oven; and all the proud, yea, and all that do wickedly, shall be stubble: and the day that cometh shall burn them up, saith the LORD of hosts, that it shall leave them neither root nor branch. But unto you that fear my name shall the Sun of righteousness arise with healing in his wings; and ye shall go forth, and grow up as calves of the stall. And ye shall tread down the wicked; for they shall be ashes under the soles of your feet in the day that I shall do this, saith the LORD of hosts. (Malachi 4:1-3)

But, beloved, be not ignorant of this one thing, that one day *is* with the Lord as a thousand years, and a thousand years as one day. The Lord is not slack concerning his promise, as some men count slackness; but is longsuffering to us-ward, not willing that any should perish, but that all should come to repentance. But the day of the Lord will come as a thief in the night; in the which the heavens shall pass away with a great noise, and the elements shall melt with fervent heat, the earth also and the works that are therein shall be burned up. (2Peter 3:8-10)

[186] And if thy hand offend thee, cut it off: it is better for thee to enter into life maimed, than having two hands to go into hell, into the fire that never shall be quenched: Where their worm dieth not, and the fire is not quenched. And if thy foot offend thee, cut it off: it is better for thee to enter halt into life, than having two feet to be cast into hell, into the fire that never shall be quenched: Where their worm dieth not, and the fire is not quenched. And if thine eye offend thee, pluck it out: it is better for thee to enter into the kingdom of God with one eye, than having two eyes to be cast into hell fire: Where their worm dieth not, and the fire is not quenched. (Mark 9:43-48)

[187] For the living know that they shall die: but the dead know not any thing, neither have they any more a reward; for the memory of them is forgotten. Also their love, and their hatred, and their envy, is now perished; neither have they any more a portion for ever in any thing that is done under the sun. (Ecclesiastes 9:5; 6)

[188] The Son of man shall send forth his angels, and they shall gather out of his kingdom all things that offend, and them which do iniquity; And shall cast them into a furnace of fire: there shall be wailing and gnashing of teeth. (Matthew 13:42)

[189] But, beloved, be not ignorant of this one thing, that one day is with the Lord as a thousand years, and a thousand years as one day. (2Peter 3:8)

[190] It is a fearful thing to fall into the hands of the living God. (Hebrews 10:31)

[191] And the Spirit and the bride say, Come. And let him that heareth say, Come. And let him that is athirst come. And whosoever will, let him take the water of life freely. (Revelation 22:17)

[192] All that the Father giveth me shall come to me; and him that cometh to me I will in no wise cast out. (John 6:37)

No man can come to me, except the Father which hath sent me draw him: and I will raise him up at the last day. (John 6:44)

[193] For God so loved the world, that he gave his only begotten Son, that whosoever believeth in him should not perish, but have everlasting life. (John 3:16)

[194] And beside all this, between us and you there is a great gulf fixed: so that they which would pass from hence to you cannot; neither can they pass to us, that would come from thence. (Luke 16:26)

[195] Then said Jesus unto them again, Verily, verily, I say unto you, I am the door of the sheep. (John 10:7)

[196] (Now that he ascended, what is it but that he also descended first into the lower parts of the earth? (Ephesians 4:9)

[197] And one of the malefactors which were hanged railed on him, saying, If thou be Christ, save thyself and us. But the other answering rebuked him, saying, Dost not thou fear God, seeing thou art in the same condemnation? And we indeed justly; for we receive the due reward of our deeds: but this man hath done nothing amiss. And he said unto Jesus, Lord, remember me when thou comest into thy

kingdom. And Jesus said unto him, Verily I say unto thee, To day shalt thou be with me in paradise. (Luke 23:39-43)

[198] Saying, The Lord is risen indeed, and hath appeared to Simon. (Luke 24:34)

[199] He that descended is the same also that ascended up far above all heavens, that he might fill all things. (Ephesians 4:10)

[200] Jesus saith unto her, Touch me not; for I am not yet ascended to my Father: but go to my brethren, and say unto them, I ascend unto my Father, and your Father; and to my God, and your God. (John 20:17)

[201] I am Alpha and Omega, the beginning and the ending, saith the Lord, which is, and which was, and which is to come, the Almighty. (Revelation 1:8)

CHAPTER FIVE

[1] There is no remembrance of former things; neither shall there be any remembrance of things that are to come with those that shall come after. (Ecclesiastes 1:11)

[2] Remember the former things of old: for I am God, and there is none else; I am God, and there is none like me. (Isaiah 46:9)

[3] He that descended is the same also that ascended up far above all heavens, that he might fill all things.) And he gave some, apostles; and some, prophets; and some, evangelists; and some, pastors and teachers; For the perfecting of the saints, for the work of the ministry, for the edifying of the body of Christ: Till we all come in the unity of the faith, and of the knowledge of the Son of God, unto a perfect man, unto the measure of the stature of the fulness of Christ: That we henceforth be no more children, tossed to and fro, and carried about with every wind of doctrine, by the sleight of men, and cunning craftiness, whereby they lie in wait to deceive; But speaking the truth in love, may grow up into him in all things, which is the head, even Christ: (Ephesians 4:10-15)

[4] For whom he did foreknow, he also did predestinate to be conformed to the image of his Son, that he might be the firstborn among many brethren. Moreover whom he did predestinate, them he also called: and whom he called, them he also justified: and whom he justified, them he also glorified. (Romans 8:29; 30)

[5] And he is before all things, and by him all things consist. And he is the head of the body, the church: who is the beginning, the firstborn from the dead; that in all things he might have the preeminence. (Colossians 1:17; 18)

[6] For the Son of man is come to save that which was lost. (Matthew 18:11)

[7] He hath made every thing beautiful in his time: also he hath set the world in their heart, so that no man can find out the work that God maketh from the beginning to the end. I know that, whatsoever God doeth, it shall be for ever: nothing can be put to it, nor any thing taken from it: and God doeth it, that men should fear before him. (Ecclesiastes 3:11; 14)

[8] Even so we, when we were children, were in bondage under the elements of the world: But when the fulness of the time was come, God sent forth his Son, made of a woman, made under the law, To redeem them that were under the law, that we might receive the adoption of sons. (Galatians 4:3-5)

[9] There is no remembrance of former things; neither shall there be any remembrance of things that are to come with those that shall come after. (Ecclesiastes 1:11)

[10] I know that, whatsoever God doeth, it shall be for ever: nothing can be put to it, nor any thing taken from it: and God doeth it, that men should fear before him. (Ecclesiastes 3:14)

[11] Thou knowest my downsitting and mine uprising, thou understandest my thought afar off. Thou compassest my path and my lying down, and art acquainted with all my ways. For there is not a word in my tongue, but, lo, O LORD, thou knowest it altogether. (Psalm 139:2; 4)

And it shall come to pass, that before they call, I will answer; and while they are yet speaking, I will hear. (Isaiah 65:24)

[12] I know that, whatsoever God doeth, it shall be for ever: nothing can be put to it, nor any thing taken from it: and God doeth it, that men should fear before him. (Ecclesiastes 3:14)

[13] That which hath been is now; and that which is to be hath already been; and God requireth that which is past. (Ecclesiastes 3:15)

[14] The thing that hath been, it is that which shall be; and that which is done is that which shall be done: and there is no new thing under the sun. Is there any thing whereof it may be said, See, this is new? it hath been already of old time, which was before us. (Ecclesiastes 1:9; 10)

I know that, whatsoever God doeth, it shall be for ever: nothing can be put to it, nor any thing taken from it: and God doeth it, that men should fear before him. That which hath been is now; and that which is to be hath already been; and God requireth that which is past. (Ecclesiastes 3:14; 15)

The LORD of hosts hath sworn, saying, Surely as I have thought, so shall it come to pass; and as I have purposed, so shall it stand: (Isaiah 14:24)

Remember the former things of old: for I am God, and there is none else; I am God, and there is none like me, Declaring the end from the beginning, and from ancient times the things that are not yet done, saying, My counsel shall stand, and I will do all my pleasure: (Isaiah 46:9; 10)

[15] God forbid: yea, let God be true, but every man a liar; as it is written, That thou mightest be justified in thy sayings, and mightest overcome when thou art judged. (Romans 3:4)

[16] For whom he did foreknow, he also did predestinate to be conformed to the image of his Son, that he might be the firstborn among many brethren. Moreover whom he did predestinate, them he also called: and whom he called, them he also justified: and whom he justified, them he also glorified. (Romans 8:29; 30)

[17] The counsel of the LORD standeth for ever, the thoughts of his heart to all generations. (Psalm 33:11)

The LORD of hosts hath sworn, saying, Surely as I have thought, so shall it come to pass; and as I have purposed, so shall it stand: (Isaiah 14:24)

For my thoughts are not your thoughts, neither are your ways my ways, saith the LORD. For as the heavens are higher than the earth, so are my ways higher than your ways, and my thoughts than your thoughts. (Isaiah 55:8; 9)

The anger of the LORD shall not return, until he have executed, and till he have performed the thoughts of his heart: in the latter days ye shall consider it perfectly. (Jeremiah 23:20)

For I know the thoughts that I think toward you, saith the LORD, thoughts of peace, and not of evil, to give you an expected end. (Jeremiah 29:11)

But they know not the thoughts of the LORD, neither understand they his counsel: for he shall gather them as the sheaves into the floor. (Micah 4:12)

[18] Howbeit when he, the Spirit of truth, is come, he will guide you into all truth: for he shall not speak of himself; but whatsoever he shall hear, that shall he speak: and he will shew you things to come. (John 16:13)

[19] But as it is written, Eye hath not seen, nor ear heard, neither have entered into the heart of man, the things which God hath prepared for them that love him. But God hath revealed them unto us by his Spirit: for the Spirit searcheth all things, yea, the deep things of God. (1Corinthians 2:9; 10)

[20] And his disciples asked him, saying, What might this parable be? And he said, Unto you it is given to know the mysteries of the kingdom of God: but to others in parables; that seeing they might not see, and hearing they might not understand. (Luke 8:9; 10)

[21] Unto me, who am less than the least of all saints, is this grace given, that I should preach among the Gentiles the unsearchable

riches of Christ; And to make all men see what is the fellowship of the mystery, which from the beginning of the world hath been hid in God, who created all things by Jesus Christ: To the intent that now unto the principalities and powers in heavenly places might be known by the church the manifold wisdom of God, According to the eternal purpose which he purposed in Christ Jesus our Lord: (Ephesians 3:8-11)

22 Where wast thou when I laid the foundations of the earth? declare, if thou hast understanding. Who hath laid the measures thereof, if thou knowest? or who hath stretched the line upon it? Whereupon are the foundations thereof fastened? or who laid the corner stone thereof; When the morning stars sang together, and all the sons of God shouted for joy? (Job 38:4-7)

23 Blessed be the God and Father of our Lord Jesus Christ, who hath blessed us with all spiritual blessings in heavenly places in Christ: According as he hath chosen us in him before the foundation of the world, that we should be holy and without blame before him in love: Having predestinated us unto the adoption of children by Jesus Christ to himself, according to the good pleasure of his will, To the praise of the glory of his grace, wherein he hath made us accepted in the beloved. (Ephesians 1:3-6)

24 In the beginning was the Word, and the Word was with God, and the Word was God. The same was in the beginning with God. All things were made by him; and without him was not any thing made that was made. (John 1:1-3)

25 And the LORD God caused a deep sleep to fall upon Adam, and he slept: and he took one of his ribs, and closed up the flesh instead thereof; And the rib, which the LORD God had taken from man, made he a woman, and brought her unto the man. And Adam said, This is now bone of my bones, and flesh of my flesh: she shall be called Woman, because she was taken out of Man. (Genesis 2: 21-23)

26 But he that is joined unto the Lord is one spirit. (1Corinthians 6:17)

According as he hath chosen us in him before the foundation of the world, that we should be holy and without blame before him in love: (Ephesians 1:4)

²⁷ That which hath been is now; and that which is to be hath already been; and God requireth that which is past. (Ecclesiastes 3:15)

²⁸ Ye also, as lively stones, are built up a spiritual house, an holy priesthood, to offer up spiritual sacrifices, acceptable to God by Jesus Christ. (1Peter 2:5)

²⁹ Go ye therefore, and teach all nations, baptizing them in the name of the Father, and of the Son, and of the Holy Ghost: Teaching them to observe all things whatsoever I have commanded you: and, lo, I am with you alway, even unto the end of the world. Amen. (Matthew 28:19; 20)

³⁰ But as many as received him, to them gave he power to become the sons of God, even to them that believe on his name: (John 1:12)

Behold, what manner of love the Father hath bestowed upon us, that we should be called the sons of God: therefore the world knoweth us not, because it knew him not. Beloved, now are we the sons of God, and it doth not yet appear what we shall be: but we know that, when he shall appear, we shall be like him; for we shall see him as he is. And every man that hath this hope in him purifieth himself, even as he is pure. (1John 3:1-3)

³¹ What? know ye not that your body is the temple of the Holy Ghost which is in you, which ye have of God, and ye are not your own? (1Corinthians 6:19)

³² And let us consider one another to provoke unto love and to good works: Not forsaking the assembling of ourselves together, as the manner of some is; but exhorting one another: and so much the more, as ye see the day approaching. (Hebrews 10:24; 25)

³³ For this cause I bow my knees unto the Father of our Lord Jesus Christ, Of whom the whole family in heaven and earth is named. (Ephesians 3:14; 15)

[34] Be ye not unequally yoked together with unbelievers: for what fellowship hath righteousness with unrighteousness? and what communion hath light with darkness? And what concord hath Christ with Belial? or what part hath he that believeth with an infidel? And what agreement hath the temple of God with idols? for ye are the temple of the living God; as God hath said, I will dwell in them, and walk in them; and I will be their God, and they shall be my people. Wherefore come out from among them, and be ye separate, saith the Lord, and touch not the unclean thing; and I will receive you, And will be a Father unto you, and ye shall be my sons and daughters, saith the Lord Almighty. (2Corinthians 6:14-18)

[35] Know ye not that your bodies are the members of Christ? shall I then take the members of Christ, and make them the members of an harlot? God forbid. What? know ye not that he which is joined to an harlot is one body? for two, saith he, shall be one flesh. (1Corinthians 6:15-16)

Wherefore whosoever shall eat this bread, and drink this cup of the Lord, unworthily, shall be guilty of the body and blood of the Lord. But let a man examine himself, and so let him eat of that bread, and drink of that cup. For he that eateth and drinketh unworthily, eateth and drinketh damnation to himself, not discerning the Lord's body. (1Corinthians 11:27-29)

[36] For I am jealous over you with godly jealousy: for I have espoused you to one husband, that I may present you as a chaste virgin to Christ. (2Corinthians 11:2)

These are they which were not defiled with women; for they are virgins. These are they which follow the Lamb whithersoever he goeth. These were redeemed from among men, being the firstfruits unto God and to the Lamb. And in their mouth was found no guile: for they are without fault before the throne of God. (Revelation 14:4; 5)

And the Spirit and the bride say, Come. And let him that heareth say, Come. And let him that is athirst come. And whosoever will, let him take the water of life freely. (Revelation 22:17)

[37] Wherefore I also, after I heard of your faith in the Lord Jesus, and love unto all the saints, Cease not to give thanks for you, making mention of you in my prayers; That the God of our Lord Jesus Christ, the Father of glory, may give unto you the spirit of wisdom and revelation in the knowledge of him: The eyes of your understanding being enlightened; that ye may know what is the hope of his calling, and what the riches of the glory of his inheritance in the saints, And what is the exceeding greatness of his power to us-ward who believe, according to the working of his mighty power, Which he wrought in Christ, when he raised him from the dead, and set him at his own right hand in the heavenly places, Far above all principality, and power, and might, and dominion, and every name that is named, not only in this world, but also in that which is to come: And hath put all things under his feet, and gave him to be the head over all things to the church, Which is his body, the fulness of him that filleth all in all. (Ephesians 1:15-23)

But God, who is rich in mercy, for his great love wherewith he loved us, Even when we were dead in sins, hath quickened us together with Christ, (by grace ye are saved;) And hath raised us up together, and made us sit together in heavenly places in Christ Jesus: That in the ages to come he might shew the exceeding riches of his grace in his kindness toward us through Christ Jesus. For by grace are ye saved through faith; and that not of yourselves: it is the gift of God: (Ephesians 2:4-8)

And he that overcometh, and keepeth my works unto the end, to him will I give power over the nations: And he shall rule them with a rod of iron; as the vessels of a potter shall they be broken to shivers: even as I received of my Father. And I will give him the morning star. He that hath an ear, let him hear what the Spirit saith unto the churches. (Revelation 2:26-29)

To him that overcometh will I grant to sit with me in my throne, even as I also overcame, and am set down with my Father in his throne. (Revelation 3:21)

[38] I know that, whatsoever God doeth, it shall be for ever: nothing can be put to it, nor any thing taken from it: and God doeth it, that men should fear before him. (Ecclesiastes 3:14)

[39] Jesus Christ the same yesterday, and to day, and for ever. (Hebrews 13:8)

[40] Nevertheless I tell you the truth; It is expedient for you that I go away: for if I go not away, the Comforter will not come unto you; but if I depart, I will send him unto you. And when he is come, he will reprove the world of sin, and of righteousness, and of judgment: Of sin, because they believe not on me; Of righteousness, because I go to my Father, and ye see me no more; Of judgment, because the prince of this world is judged. (John 16:7-16)

[41] (For the children being not yet born, neither having done any good or evil, that the purpose of God according to election might stand, not of works, but of him that calleth;) It was said unto her, The elder shall serve the younger. As it is written, Jacob have I loved, but Esau have I hated. What shall we say then? Is there unrighteousness with God? God forbid. For he saith to Moses, I will have mercy on whom I will have mercy, and I will have compassion on whom I will have compassion. So then it is not of him that willeth, nor of him that runneth, but of God that sheweth mercy. (Romans 9:11-16)

[42] Ye have heard that it was said by them of old time, Thou shalt not commit adultery: But I say unto you, That whosoever looketh on a woman to lust after her hath committed adultery with her already in his heart. (Matthew 5:37-28)

[43] And, behold, one came and said unto him, Good Master, what good thing shall I do, that I may have eternal life? And he said unto him, Why callest thou me good? there is none good but one, that is, God: but if thou wilt enter into life, keep the commandments. (Matthew 19:16-17)

[44] He hath made every thing beautiful in his time: also he hath set the world in their heart, so that no man can find out the work that God maketh from the beginning to the end. (Ecclesiastes 3:11)

[45] For whom he did foreknow, he also did predestinate to be conformed to the image of his Son, that he might be the firstborn among many brethren. Moreover whom he did predestinate, them he also called: and whom he called, them he also justified: and whom he justified, them he also glorified. (Romans 8:29-30)

[46] Nevertheless I tell you the truth; It is expedient for you that I go away: for if I go not away, the Comforter will not come unto you; but if I depart, I will send him unto you. And when he is come, he will reprove the world of sin, and of righteousness, and of judgment: Of sin, because they believe not on me; Of righteousness, because I go to my Father, and ye see me no more; Of judgment, because the prince of this world is judged. (John 16:7-11)

[47] "I have much more to tell you, but now it would be too much for you to bear. When, however, the Spirit comes, who reveals the truth about God, he will lead you into all the truth. He will not speak on his own authority, but he will speak of what he hears and will tell you of things to come". (John 16:12; 13)

[48] Unto me, who am less than the least of all saints, is this grace given, that I should preach among the Gentiles the unsearchable riches of Christ; And to make all men see what is the fellowship of the mystery, which from the beginning of the world hath been hid in God, who created all things by Jesus Christ: To the intent that now unto the principalities and powers in heavenly places might be known by the church the manifold wisdom of God, According to the eternal purpose which he purposed in Christ Jesus our Lord: (Ephesians 3:8-11)

[49] Howbeit we speak wisdom among them that are perfect: yet not the wisdom of this world, nor of the princes of this world, that come to nought: But we speak the wisdom of God in a mystery, even the hidden wisdom, which God ordained before the world unto our glory: Which none of the princes of this world knew: for had they known it, they would not have crucified the Lord of glory. But as it is written, Eye hath not seen, nor ear heard, neither have entered into the heart of man, the things which God hath prepared for them that love him. But God hath revealed them unto us by his Spirit: for the Spirit searcheth all things, yea, the deep things of God. (1Corinthians 2:6-10)

[50] He that hath an ear, let him hear what the Spirit saith unto the churches; To him that overcometh will I give to eat of the hidden manna, and will give him a white stone, and in the stone a new name written, which no man knoweth saving he that receiveth it. (Revelation 2:17)

[51] When the Son of man shall come in his glory, and all the holy angels with him, then shall he sit upon the throne of his glory: And before him shall be gathered all nations: and he shall separate them one from another, as a shepherd divideth his sheep from the goats: (Matthew 25:31; 32)

I charge thee therefore before God, and the Lord Jesus Christ, who shall judge the quick and the dead at his appearing and his kingdom; (2Timothy 4:1)

And the devil that deceived them was cast into the lake of fire and brimstone, where the beast and the false prophet are, and shall be tormented day and night for ever and ever. And I saw a great white throne, and him that sat on it, from whose face the earth and the heaven fled away; and there was found no place for them. And I saw the dead, small and great, stand before God; and the books were opened: and another book was opened, which is the book of life: and the dead were judged out of those things which were written in the books, according to their works. And the sea gave up the dead which were in it; and death and hell delivered up the dead which were in them: and they were judged every man according to their works. And death and hell were cast into the lake of fire. This is the second death. And whosoever was not found written in the book of life was cast into the lake of fire. (Revelation 20:15)

And, behold, I come quickly; and my reward is with me, to give every man according as his work shall be. (Revelation 22:12)

[52] For in him we live, and move, and have our being; as certain also of your own poets have said, For we are also his offspring. (Acts 17:28)

[53] And he said unto them, It is not for you to know the times or the seasons, which the Father hath put in his own power. (Acts 1:7)

[54] Wherefore he saith, Awake thou that sleepest, and arise from the dead, and Christ shall give thee light. (Ephesians 5:14)

[55] But unto the Son he saith, Thy throne, O God, is for ever and ever: a sceptre of righteousness is the sceptre of thy kingdom. Thou hast loved righteousness, and hated iniquity; therefore God, even thy

God, hath anointed thee with the oil of gladness above thy fellows. (Hebrews 1:8-9)

[56] Husbands, love your wives, even as Christ also loved the church, and gave himself for it; That he might sanctify and cleanse it with the washing of water by the word, That he might present it to himself a glorious church, not having spot, or wrinkle, or any such thing; but that it should be holy and without blemish. So ought men to love their wives as their own bodies. He that loveth his wife loveth himself. For no man ever yet hated his own flesh; but nourisheth and cherisheth it, even as the Lord the church: For we are members of his body, of his flesh, and of his bones. For this cause shall a man leave his father and mother, and shall be joined unto his wife, and they two shall be one flesh. This is a great mystery: but I speak concerning Christ and the church. (Ephesians 5: 25-32)

[57] Ye men of Israel, hear these words; Jesus of Nazareth, a man approved of God among you by miracles and wonders and signs, which God did by him in the midst of you, as ye yourselves also know: Him, being delivered by the determinate counsel and foreknowledge of God, ye have taken, and by wicked hands have crucified and slain: (Act 2: 22; 23)

[58] (For the children being not yet born, neither having done any good or evil, that the purpose of God according to election might stand, not of works, but of him that calleth;) It was said unto her, The elder shall serve the younger. As it is written, Jacob have I loved, but Esau have I hated. What shall we say then? Is there unrighteousness with God? God forbid. For he saith to Moses, I will have mercy on whom I will have mercy, and I will have compassion on whom I will have compassion. So then it is not of him that willeth, nor of him that runneth, but of God that sheweth mercy. For the scripture saith unto Pharaoh, Even for this same purpose have I raised thee up, that I might shew my power in thee, and that my name might be declared throughout all the earth. Therefore hath he mercy on whom he will have mercy, and whom he will he hardeneth. Thou wilt say then unto me, Why doth he yet find fault? For who hath resisted his will? Nay but, O man, who art thou that repliest against God? Shall the thing formed say to him that formed it, Why hast thou made me thus? Hath

not the potter power over the clay, of the same lump to make one vessel unto honour, and another unto dishonour? (Romans 9:11-21)

[59] Thou knowest my downsitting and mine uprising, thou understandest my thought afar off. Thou compassest my path and my lying down, and art acquainted with all my ways. For there is not a word in my tongue, but, lo, O LORD, thou knowest it altogether. (Psalm 139:2-4)

And it shall come to pass, that before they call, I will answer; and while they are yet speaking, I will hear. (Isaiah 65:24)

[60] Then answered Jesus and said unto them, Verily, verily, I say unto you, The Son can do nothing of himself, but what he seeth the Father do: for what things soever he doeth, these also doeth the Son likewise. (John 5:19)

I can of mine own self do nothing: as I hear, I judge: and my judgment is just; because I seek not mine own will, but the will of the Father which hath sent me. (John 5:30)

If ye shall ask any thing in my name, I will do it. (John 14:14)

And in that day ye shall ask me nothing. Verily, verily, I say unto you, Whatsoever ye shall ask the Father in my name, he will give it you. (John 16:23)

Jesus saith unto him, I am the way, the truth, and the life: no man cometh unto the Father, but by me. If ye had known me, ye should have known my Father also: and from henceforth ye know him, and have seen him. Philip saith unto him, Lord, shew us the Father, and it sufficeth us. Jesus saith unto him, Have I been so long time with you, and yet hast thou not known me, Philip? he that hath seen me hath seen the Father; and how sayest thou then, Shew us the Father? Believest thou not that I am in the Father, and the Father in me? the words that I speak unto you I speak not of myself: but the Father that dwelleth in me, he doeth the works. Believe me that I am in the Father, and the Father in me: or else believe me for the very works' sake. (John 14:11-16)

[61] For the gifts and calling of God are without repentance. (Romans 11:29)

CHAPTER SIX

[1] And ye shall know the truth, and the truth shall make you free. (John 8:32)

[2] This people draweth nigh unto me with their mouth, and honoureth me with their lips; but their heart is far from me. But in vain they do worship me, teaching for doctrines the commandments of men. (Matthew 15:8; 9)

[3] Wherefore if ye be dead with Christ from the rudiments of the world, why, as though living in the world, are ye subject to ordinances, (Touch not; taste not; handle not; Which all are to perish with the using;) after the commandments and doctrines of men? Which things have indeed a shew of wisdom in will worship, and humility, and neglecting of the body; not in any honour to the satisfying of the flesh. (Colossians 2:20-23)

[4] Who also hath made us able ministers of the new testament; not of the letter, but of the spirit: for the letter killeth, but the spirit giveth life. (2Corinthians 3:6)

[5] Study to shew thyself approved unto God, a workman that needeth not to be ashamed, rightly dividing the word of truth. (2Timothy 2:15)

[6] For I reckon that the sufferings of this present time are not worthy to be compared with the glory which shall be revealed in us. For the earnest expectation of the creature waiteth for the manifestation of the sons of God. For the creature was made subject to vanity, not willingly, but by reason of him who hath subjected the same in hope, Because the creature itself also shall be delivered from the bondage of corruption into the glorious liberty of the children of God. (Romans 8:18-21)

[7] And he answered and said unto them, Have ye not read, that he which made them at the beginning made them male and female, And said, For this cause shall a man leave father and mother, and shall cleave to his wife: and they twain shall be one flesh? Wherefore they

are no more twain, but one flesh. What therefore God hath joined together, let not man put asunder. (Matthew 19:4-6)

[8] But he that is joined unto the Lord is one spirit. (1Corinthians 6:16)

[9] And God said, Let us make man in our image, after our likeness: and let them have dominion over the fish of the sea, and over the fowl of the air, and over the cattle, and over all the earth, and over every creeping thing that creepeth upon the earth. So God created man in his own image, in the image of God created he him; male and female created he them. (Genesis 1:26; 27)

[10] And the Spirit and the bride say, Come. And let him that heareth say, Come. And let him that is athirst come. And whosoever will, let him take the water of life freely. (Revelation 22:17)

[11] And if children, then heirs; heirs of God, and joint-heirs with Christ; if so be that we suffer with *him*, that we may be also glorified together. (Romans 8:17)

[12] And they sung a new song, saying, Thou art worthy to take the book, and to open the seals thereof: for thou wast slain, and hast redeemed us to God by thy blood out of every kindred, and tongue, and people, and nation; (Revelation 5:9)

[13] Who also hath made us able ministers of the new testament; not of the letter, but of the spirit: for the letter killeth, but the spirit giveth life. (2Corintians 3:6)

[14] Thy word is a lamp (the Body) unto my feet, and a light (the Spirit) unto my path. (Psalm 119:105)

[15] And the Spirit and the bride say, Come. And let him that heareth say, Come. And let him that is athirst come. And whosoever will, let him take the water of life freely. (Revelation 22:17)

[16] There is one body, and one Spirit, even as ye are called in one hope of your calling; (Ephesians 4:4)

[17] For we are members of his body, of his flesh, and of his bones. For this cause shall aman leave his father and mother, and shall be joined

unto his wife, and they two shall be one flesh. This is a great mystery: but I speak concerning Christ and the church. (Ephesians 5:30-32)

[18] Thy word is a lamp unto my feet, and a light unto my path. (Psalm 119:105)

[19] It is the spirit that quickeneth; the flesh profiteth nothing: the words that I speak unto you, they are spirit, and they are life. (John 6:63)

[20] Jesus answered and said unto him, Art thou a master of Israel, and knowest not these things? Verily, verily, I say unto thee, We speak that we do know, and testify that we have seen; and ye receive not our witness. (John 3:10; 11)

[21] But if I do, though ye believe not me, believe the works: that ye may know, and believe, that the Father is in me, and I in him. (John 10:38)

[22] According as he hath chosen us in him before the foundation of the world, that we should be holy and without blame before him in love: (Ephesians 1:4)

[23] Wherefore seeing we also are compassed about with so great a cloud of witnesses, let us lay aside every weight, and the sin which doth so easily beset us, and let us run with patience the race that is set before us, (Hebrews 12:1)

[24] What therefore God hath joined together, let not man put asunder. (Mark 10:9)

[25] Him, being delivered by the determinate counsel and foreknowledge of God, ye have taken, and by wicked hands have crucified and slain: (Acts 2:23)

[26] And all things are of God, who hath reconciled us to himself by Jesus Christ, and hath given to us the ministry of reconciliation; To wit, that God was in Christ, reconciling the world unto himself, not imputing their trespasses unto them; and hath committed unto us the word of reconciliation. (2Corinthians 5:18; 19)

[27] I know that, whatsoever God doeth, it shall be for ever: nothing can be put to it, nor any thing taken from it: and God doeth it, that men should fear before him. (Ecclesiastes 3:14)

²⁸ And all that dwell upon the earth shall worship him, whose names are not written in the book of life of the Lamb slain from the foundation of the world. (Revelation 13:8)

²⁹ According as he hath chosen us in him before the foundation of the world, that we should be holy and without blame before him in love: (Ephesians 1:4)

³⁰ But he that is joined unto the Lord is one spirit. (1Corinthians 6:17)

³¹ Jesus Christ the same yesterday, and to day, and for ever. (Hebrews 13:8)

³² According as he hath chosen us in him before the foundation of the world, that we should be holy and without blame before him in love: (Ephesians 1:4)

³³ Know ye not that ye are the temple of God, and that the Spirit of God dwelleth in you? (1Corinthians 3:16)

³⁴ I know that, whatsoever God doeth, it shall be for ever: nothing can be put to it, nor any thing taken from it: and God doeth it, that men should fear before him. That which hath been is now; and that which is to be hath already been; and God requireth that which is past. (Ecclesiastes 3:14; 15)

³⁵ Even the mystery which hath been hid from ages and from generations, but now is made manifest to his saints: To whom God would make known what is the riches of the glory of this mystery among the Gentiles; which is Christ in you, the hope of glory: (Colossians 1:26; 27)

³⁶ Moreover he sprinkled with blood both the tabernacle, and all the vessels of the ministry. And almost all things are by the law purged with blood; and without shedding of blood is no remission. (Hebrews 9:21; 22)

³⁷ And as they were eating, Jesus took bread, and blessed it, and brake it, and gave it to the disciples, and said, Take, eat; this is my body. And he took the cup, and gave thanks, and gave it to them, saying,

Drink ye all of it; For this is my blood of the new testament, which is shed for many for the remission of sins. (Matthew 26:26-28)

[38] For the life of the flesh is in the blood: and I have given it to you upon the altar to make an atonement for your souls: for it is the blood that maketh an atonement for the soul. For it is the life of all flesh; the blood of it is for the life thereof: therefore I said unto the children of Israel, Ye shall eat the blood of no manner of flesh: for the life of all flesh is the blood thereof: whosoever eateth it shall be cut off. (Leviticus 17:11; 14)

[39] And if any mischief follow, then thou shalt give life for life, Eye for eye, tooth for tooth, hand for hand, foot for foot, Burning for burning, wound for wound, stripe for stripe. (Exodus 21:23-25)

[40] For the life of the flesh is in the blood: and I have given it to you upon the altar to make an atonement for your souls: for it is the blood that maketh an atonement for the soul. (Leviticus 17:11)

[41] We have an altar, whereof they have no right to eat which serve the tabernacle. For the bodies of those beasts, whose blood is brought into the sanctuary by the high priest for sin, are burned without the camp. (Hebrews 13:10; 11)

[42] And the skin of the bullock, and all his flesh, with his head, and with his legs, and his inwards, and his dung, Even the whole bullock shall he carry forth without the camp unto a clean place, where the ashes are poured out, and burn him on the wood with fire: where the ashes are poured out shall he be burnt. And if the whole congregation of Israel sin through ignorance, and the thing be hid from the eyes of the assembly, and they have done somewhat against any of the commandments of the LORD concerning things which should not be done, and are guilty; When the sin, which they have sinned against it, is known, then the congregation shall offer a young bullock for the sin, and bring him before the tabernacle of the congregation. And the elders of the congregation shall lay their hands upon the head of the bullock before the LORD: and the bullock shall be killed before the LORD. And the priest that is anointed shall bring of the bullock's blood to the tabernacle of the congregation: (Leviticus 4:11-16)

[43] Wherefore Jesus also, that he might sanctify the people with his own blood, suffered without the gate. Let us go forth therefore unto him without the camp, bearing his reproach. (Hebrews 13:12; 13)

[44] I am poured out like water, and all my bones are out of joint: my heart is like wax; it is melted in the midst of my bowels. My strength is dried up like a potsherd; and my tongue cleaveth to my jaws; and thou hast brought me into the dust of death. For dogs have compassed me: the assembly of the wicked have inclosed me: they pierced my hands and my feet. I may tell all my bones: they look and stare upon me. They part my garments among them, and cast lots upon my vesture. (Psalm 22:14-18)

[45] And Adam was not deceived, but the woman being deceived was in the transgression. (1Timothy 2:14)

[46] For he hath made him to be sin for us, who knew no sin; that we might be made the righteousness of God in him. (2Corinthians 5:21)

[47] Wherefore, as by one man sin entered into the world, and death by sin; and so death passed upon all men, for that all have sinned: (For until the law sin was in the world: but sin is not imputed when there is no law. Nevertheless death reigned from Adam to Moses, even over them that had not sinned after the similitude of Adam's transgression, who is the figure of him that was to come. (Romans 5:12-14)

[48] But I would have you know, that the head of every man is Christ; and the head of the woman is the man; and the head of Christ is God. (1Corinthians 11:3)

That we henceforth be no more children, tossed to and fro, and carried about with every wind of doctrine, by the sleight of men, and cunning craftiness, whereby they lie in wait to deceive; But speaking the truth in love, may grow up into him in all things, which is the head, even Christ: (Ephesians 4:14; 15)

For the husband is the head of the wife, even as Christ is the head of the church: and he is the saviour of the body. (Ephesians 5:23)

[49] For as the body without the spirit is dead, so faith without works is dead also. (James 2:26)

[50] And if he bring a lamb for a sin offering, he shall bring it a female without blemish. And he shall lay his hand upon the head of the sin offering, and slay it for a sin offering in the place where they kill the burnt offering. And the priest shall take of the blood of the sin offering with his finger, and put it upon the horns of the altar of burnt offering, and shall pour out all the blood thereof at the bottom of the altar: And he shall take away all the fat thereof, as the fat of the lamb is taken away from the sacrifice of the peace offerings; and the priest shall burn them upon the altar, according to the offerings made by fire unto the LORD: and the priest shall make an atonement for his sin that he hath committed, and it shall be forgiven him. (Leviticus 4:32-35)

[51] They said unto him, Grant unto us that we may sit, one on thy right hand, and the other on thy left hand, in thy glory. But Jesus said unto them, Ye know not what ye ask: can ye drink of the cup that I drink of? and be baptized with the baptism that I am baptized with? And they said unto him, We can. And Jesus said unto them, Ye shall indeed drink of the cup that I drink of; and with the baptism that I am baptized withal shall ye be baptized: (Mark 10:37-39)

[52] Buried with him in baptism, wherein also ye are risen with him through the faith of the operation of God, who hath raised him from the dead. (Colossians 2:12)

Even when we were dead in sins, hath quickened us together with Christ, (by grace ye are saved;) And hath raised us up together, and made us sit together in heavenly places in Christ Jesus: (Ephesians 2:5)

[53] And all that dwell upon the earth shall worship him, whose names are not written in the book of life of the Lamb slain from the foundation of the world. (Revelation 13:8)

[54] Behold, thou desirest truth in the inward parts: and in the hidden part thou shalt make me to know wisdom. Purge me with hyssop, and I shall be clean: wash me, and I shall be whiter than snow. Make me to hear joy and gladness; that the bones which thou hast broken may rejoice. Hide thy face from my sins, and blot out all mine iniquities. Create in me a clean heart, O God; and renew a right spirit within me. Cast me not away from thy presence; and take not thy holy spirit

from me. Restore unto me the joy of thy salvation; and uphold me with thy free spirit. Then will I teach transgressors thy ways; and sinners shall be converted unto thee. (Psalm 51:6-13)

[55] And one of the elders answered, saying unto me, What are these which are arrayed in white robes? and whence came they? And I said unto him, Sir, thou knowest. And he said to me, These are they which came out of great tribulation, and have washed their robes, and made them white in the blood of the Lamb. Therefore are they before the throne of God, and serve him day and night in his temple: and he that sitteth on the throne shall dwell among them. They shall hunger no more, neither thirst any more; neither shall the sun light on them, nor any heat. For the Lamb which is in the midst of the throne shall feed them, and shall lead them unto living fountains of waters: and God shall wipe away all tears from their eyes. (Revelation 7:13-17)

[56] The Spirit itself beareth witness with our spirit, that we are the children of God: And if children, then heirs; heirs of God, and joint-heirs with Christ; if so be that we suffer with him, that we may be also glorified together. For I reckon that the sufferings of this present time are not worthy to be compared with the glory which shall be revealed in us. (Romans 8:16-18)

[57] And the very God of peace sanctify you wholly; and I pray God your whole spirit and soul and body be preserved blameless unto the coming of our Lord Jesus Christ. (1Thessalonoians 5:23)

[58] And the priest shall put some of the blood upon the horns of the altar of sweet incense before the LORD, which is in the tabernacle of the congregation; and shall pour all the blood of the bullock at the bottom of the altar of the burnt offering, which is at the door of the tabernacle of the congregation. (Leviticus 4:7)

[59] For the wages of sin is death; but the gift of God is eternal life through Jesus Christ our Lord. (Romans 6:23)

[60] And he that killeth any man shall surely be put to death. And he that killeth a beast shall make it good; beast for beast. And if a man cause a blemish in his neighbour; as he hath done, so shall it be done to him; Breach for breach, eye for eye, tooth for tooth: as he hath caused a blemish in a man, so shall it be done to him again. And he

that killeth a beast, he shall restore it: and he that killeth a man, he shall be put to death. (Leviticus 24: 17-21)

[61] Even as the Son of man came not to be ministered unto, but to minister, and to give his life a ransom for many. (Matthew 20:28)

[62] But we have this treasure in earthen vessels, that the excellency of the power may be of God, and not of us. (2Corinthians 4:7)

[63] To wit, that God was in Christ, reconciling the world unto himself, not imputing their trespasses unto them; and hath committed unto us the word of reconciliation. (2 Corinthians 5:19)

[64] For the earnest expectation of the creature waiteth for the manifestation of the sons of God. (Romans 8:19)

[65] The eyes of your understanding being enlightened; that ye may know what is the hope of his calling, and what the riches of the glory of his inheritance in the saints. (Ephesians 1:18)

To whom God would make known what is the riches of the glory of this mystery among the Gentiles; which is Christ in you, the hope of glory: (Colossians 1:27)

[66] When he shall come to be glorified in his saints, and to be admired in all them that believe (because our testimony among you was believed) in that day. (2Thessalonians 1:10)

[67] For the Son of man shall come in the glory of his Father with his angels; and then he shall reward every man according to his works. (Matthew 16:27)

And he shall send his angels with a great sound of a trumpet, and they shall gather together his elect from the four winds, from one end of heaven to the other. (Mathew 24:31)

For a man indeed ought not to cover his head, forasmuch as he is the image and glory of God: but the woman is the glory of the man. (1Corinthians 11:7)

And to you who are troubled rest with us, when the Lord Jesus shall be revealed from heaven with his mighty angels, (2Thessalonians 1:7)

To the end he may stablish your hearts unblameable in holiness before God, even our Father, at the coming of our Lord Jesus Christ with all his saints. (1Thessalonians 3:13)

To whom God would make known what *is* the riches of the glory of this mystery among the Gentiles; which is Christ in you, the hope of glory: (Colossians 1:27)

And Enoch also, the seventh from Adam, prophesied of these, saying, Behold, the Lord cometh with ten thousands of his saints, (Jude 1:14)

And when he was demanded of the Pharisees, when the kingdom of God should come, he answered them and said, The kingdom of God cometh not with observation: Neither shall they say, Lo here! or, lo there! for, behold, the kingdom of God is within you. (Luke 17:20; 21)

Wherefore if they shall say unto you, Behold, he is in the desert; go not forth: behold, he is in the secret chambers; believe it not. For as the lightning cometh out of the east, and shineth even unto the west; so shall also the coming of the Son of man be. (Matthew 24:26; 27)

[68] Then we which are alive and remain shall be caught up together with them in the clouds, to meet the Lord in the air: and so shall we ever be with the Lord. (1Thessalonians 4:17)

[69] And he said, Unto you it is given to know the mysteries of the kingdom of God: but to others in parables; that seeing they might not see, and hearing they might not understand. (Luke 8:10)

[70] But he answered and said, It is not meet to take the children's bread, and to cast it to dogs. (Matthew 15:26)

Fear not, little flock; for it is your Father's good pleasure to give you the kingdom. (Luke 12:32)

Ye are of your father the devil, and the lusts of your father ye will do. He was a murderer from the beginning, and abode not in the truth, because there is no truth in him. When he speaketh a lie, he speaketh of his own: for he is a liar, and the father of it. (John 8:44)

[71] But we speak the wisdom of God in a mystery, even the hidden wisdom, which God ordained before the world unto our glory: (1Corinthians 2:7)

[72] Another parable put he forth unto them, saying, The kingdom of heaven is likened unto a man which sowed good seed in his field: But while men slept, his enemy came and sowed tares among the wheat, and went his way. But when the blade was sprung up, and brought forth fruit, then appeared the tares also. (Matthew 13:34-26)

Then shall the kingdom of heaven be likened unto ten virgins, which took their lamps, and went forth to meet the bridegroom. And five of them were wise, and five *were* foolish. They that *were* foolish took their lamps, and took no oil with them: But the wise took oil in their vessels with their lamps. While the bridegroom tarried, they all slumbered and slept. (Matthew 25:1-5)

Wherefore he saith, Awake thou that sleepest, and arise from the dead, and Christ shall give thee light. (Ephesians 5:14)

[73] But while men slept, his enemy came and sowed tares among the wheat, and went his way. (Matthew 13:25)

[74] Then Jesus said unto them, Take heed and beware of the leaven of the Pharisees and of the Sadducees. (Matthew 16:6)

[75] Because thou sayest, I am rich, and increased with goods, and have need of nothing; and knowest not that thou art wretched, and miserable, and poor, and blind, and naked: (Revelation 3:17)

[76] And he cried mightily with a strong voice, saying, Babylon the great is fallen, is fallen, and is become the habitation of devils, and the hold of every foul spirit, and a cage of every unclean and hateful bird. For all nations have drunk of the wine of the wrath of her fornication, and the kings of the earth have committed fornication with her, and the merchants of the earth are waxed rich through the abundance of her delicacies. And I heard another voice from heaven, saying, Come out of her, my people, that ye be not partakers of her sins, and that ye receive not of her plagues. Revelation 18:2-4)

[77] Will a man rob God? Yet ye have robbed me. But ye say, Wherein have we robbed thee? In tithes and offerings. Ye are cursed with a

curse: for ye have robbed me, even this whole nation. Bring ye all the tithes into the storehouse, that there may be meat in mine house, and prove me now herewith, saith the LORD of hosts, if I will not open you the windows of heaven, and pour you out a blessing, that there shall not be room enough to receive it. (Malachi 3:8-10)

[78] And in the same house remain, eating and drinking such things as they give: for the labourer is worthy of his hire. Go not from house to house. (Luke 10:7)

[79] Who goeth a warfare any time at his own charges? who planteth a vineyard, and eateth not of the fruit thereof? or who feedeth a flock, and eateth not of the milk of the flock? (1Corinthians 9:7)

[80] Ye eat the fat, and ye clothe you with the wool, ye kill them that are fed: but ye feed not the flock. (Ezekiel 34:3)

[81] And as for you, O my flock, thus saith the Lord GOD; Behold, I judge between cattle and cattle, between the rams and the he goats. Seemeth it a small thing unto you to have eaten up the good pasture, but ye must tread down with your feet the residue of your pastures? and to have drunk of the deep waters, but ye must foul the residue with your feet? And as for my flock, they eat that which ye have trodden with your feet; and they drink that which ye have fouled with your feet. Therefore thus saith the Lord GOD unto them; Behold, I, even I, will judge between the fat cattle and between the lean cattle. (Ezekiel 34:17—20)

Go to now, ye rich men, weep and howl for your miseries that shall come upon you. Your riches are corrupted, and your garments are motheaten. Your gold and silver is cankered; and the rust of them shall be a witness against you, and shall eat your flesh as it were fire. Ye have heaped treasure together for the last days. Behold, the hire of the labourers who have reaped down your fields, which is of you kept back by fraud, crieth: and the cries of them which have reaped are entered into the ears of the Lord of sabaoth. Ye have lived in pleasure on the earth, and been wanton; ye have nourished your hearts, as in a day of slaughter. Ye have condemned and killed the just; and he doth not resist you. (James 5:1-6)

[82] Now concerning the collection for the saints, as I have given order to the churches of Galatia, even so do ye. Upon the first day of the week let every one of you lay by him in store, as God hath prospered him, that there be no gatherings when I come. (1Corinthians 16:1; 2)

[83] Therefore I thought it necessary to exhort the brethren, that they would go before unto you, and make up beforehand your bounty, whereof ye had notice before, that the same might be ready, as a matter of bounty, and not as of covetousness. But this I say, He which soweth sparingly shall reap also sparingly; and he which soweth bountifully shall reap also bountifully. Every man according as he purposeth in his heart, so let him give; not grudgingly, or of necessity: for God loveth a cheerful giver. (2Corinthians 9:5-7)

[84] For even that which was made glorious had no glory in this respect, by reason of the glory that excelleth. For if that which is done away was glorious, much more that which remaineth is glorious. Seeing then that we have such hope, we use great plainness of speech: And not as Moses, which put a vail over his face, that the children of Israel could not stedfastly look to the end of that which is abolished: But their minds were blinded: for until this day remaineth the same vail untaken away in the reading of the old testament; which vail is done away in Christ. But even unto this day, when Moses is read, the vail is upon their heart. Nevertheless when it shall turn to the Lord, the vail shall be taken away. (2Corinthians 3:10-16)

[85] For Christ is the end of the law for righteousness to every one that believeth. (Romans 10:4)

[86] Christ is become of no effect unto you, whosoever of you are justified by the law; ye are fallen from grace. (Galatians 5:4)

[87] So he carried me away in the spirit into the wilderness: and I saw a woman sit upon a scarlet coloured beast, full of names of blasphemy, having seven heads and ten horns. And the woman was arrayed in purple and scarlet colour, and decked with gold and precious stones and pearls, having a golden cup in her hand full of abominations and filthiness of her fornication: And upon her forehead was a name written, MYSTERY, BABYLON THE GREAT, THE MOTHER OF HARLOTS AND ABOMINATIONS OF THE EARTH. And I saw

the woman drunken with the blood of the saints, and with the blood of the martyrs of Jesus: and when I saw her, I wondered with great admiration. (Revelation 17:3-6)

[88] And the word of the LORD came unto me, saying, Son of man, prophesy against the shepherds of Israel, prophesy, and say unto them, Thus saith the Lord GOD unto the shepherds; Woe be to the shepherds of Israel that do feed themselves! should not the shepherds feed the flocks? Ye eat the fat, and ye clothe you with the wool, ye kill them that are fed: but ye feed not the flock. (Ezekiel 34:1-3)

[89] He answered and said unto them, Well hath Esaias prophesied of you hypocrites, as it is written, This people honoureth me with their lips, but their heart is far from me. Howbeit in vain do they worship me, teaching for doctrines the commandments of men. For laying aside the commandment of God, ye hold the tradition of men, as the washing of pots and cups: and many other such like things ye do. And he said unto them, Full well ye reject the commandment of God, that ye may keep your own tradition. (Mark 7:6-9)

[90] But what saith the answer of God unto him? I have reserved to myself seven thousand men, who have not bowed the knee to the image of Baal. Even so then at this present time also there is a remnant according to the election of grace. (Romans 11:4; 5)

[91] Woe unto them! for they have gone in the way of Cain, and ran greedily after the error of Balaam for reward, and perished in the gainsaying of Core. (Jude 1:11)

[92] People of Israel, listen to the message that the LORD has for you. He says, "Do not follow the ways of other nations; do not be disturbed by unusual sights in the sky, even though other nations are terrified. The religion of these people is worthless. A tree is cut down in the forest; it is carved by the tools of the woodworker and decorated with silver and gold. It is fastened down with nails to keep it from falling over. Such idols are like scarecrows in a field of melons; they cannot speak; they have to be carried because they cannot walk. Do not be afraid of them: they can cause you no harm, and they can do you no good." LORD, there is no one like you; you are mighty, and your name is great and powerful. (Jeremiah 10:1-6)

[93] For the wrath of God is revealed from heaven against all ungodliness and unrighteousness of men, who hold the truth in unrighteousness; Because that which may be known of God is manifest in them; for God hath shewed it unto them. For the invisible things of him from the creation of the world are clearly seen, being understood by the things that are made, even his eternal power and Godhead; so that they are without excuse: Because that, when they knew God, they glorified him not as God, neither were thankful; but became vain in their imaginations, and their foolish heart was darkened. Professing themselves to be wise, they became fools, And changed the glory of the uncorruptible God into an image made like to corruptible man, and to birds, and fourfooted beasts, and creeping things. Wherefore God also gave them up to uncleanness through the lusts of their own hearts, to dishonour their own bodies between themselves: Who changed the truth of God into a lie, and worshipped and served the creature more than the Creator, who is blessed for ever. Amen. (Romans 1:18-25)

[94] But while men slept, his enemy came and sowed tares among the wheat, and went his way. (Matthew 13:25)

Be ye not unequally yoked together with unbelievers: for what fellowship hath righteousness with unrighteousness? and what communion hath light with darkness? And what concord hath Christ with Belial? or what part hath he that believeth with an infidel? And what agreement hath the temple of God with idols? for ye are the temple of the living God; as God hath said, I will dwell in them, and walk in them; and I will be their God, and they shall be my people. Wherefore come out from among them, and be ye separate, saith the Lord, and touch not the unclean thing; and I will receive you, And will be a Father unto you, and ye shall be my sons and daughters, saith the Lord Almighty. (2Corinthians 6:14-18)

And I heard another voice from heaven, saying, Come out of her, my people, that ye be not partakers of her sins, and that ye receive not of her plagues. (Revelation 18:4)

[95] For God, who commanded the light to shine out of darkness, hath shined in our hearts, to give the light of the knowledge of the glory of God in the face of Jesus Christ. (2Corinthians 4:6)

Forasmuch as thou sawest that the stone was cut out of the mountain without hands, and that it brake in pieces the iron, the brass, the clay, the silver, and the gold; the great God hath made known to the king what shall come to pass hereafter: and the dream is certain, and the interpretation thereof sure. (Daniel 2:45)

And when they were departed, behold, the angel of the Lord appeareth to Joseph in a dream, saying, Arise, and take the young child and his mother, and flee into Egypt, and be thou there until I bring thee word: for Herod will seek the young child to destroy him. When he arose, he took the young child and his mother by night, and departed into Egypt: And was there until the death of Herod: that it might be fulfilled which was spoken of the Lord by the prophet, saying, Out of Egypt have I called my son. (Matthew 2:13-15)

[96] Wherefore come out from among them, and be ye separate, saith the Lord, and touch not the unclean thing; and I will receive you, And will be a Father unto you, and ye shall be my sons and daughters, saith the Lord Almighty. (2Corinthians 6:17; 18)

And I heard another voice from heaven, saying, Come out of her, my people, that ye be not partakers of her sins, and that ye receive not of her plagues. (Revelation 18:4)

[97] And he shall send his angels with a great sound of a trumpet, and they shall gather together his elect from the four winds, from one end of heaven to the other. (Matthew 24:31)

And I will give you pastors according to mine heart, which shall feed you with knowledge and understanding. (Jeremiah 3:15)

[98] As it is written, There is none righteous, no, not one: There is none that understandeth, there is none that seeketh after God. They are all gone out of the way, they are together become unprofitable; there is none that doeth good, no, not one. Their throat is an open sepulchre; with their tongues they have used deceit; the poison of asps is under their lips: Whose mouth is full of cursing and bitterness: Their feet are swift to shed blood: Destruction and misery are in their ways: And the way of peace have they not known: There is no fear of God before their eyes. (Romans 3:10-18)

[99] And he said, Unto you it is given to know the mysteries of the kingdom of God: but to others in parables; that seeing they might not see, and hearing they might not understand. (Luke 8:10)

[100] He that overcometh shall inherit all things; and I will be his God, and he shall be my son. (Revelation 21:7)

[101] And he shall rule them with a rod of iron; as the vessels of a potter shall they be broken to shivers: even as I received of my Father. (Revelation 2:27)

CHAPTER SEVEN

[1] Knowing this first, that no prophecy of the scripture is of any private interpretation. (2Peter 1:20)

[2] The Revelation of Jesus Christ, which God gave unto him, to shew unto his servants things which must shortly come to pass; and he sent and signified it by his angel unto his servant John: (Revelation 1:1)

[3] And I saw an angel come down from heaven, having the key of the bottomless pit and a great chain in his hand. (Revelation 20:1)

[4] I was in the Spirit on the Lord's day, and heard behind me a great voice, as of a trumpet. (Revelation 1:10)

[5] And Elisha prayed, and said, LORD, I pray thee, open his eyes, that he may see. And the LORD opened the eyes of the young man; and he saw: and, behold, the mountain was full of horses and chariots of fire round about Elisha. (2Kings 6:17)

[6] And there came two angels to Sodom at even; and Lot sat in the gate of Sodom: and Lot seeing them rose up to meet them; and he bowed himself with his face toward the ground . . . And they (the people of Sodom and Gomorrah) called unto Lot, and said unto him, Where are the men which came in to thee this night? bring them out unto us, that we may know them. (Genesis 19:1; 5)

[7] No man can enter into a strong man's house, and spoil his goods, except he will first bind the strong man; and then he will spoil his house. (Mark 3:27)

[8] But if I with the finger of God cast out devils, no doubt the kingdom of God is come upon you. (Luke 11:20)

[9] But if I cast out devils by the Spirit of God, then the kingdom of God is come unto you. (Matthew 12:28)

[10] And I will give unto thee the keys of the kingdom of heaven: and whatsoever thou shalt bind on earth shall be bound in heaven: and whatsoever thou shalt loose on earth shall be loosed in heaven. (Matthew 16:19)

[11] And, being assembled together with them, commanded them that they should not depart from Jerusalem, but wait for the promise of the Father, which, saith he, ye have heard of me. For John truly baptized with water; but ye shall be baptized with the Holy Ghost not many days hence. (Acts 1:4; 5)

But ye shall receive power, after that the Holy Ghost is come upon you: and ye shall be witnesses unto me both in Jerusalem, and in all Judaea, and in Samaria, and unto the uttermost part of the earth. (Acts 1:8)

[12] And they were all amazed, and spake among themselves, saying, What a word is this! for with authority and power he commandeth the unclean spirits, and they come out. (Luke 4:36)

[13] Verily, verily, I say unto you, He that believeth on me, the works that I do shall he do also; and greater works than these shall he do; because I go unto my Father. (John 14:12)

[14] No man can enter into a strong man's house, and spoil his goods, except he will first bind the strong man; and then he will spoil his house. (Mark 3:27)

[15] The Spirit of the Lord is upon me, because he hath anointed me to preach the gospel to the poor; he hath sent me to heal the brokenhearted, to preach deliverance to the captives, and recovering of sight to the blind, to set at liberty them that are bruised. (Luke 4:18)

But now we are delivered from the law, that being dead wherein we were held; that we should serve in newness of spirit, and not in the oldness of the letter. (Romans 7:6)

By which also he went and preached unto the spirits in prison. (1Peter 3:19)

For this cause was the gospel preached also to them that are dead, that they might be judged according to men in the flesh, but live according to God in the spirit. (1Peter 4:6)

[16] And this gospel of the kingdom shall be preached in all the world for a witness unto all nations; and then shall the end come. (Mathew 24:14)

[17] For a thousand years in thy sight are but as yesterday when it is past, and as a watch in the night. (Psalm 90:4)

But, beloved, be not ignorant of this one thing, that one day is with the Lord as a thousand years, and a thousand years as one day. (2Peter 3:8)

[18] Then cometh the end, when he shall have delivered up the kingdom to God, even the Father; when he shall have put down all rule and all authority and power; For he must reign, till he hath put all enemies under his feet. (1Corintians 15:24; 25)

[19] Whom the heaven must receive until the times of restitution of all things, which God hath spoken by the mouth of all his holy prophets since the world began. (Acts 3:21)

[20] Let no man deceive you by any means: for that day shall not come, except there come a falling away first, and that man of sin be revealed, the son of perdition; Who opposeth and exalteth himself above all that is called God, or that is worshipped; so that he as God sitteth in the temple of God, shewing himself that he is God. (2Thessalonians 2:3-4)

[21] Another parable put he forth unto them, saying, The kingdom of heaven is likened unto a man which sowed good seed in his field: But while men slept, his enemy came and sowed tares among the wheat, and went his way. But when the blade was sprung up, and

brought forth fruit, then appeared the tares also. So the servants of the householder came and said unto him, Sir, didst not thou sow good seed in thy field? from whence then hath it tares? He said unto them, An enemy hath done this. The servants said unto him, Wilt thou then that we go and gather them up? But he said, Nay; lest while ye gather up the tares, ye root up also the wheat with them. Let both grow together until the harvest: and in the time of harvest I will say to the reapers, Gather ye together first the tares, and bind them in bundles to burn them: but gather the wheat into my barn. (Mat 13:24-30)

[22] Thou sawest till that a stone was cut out without hands, which smote the image upon his feet that were of iron and clay, and brake them to pieces. Forasmuch as thou sawest that the stone was cut out of the mountain without hands, and that it brake in pieces the iron, the brass, the clay, the silver, and the gold; the great God hath made known to the king what shall come to pass hereafter: and the dream is certain, and the interpretation thereof sure. (Daniel 2:34; 45)

[23] For who maketh thee to differ from another? and what hast thou that thou didst not receive? now if thou didst receive it, why dost thou glory, as if thou hadst not received it? Now ye are full, now ye are rich, ye have reigned as kings without us: and I would to God ye did reign, that we also might reign with you. (Corinthians 4:7; 8)

[24] And when he had called unto him his twelve disciples, he gave them power against unclean spirits, to cast them out, and to heal all manner of sickness and all manner of disease. (Matthew 10:1)

[25] Blessed and holy is he that hath part in the first resurrection: on such the second death hath no power, but they shall be priests of God and of Christ, and shall reign with him a thousand years. (Revelation 20:6)

Praying always with all prayer and supplication in the Spirit, and watching thereunto with all perseverance and supplication for all saints. (Ephesians 6:18)

[26] And the seventh angel sounded; and there were great voices in heaven, saying, The kingdoms of this world are become the kingdoms of our Lord, and of his Christ; and he shall reign for ever and ever. (Revelation 11:15)

[27] And hath made us kings and priests unto God and his Father; to him be glory and dominion for ever and ever. Amen. (Revelation 1:6)

And hast made us unto our God kings and priests: and we shall reign on the earth. (Revelation 5:10)

[28] Whither the forerunner is for us entered, even Jesus, made an high priest for ever after the order of Melchisedec. (Hebrews 6:20)

[29] And to you who are troubled rest with us, when the Lord Jesus shall be revealed from heaven with his mighty angels. (2Thessalonians 1:7)

[30] And the seventh angel sounded; and there were great voices in heaven, saying, The kingdoms of this world are become the kingdoms of our Lord, and of his Christ; and he shall reign for ever and ever. (Revelation 11:15)

And there shall be no night there; and they need no candle, neither light of the sun; for the Lord God giveth them light: and they shall reign for ever and ever. (Revelation 22:5)

[31] And he shall send Jesus Christ, which before was preached unto you: Whom the heaven must receive until the times of restitution of all things, which God hath spoken by the mouth of all his holy prophets since the world began. (Acts 3:20; 21)

[32] Peace I leave with you, my peace I give unto you: not as the world giveth, give I unto you. Let not your heart be troubled, neither let it be afraid. (John 14:27)

[33] Salt is good: but if the salt have lost his saltness, wherewith will ye season it? Have salt in yourselves, and have peace one with another. (Mark 9:50)

And when ye come into an house, salute it. And if the house be worthy, let your peace come upon it: but if it be not worthy, let your peace return to you. (Matthew 10:12)

[34] Who also hath made us able ministers of the new testament; not of the letter, but of the spirit: for the letter killeth, but the spirit giveth life. (2Corinthians 3:6)

[35] For though we walk in the flesh, we do not war after the flesh: For the weapons of our warfare are not carnal, but mighty through God to the pulling down of strong holds; Casting down imaginations, and every high thing that exalteth itself against the knowledge of God, and bringing into captivity every thought to the obedience of Christ, (Corinthians 10:3-5)

Put on the whole armour of God, that ye may be able to stand against the wiles of the devil. For we wrestle not against flesh and blood, but against principalities, against powers, against the rulers of the darkness of this world, against spiritual wickedness in high places. (Ephesians 6:11; 12)

[36] For the flesh lusteth against the Spirit, and the Spirit against the flesh: and these are contrary the one to the other: so that ye cannot do the things that ye would. (Galatians 5:17)

[37] For though we walk in the flesh, we do not war after the flesh: (For the weapons of our warfare are not carnal, but mighty through God to the pulling down of strong holds;) Casting down imaginations, and every high thing that exalteth itself against the knowledge of God, and bringing into captivity every thought to the obedience of Christ; (2Corinthians 10:3-5)

[38] And he had in his right hand seven stars: and out of his mouth went a sharp twoedged sword: and his countenance was as the sun shineth in his strength. (Revelation 1:16)

These shall make war with the Lamb, and the Lamb shall overcome them: for he is Lord of lords, and King of kings: and they that are with him are called, and chosen, and faithful. (Revelation 17:14)

[39] And out of his mouth goeth a sharp sword, that with it he should smite the nations: and he shall rule them with a rod of iron: and he treadeth the winepress of the fierceness and wrath of Almighty God. (Revelation 19:15)

[40] Therefore, brethren, we are debtors, not to the flesh, to live after the flesh. For if ye live after the flesh, ye shall die: but if ye through the Spirit do mortify the deeds of the body, ye shall live. (Romans 8:12; 13)

Mortify therefore your members which are upon the earth; fornication, uncleanness, inordinate affection, evil concupiscence, and covetousness, which is idolatry: (Colossians 3:5)

And take the helmet of salvation, and the sword of the Spirit, which is the word of God: (Ephesians 6:17)

[41] No man that warreth entangleth himself with the affairs of this life; that he may please him who hath chosen him to be a soldier. (2Timothy 2:4)

[42] Fight the good fight of faith, lay hold on eternal life, whereunto thou art also called, and hast professed a good profession before many witnesses. (1Timothy 6:12)

[43] I have fought a good fight, I have finished my course, I have kept the faith. (2Timothy 4:7)

[44] Proclaim ye this among the Gentiles; Prepare war, wake up the mighty men, let all the men of war draw near; let them come up: Beat your plowshares into swords, and your pruninghooks into spears: let the weak say, I am strong. Assemble yourselves, and come, all ye heathen, and gather yourselves together round about: thither cause thy mighty ones to come down, O LORD. Let the heathen be wakened, and come up to the valley of Jehoshaphat: for there will I sit to judge all the heathen round about. Put ye in the sickle, for the harvest is ripe: come, get you down; for the press is full, the fats overflow; for their wickedness is great. Multitudes, multitudes in the valley of decision: for the day of the LORD is near in the valley of decision. (Joel 3:9-14)

[45] And be not conformed to this world: but be ye transformed by the renewing of your mind, that ye may prove what is that good, and acceptable, and perfect, will of God. (Romans 12:2)

[46] For the flesh lusteth against the Spirit, and the Spirit against the flesh: and these are contrary the one to the other: so that ye cannot do the things that ye would. (Galatians 5:17)

[47] He that believeth on the Son hath everlasting life: and he that believeth not the Son shall not see life; but the wrath of God abideth on him. (John 3:36)

[48] And many of them that sleep in the dust of the earth shall awake, some to everlasting life, and some to shame and everlasting contempt. (Daniel 12:2)

But the rest of the dead lived not again until the thousand years were finished. This is the first resurrection. (Revelation 20:5)

[49] Verily, verily, I say unto you, The hour is coming, and now is, when the dead shall hear the voice of the Son of God: and they that hear shall live. (John 5:25)

[50] And not only they, but ourselves also, which have the first fruits of the Spirit, even we ourselves groan within ourselves, waiting for the adoption, to wit, the redemption of our body. (Romans 8:23)

[51] But these, as natural brute beasts, made to be taken and destroyed, speak evil of the things that they understand not; and shall utterly perish in their own corruption. (2Peter 2:12)

[52] Who hath delivered us from the power of darkness, and hath translated us into the kingdom of his dear Son: (Colossians 1:13)

[53] And the priests that bare the ark of the covenant of the LORD stood firm on dry ground in the midst of Jordan, and all the Israelites passed over on dry ground, until all the people were passed clean over Jordan. (Joshua 3:17)

[54] And account that the longsuffering of our Lord is salvation; even as our beloved brother Paul also according to the wisdom given unto him hath written unto you; As also in all his epistles, speaking in them of these things; in which are some things hard to be understood, which they that are unlearned and unstable wrest, as they do also the other scriptures, unto their own destruction. (2Peter 3:15; 16)

[55] How that by revelation he made known unto me the mystery; (as I wrote afore in few words, Whereby, when ye read, ye may understand my knowledge in the mystery of Christ) Which in other ages was not made known unto the sons of men, as it is now revealed unto his holy apostles and prophets by the Spirit. (Ephesians 3:3-5)

[56] But ye are a chosen generation, a royal priesthood, an holy nation, a peculiar people; that ye should shew forth the praises of him who hath called you out of darkness into his marvellous light: (1Peter 2:9)

[57] And unto the angel of the church of the Laodiceans write; These things saith the Amen, the faithful and true witness, the beginning of the creation of God; I know thy works, that thou art neither cold nor hot: I would thou wert cold or hot. So then because thou art lukewarm, and neither cold nor hot, I will spue thee out of my mouth. Because thou sayest, I am rich, and increased with goods, and have need of nothing; and knowest not that thou art wretched, and miserable, and poor, and blind, and naked: I counsel thee to buy of me gold tried in the fire, that thou mayest be rich; and white raiment, that thou mayest be clothed, and that the shame of thy nakedness do not appear; and anoint thine eyes with eyesalve, that thou mayest see. As many as I love, I rebuke and chasten: be zealous therefore, and repent. Behold, I stand at the door, and knock: if any man hear my voice, and open the door, I will come in to him, and will sup with him, and he with me. To him that overcometh will I grant to sit with me in my throne, even as I also overcame, and am set down with my Father in his throne. He that hath an ear, let him hear what the Spirit saith unto the churches. (Revelation 3:14-22)

And after these things I saw another angel come down from heaven, having great power; and the earth was lightened with his glory. And he cried mightily with a strong voice, saying, Babylon the great is fallen, is fallen, and is become the habitation of devils, and the hold of every foul spirit, and a cage of every unclean and hateful bird. For all nations have drunk of the wine of the wrath of her fornication, and the kings of the earth have committed fornication with her, and the merchants of the earth are waxed rich through the abundance of her delicacies. And I heard another voice from heaven, saying, Come out of her, my people, that ye be not partakers of her sins, and that ye receive not of her plagues. For her sins have reached unto heaven, and God hath remembered her iniquities. (Revelation 18:1-5)

[58] The beast that thou sawest was, and is not; and shall ascend out of the bottomless pit, and go into perdition: and they that dwell on the earth shall wonder, whose names were not written in the book of life from the foundation of the world, when they behold the beast that

was, and is not, and yet is. And here is the mind which hath wisdom. The seven heads are seven mountains, on which the woman sitteth. And there are seven kings: five are fallen, and one is, and the other is not yet come; and when he cometh, he must continue a short space. And the beast that was, and is not, even he is the eighth, and is of the seven, and goeth into perdition. And the ten horns which thou sawest are ten kings, which have received no kingdom as yet; but receive power as kings one hour with the beast. These have one mind, and shall give their power and strength unto the beast. These shall make war with the Lamb, and the Lamb shall overcome them: for he is Lord of lords, and King of kings: and they that are with him are called, and chosen, and faithful. (Revelation 17:8-14)

[59] And after these things I saw four angels standing on the four corners of the earth, holding the four winds of the earth, that the wind should not blow on the earth, nor on the sea, nor on any tree. And I saw another angel ascending from the east, having the seal of the living God: and he cried with a loud voice to the four angels, to whom it was given to hurt the earth and the sea, Saying, Hurt not the earth, neither the sea, nor the trees, till we have sealed the servants of our God in their foreheads. (Rev 7:1-3)

And the fifth angel sounded, and I saw a star fall from heaven unto the earth: and to him was given the key of the bottomless pit. And he opened the bottomless pit; and there arose a smoke out of the pit, as the smoke of a great furnace; and the sun and the air were darkened by reason of the smoke of the pit. And there came out of the smoke locusts upon the earth: and unto them was given power, as the scorpions of the earth have power. And it was commanded them that they should not hurt the grass of the earth, neither any green thing, neither any tree; but only those men which have not the seal of God in their foreheads. (Revelation 9:1-4)

But of the times and the seasons, brethren, ye have no need that I write unto you. For yourselves know perfectly that the day of the Lord so cometh as a thief in the night. For when they shall say, Peace and safety; then sudden destruction cometh upon them, as travail upon a woman with child; and they shall not escape. (1Thessalonians 5:1-3)

But the heavens and the earth, which are now, by the same word are kept in store, reserved unto fire against the day of judgment and perdition of ungodly men. (2Peter 3:7)

And Enoch also, the seventh from Adam, prophesied of these, saying, Behold, the Lord cometh with ten thousands of his saints, To execute judgment upon all, and to convince all that are ungodly among them of all their ungodly deeds which they have ungodly committed, and of all their hard speeches which ungodly sinners have spoken against him. (Jude 1: 14; 15)

[60] Likewise also as it was in the days of Lot; they did eat, they drank, they bought, they sold, they planted, they builded; But the same day that Lot went out of Sodom it rained fire and brimstone from heaven, and destroyed them all. (Luke 17:28; 29)

[61] But there were false prophets also among the people, even as there shall be false teachers among you, who privily shall bring in damnable heresies, even denying the Lord that bought them, and bring upon themselves swift destruction. And many shall follow their pernicious ways; by reason of whom the way of truth shall be evil spoken of. And through covetousness shall they with feigned words make merchandise of you: whose judgment now of a long time lingereth not, and their damnation slumbereth not. For if God spared not the angels that sinned, but cast them down to hell, and delivered them into chains of darkness, to be reserved unto judgment; And spared not the old world, but saved Noah the eighth person, a preacher of righteousness, bringing in the flood upon the world of the ungodly; And turning the cities of Sodom and Gomorrha into ashes condemned them with an overthrow, making them an ensample unto those that after should live ungodly; And delivered just Lot, vexed with the filthy conversation of the wicked: (For that righteous man dwelling among them, in seeing and hearing, vexed his righteous soul from day to day with their unlawful deeds;) The Lord knoweth how to deliver the godly out of temptations, and to reserve the unjust unto the day of judgment to be punished: (2Peter 2:1-9)

And I heard another voice from heaven, saying, Come out of her, my people, that ye be not partakers of her sins, and that ye receive not of her plagues. (Revelation 18:4)

A SPECIAL MESSAGE TO CHRISTIAN HUSBANDS AND WIVES

[1] But I would have you know, that the head of every man is Christ; and the head of the woman is the man; and the head of Christ is God. (1Corinthians 11:3)

[2] For this cause ought the woman to have power on her head because of the angels. (1Corinthians 11:10)

[3] But if a woman have long hair, it is a glory to her: for her hair is given her for a covering. (1Corinthians 11:15)

[4] For this is my blood of the new testament, which is shed for many for the remission of sins. (Matthew 26:28)

[5] And all things are of God, who hath reconciled us to himself by Jesus Christ, and hath given to us the ministry of reconciliation; To wit, that God was in Christ, reconciling the world unto himself, not imputing their trespasses unto them; and hath committed unto us the word of reconciliation. (2Corinthians 5:18, 19)

[6] For the life of the flesh is in the blood: and I have given it to you upon the altar to make an atonement for your souls: for it is the blood that maketh an atonement for the soul. (Leviticus 17:11)

[7] But every woman that prayeth or prophesieth with her head uncovered dishonoureth her head: for that is even all one as if she were shaven. (1Corinthians 11:5)

[8] For by grace are ye saved through faith; and that not of yourselves: it is the gift of God: Not of works, lest any man should boast. For we are his workmanship, created in Christ Jesus unto good works, which God hath before ordained that we should walk in them. (Ephesians 2:8, 10)

Knowing that a man is not justified by the works of the law, but by the faith of Jesus Christ, even we have believed in Jesus Christ, that we might be justified by the faith of Christ, and not by the works of the law: for by the works of the law shall no flesh be justified. (Galatians 2:16)

[9] Unto the woman he said, I will greatly multiply thy sorrow and thy conception; in sorrow thou shalt bring forth children; and thy desire shall be to thy husband, and he shall rule over thee. (Genesis 3:16)

[10] Not by works of righteousness which we have done, but according to his mercy he saved us, by the washing of regeneration, and renewing of the Holy Ghost; (Titus 3:5)

[11] Brethren, if a man be overtaken in a fault, ye which are spiritual, restore such an one in the spirit of meekness; considering thyself, lest thou also be tempted. (Galatians 6:1)

Not rendering evil for evil, or railing for railing: but contrariwise blessing; knowing that ye are thereunto called, that ye should inherit a blessing. (1Peter 3:9)

[12] For a man indeed ought not to cover his head, forasmuch as he is the image and glory of God: but the woman is the glory of the man. (1Corinthians 11:7)

[13] Wives, submit yourselves unto your own husbands, as unto the Lord. (Ephesians 5:22)

Therefore as the church is subject unto Christ, so let the wives be to their own husbands in every thing. (Ephesians 5:24)

Wives, submit yourselves unto your own husbands, as it is fit in the Lord. (Colossians 3:18)

For after this manner in the old time the holy women also, who trusted in God, adorned themselves, being in subjection unto their own husbands: (1Peter 3:5)

[14] For this cause ought the woman to have power on her head because of the angels. (1Corinthians 11:10)

[15] Husbands, love your wives, even as Christ also loved the church, and gave himself for it; (Ephesians 5:2)5

[16] Likewise, ye wives, be in subjection to your own husbands; that, if any obey not the word, they also may without the word be won by the conversation of the wives; (1Peter 3:1)

¹⁷ But I would have you know, that the head of every man is Christ; and the head of the woman is the man; and the head of Christ is God. (1Corinthians 11:3)

¹⁸ But I suffer not a woman to teach, nor to usurp authority over the man, but to be in silence. (1Timothy 2:12)

Obey them that have the rule over you, and submit yourselves: for they watch for your souls, as they that must give account, that they may do it with joy, and not with grief: for that is unprofitable for you. (Hebrews 13:17)

¹⁹ The woman shall not wear that which pertaineth unto a man, neither shall a man put on a woman's garment: for all that do so are abomination unto the LORD thy God. (Deuteronomy 22:5)

²⁰ For this cause ought the woman to have power on her head because of the angels. (1Corinthians 11:10)

²¹ To the intent that now unto the principalities and powers in heavenly places might be known by the church the manifold wisdom of God. (Ephesians 3:10)

²² Unto the woman he said, I will greatly multiply thy sorrow and thy conception; in sorrow thou shalt bring forth children; and thy desire shall be to thy husband, and he shall rule over thee. (Genesis 3:16)

²³ And it came to pass, when she pressed him daily with her words, and urged him, so that his soul was vexed unto death; That he told her all his heart, and said unto her, There hath not come a razor upon mine head; for I have been a Nazarite unto God from my mother's womb: if I be shaven, then my strength will go from me, and I shall become weak, and be like any other man. And when Delilah saw that he had told her all his heart, she sent and called for the lords of the Philistines, saying, Come up this once, for he hath shewed me all his heart. Then the lords of the Philistines came up unto her, and brought money in their hand. And she made him sleep upon her knees; and she called for a man, and she caused him to shave off the seven locks of his head; and she began to afflict him, and his strength went from him. And she said, The Philistines be upon thee, Samson. And he awoke out of his sleep, and said, I will go out as at other times before,

and shake myself. And he wist not that the LORD was departed from him. But the Philistines took him, and put out his eyes, and brought him down to Gaza, and bound him with fetters of brass; and he did grind in the prison house. (Judges 16:16-21)

[24] For thy Maker is thine husband; the LORD of hosts is his name; and thy Redeemer the Holy One of Israel; The God of the whole earth shall he be called. (Isaiah 54:5)

Surely as a wife treacherously departeth from her husband, so have ye dealt treacherously with me, O house of Israel, saith the LORD. (Jeremiah 3:20)

Behold, the days come, saith the LORD, that I will make a new covenant with the house of Israel, and with the house of Judah: Not according to the covenant that I made with their fathers in the day that I took them by the hand to bring them out of the land of Egypt; which my covenant they brake, although I was an husband unto them, saith the LORD: (Jeremiah 31:31)

[25] Who also hath made us able ministers of the new testament; not of the letter, but of the spirit: for the letter killeth, but the spirit giveth life. But if the ministration of death, written and engraven in stones, was glorious, so that the children of Israel could not stedfastly behold the face of Moses for the glory of his countenance; which glory was to be done away: How shall not the ministration of the spirit be rather glorious? For if the ministration of condemnation be glory, much more doth the ministration of righteousness exceed in glory. (2Corinthians 3:6-9)

[26] And almost all things are by the law purged with blood; and without shedding of blood is no remission. (Hebrews 9:22)

[27] (For not the hearers of the law are just before God, but the doers of the law shall be justified. (Romans 2:13)

Now we know that what things soever the law saith, it saith to them who are under the law: that every mouth may be stopped, and all the world may become guilty before God. Therefore by the deeds of the law there shall no flesh be justified in his sight: for by the law is the knowledge of sin. (Romans 3:19)

Being justified freely by his grace through the redemption that is in Christ Jesus: (Romans 3:24)

For sin shall not have dominion over you: for ye are not under the law, but under grace. (Romans 6:14)

Where is boasting then? It is excluded. By what law? of works? Nay: but by the law of faith. Therefore we conclude that a man is justified by faith without the deeds of the law. (Romans 3:27, 28)

[28] Because thou sayest, I am rich, and increased with goods, and have need of nothing; and knowest not that thou art wretched, and miserable, and poor, and blind, and naked: (Revelation 3:17)

[29] And the eyes of them both were opened, and they knew that they were naked; and they sewed fig leaves together, and made themselves aprons. (Genesis 3:7)

[30] Woe unto them! for they have gone in the way of Cain, and ran greedily after the error of Balaam for reward, and perished in the gainsaying of Core. (Jude 1:11)

[31] For as the body without the spirit is dead, so faith without works is dead also. (James 2:26)

[32] But I would have you know, that the head of every man is Christ; and the head of the woman is the man; and the head of Christ is God. Every man praying or prophesying, having his head covered, dishonoureth his head. (1Corinthians 11:3)

[33] For we have not an high priest which cannot be touched with the feeling of our infirmities; but was in all points tempted like as we are, yet without sin. (Hebrews 4:15)

[34] And he commanded us to preach unto the people, and to testify (witness) that it is he which was ordained of God to be the Judge of quick and dead. (Acts 10:42)

[35] All scripture is given by inspiration of God, and is profitable for doctrine, for reproof, for correction, for instruction in righteousness: (2Timothy 3:16)

³⁶ For whatsoever things were written aforetime were written for our learning, that we through patience and comfort of the scriptures might have hope. (Romans 15:4)

³⁷ Search the scriptures; for in them ye think ye have eternal life: and they are they which testify of me. (John 5:39)

³⁸ And the Spirit and the bride say, Come. And let him that heareth say, Come. And let him that is athirst come. And whosoever will, let him take the water of life freely. (Revelation 22:17)

³⁹ Then he answered and spake unto me, saying, This is the word of the LORD unto Zerubbabel, saying, Not by might, nor by power, but by my spirit, saith the LORD of hosts. (Zechariah 4:6)

⁴⁰ For the earnest expectation of the creature waiteth for the manifestation of the sons of God. (Romans 8:19)

⁴¹ I am Alpha and Omega, the beginning and the ending, saith the Lord, which is, and which was, and which is to come, the Almighty. (Revelation 1:8)

⁴² And he said unto him, Well, thou good servant: because thou hast been faithful in a very little, have thou authority over ten cities. (Luke 19:17)

⁴³ And Samuel said, Hath the LORD as great delight in burnt offerings and sacrifices, as in obeying the voice of the LORD? Behold, to obey is better than sacrifice, and to hearken than the fat of rams. (1Samuel 15:22)

⁴⁴ The sacrifices of God are a broken spirit: a broken and a contrite heart, O God, thou wilt not despise. (Psalm 51:17)

⁴⁵ Who bare record of the word of God, and of the testimony of Jesus Christ, and of all things that he saw. (Revelation 1:2)

⁴⁶ Moreover if thy brother shall trespass against thee, go and tell him his fault between thee and him alone: if he shall hear thee, thou hast gained thy brother. But if he will not hear thee, then take with thee one or two more, that in the mouth of two or three witnesses every word may be established. And if he shall neglect to hear them, tell it

unto the church: but if he neglect to hear the church, let him be unto thee as an heathen man and a publican. (Matthew 18:15—17)

Dare any of you, having a matter against another, go to law before the unjust, and not before the saints? Do ye not know that the saints shall judge the world? and if the world shall be judged by you, are ye unworthy to judge the smallest matters? Know ye not that we shall judge angels? how much more things that pertain to this life? (1Corinthians 6:1—3)

And if any man obey not our word by this epistle, note that man, and have no company with him, that he may be ashamed. Yet count him not as an enemy, but admonish him as a brother. (Thessalonians 3:14, 15)

[47] Against an elder receive not an accusation, but before two or three witnesses. (1Timothy 5:19)